GROWING UP
IN THE
THIRTIES

Grace Horseman

£8·99 12194

Cottage Publishing

© Grace Horseman 1994.

First Published in 1994 by Grace Horseman of 3 Ashburton Road, Brimley, Bovey Tracey, Devon TQ13 9BZ in association with:

Cottage Publishing
Bovey Tracey
Devon TQ13 9AE
Tel: 0626 835757

British Library Catalogue in Publication Data

A CIP Catalogue Record for this book is available from the British Library

ISBN 1-897785-03-8

Horseman, Grace
Growing up in the Thirties

Madders, Jane and Horseman, Grace
Growing up in the Twenties

Typeset by
Nick Harman of Cottage Publishing, Bovey Tracey

Printed in Great Britain by
Sprint Print Ltd, Exeter

Cover illustration and photographs
The cover illustration is from an original water colour by Miss Enid Dynes (1909-1991), a Bob and a former headmistress of Chichester High School for Girls. It shows Jane and Grace in the garden at Bude where the Bobs were together for a week in 1978: overlaid are photographs of Nina Armour and friends having tea in the garden; Betty Baden-Powell on aboard ship en-route for Kenya in 1935; unemployed demonstrators with 'the coffin'; Winston Churchill. On the reverse side are some Bobs at Marigolds; Jane Madders (centre) with leaders from the Central Council for Recreative Physical Training; an airline of the Thirties.

CONTENTS

INTRODUCTION

They have been called the Threadbare Thirties, and so they must have seemed to many. During the Twenties there had been a gradual improvement in the standard of living, with eight million houses built and unemployment down to one million, though many people were still condemned to live in slum accommodation. Then in 1929 there came the Wall Street crash in America. Unemployment there was over three million, and tariffs were imposed on imports to protect American industry. This meant many countries lost one of their best markets, and some of them put up their own tariffs, so further restricting markets. Panic followed around the world and the failure of credit caused an economic crisis. Many collapsed, leading to a trebling of unemployment in Britain. Things continued to get worse until 21.9% of working people were unemployed in 1932. The introduction of the Means Test before the granting of extra relief caused much resentment, and further hardship.

In her book *Twopence To Cross The Mersey*, Helen Forrester describes the devastating effect on her life when her father was made bankrupt in 1930. The family had to leave their comfortable home with a nanny and maids, and fight for their very existence in Liverpool. Helen was the oldest and so was made responsible for looking after the six younger children. Trying to keep them fed and their clothes clean with no soap and only cold water was an impossible task in the grimy slums of Liverpool. Many others suffered in this way.

However, conditions improved slowly during the Thirties, with less unemployment and, for those in work, there was a definite improvement in living standards. The majority of the British only wanted a peaceful life   they could not contemplate another war after the carnage of 1914-1918, so they ignored the warning signs abroad. In Russia Stalin was pursuing his brutal collectivisation -- forcing peasants to give up their own plots and work on collective farms. The richer peasants, called Kulaks, suffered most. Many of them were deported to remote areas of the country and some to labour camps, where they often disappeared. Then in 1931 Japan seized Manchuria, but no action was taken by the allies, apart from voicing disapproval of Japan's aggression, whereupon Japan left the League of Nations.

Again, when Mussolini attacked Abyssinia there was no concerted action by the League of Nations. Britain imposed commercial sanctions but had little support from other nations and, like Japan, Italy left the League and instead made a pact with her sworn enemy, Germany. Hitler had rearmed, contrary to the terms of the Treaty of Versailles, and whilst Italy was conquering Abyssinia he reoccupied the demilitarised Rhineland. Failure on the part of the allies to take any firm action at this point, when Hitler might have been stopped, led to further annexations and eventually the Second World War.

However, most Britons were much more interested in what was going on at home. That same year Amy Johnson flew solo from Croydon Airport to Australia, the first woman to do so, and the Australian Donald Bradman achieved a record score of 334 runs in the Test match against England at Leeds. The crash of the airship R101 over France was much more important to most people than what was happening elsewhere. The cinema was another form of escapism and Hollywood catered for the demand by producing extravagant new films. Ginger Rogers and Fred Astaire began their extremely successful dancing partnership with *Flying Down To Rio:* many others followed.

On January 20th 1936 King George V died at Sandringham and was succeeded by Edward VIII, who was well known and well loved as Prince of Wales. But his reign was short lived: he had fallen in love with Mrs. Ernest Simpson, who then sought a divorce from her husband. When it was learnt that the King intended to marry Mrs. Simpson this led to his enforced abdication on December 11th. His brother, Duke of York, succeeded him as George VI. He was happily married to Elizabeth, a Scotswoman of noble blood, and they and their daughters soon endeared themselves to the people.

By 1937 people in Britain, France and other countries at last began to appreciate what another war would be like, having seen the effects of Germany's bombardment of Guernica during the Spanish Civil War. Fear of gas attacks was predominant, and arrangements were made to fit every civilian with a gas mask.

That same year marked the Coronation of George VI and Queen Elizabeth (now the Queen Mother). It was a time of enthusiastic celebration, with street parties throughout the country.

Neville Chamberlain, Prime Minister of Britain, met Hitler three times during 1938 and thought that if he allowed him to take over the area of Czechoslovakia where the Sudetan Germans lived, Hitler would accept a binding agreement and go no further   he returned from Munich in September waving a piece of paper: It is peace for our time , he declared. How wrong he was was to be demonstrated less than a year later.

The following chapters contain personal accounts of many men and women of different backgrounds concerning life as it affected them during the Thirties: some experienced great poverty, others were not affected by the recession. They come from many different parts of Britain, with differing backgrounds and qualifications.

1. FAMILY LIFE

Introduction

In the early Thirties it was still obligatory for most professional women to resign when they married, and many good teachers were lost to education because of this discrimination; the same applied to many other professions. Not only did the married woman suffer the loss of her personal income, but often she had to move to a strange locality where she knew no-one. She spent much of the day alone, coping with unfamiliar domestic chores, and she was even more tied when the first baby arrived. Many husbands were parsimonious when it came to giving their wives money for housekeeping, yet alone extra for pocket money.

In former days people often lived in extended families. Fathers frequently died quite young and the widowed mother took it for granted that she would live with one of her children. So there was a baby-sitter on the spot and someone to share the work and interests. However, this could also lead to friction!

The housing boom of the Twenties increased during the Thirties. About 2,700,000 houses were built in England and Wales, the great majority without public aid. The construction of new houses in the years between the wars provided one-third of all houses existing in England and Wales at the beginning of the Second World War.

So for many the standard of living improved, but the uprooting of people from the east end of London, where they had lived happily together, left many of them feeling very lonely and isolated, especially if they lived in one of the high rise flats. In our day we have recognised the folly of placing people in buildings where there is nowhere at hand for the children to play.

Others were better off than they had ever been. Children whose fathers had died in the First World War were growing up, easing the strain on their widowed mothers. Yet the spectre of unemployment loomed large, especially during the first years of the Thirties, and the threat of the Second World War over the latter years.

Large families were not as common in the Thirties as they were in Victorian times, but Mrs, Kathleen Stirzaker of Exeter knew what it was like to be the oldest of eight children, all born between 1921 and 1929.

As I was the oldest child, I had to look after the younger ones, two boys and five girls. On Saturdays I took my youngest sisters to the park in their pushchair. They were twins, and only two years old. Sometimes we had picnics and all the family would come with us then.

Dad usually joined us in a game of rounders, and Mum did her knitting. Most families found their entertainment this way as a lot of men were unemployed at this time. I can't remember my dad being out of work (he was a storeman in the Council Offices) but we weren't able to afford to go to the cinema very often, although we all loved the pictures, as we called them. I remember my dad taking us to see the first talkies.

I think a lot of children in the Thirties were often hungry as, if the father or mother could not get work, there would be no money coming into the house. We had no Social Security then. Women did domestic work to help out, and neighbours often fed children of people who were unemployed. Men grew vegetables in their gardens and allotments to help feed their families, and often helped their neighbours with food and clothing. I remember one boy always wore his mother's shoes to school, because he had none of his own. People were kinder to each other in those days.

Bob Rutty was born in 1911, one of six children, and was just twenty-two years old when he married.

When on 4th August 1928 I attended the wedding celebration at Norfolk Road of Winnie and Charlie (the Roberts' house), I did not know that it had all been arranged so that I should meet Eve Roberts. I've never been sorry about that! One of the favourite pieces of furniture at their house was a very large armchair in the parlour, which her father, an upholsterer, had made. It took two people (not intentionally), but the two of you could sit in it comfortably if you cuddled up a bit. I was the one who turned out the light that night on 4th August: I was very popular with the other couples for doing that!

Eve and I were married on 17th September 1933 at St. Paul's Church on the corner of Essex Road and St. Paul's Road; the Rev. H. Cooper officiated. We spent our honeymoon going to theatres, cinemas and other nice places in London.

Eve was a beautiful girl and it is only sad that an accursed illness took hold of her and did what it did to her, at one stage distorting the shape of her hands and face, and then not progressing further. Eve's Father was a short wax-moustached, debonair sort with grey, white wavy hair; always smoking and always knocking back pints. He had awful teeth. His wife died shortly after I met Eve.

There was a younger sister, who was a fly-by-night. She had a tragic end after going mental following childbirth.

After living at 24 Sandmere Road, Clapham, for a little while (numbers 26 and upwards were demolished by a bomb in the war), Eve got lonely, so we moved back to North London and took a flat at Ockendon Road: top floor, two rooms. The landlord was a chap named Ager and a real old bore, so we decided when Eve became pregnant that we must move, which we did -- to 123 Englefield Road with the delightful Misses Jessie, the elder, Tee-Toe and Nellie Gee as landladies.

Firstly we had the ground floor flat - two communicating rooms and kitchen, with use of bath. Eventually we moved to the basement flat to get the use of the garden: same size. I surfaced the sloping sideway over the existing gravel to provide a proper concrete path to our flat and garden; both flats 18 shillings a week. Peter was born here on 28th June 1938: it was snowing!

In July 1939 we moved to 48 Cambridge Gardens at Winchmore Hill (once more near to the New River as at Rosebery Avenue). It was an 88 year lease, purchased for £750: ground rent £9.90 per annum. My mortgage repayments were 43/4d per month. Buying it used up every penny we had got!

When the Leasehold Enfranchisement Act came into force we bought the ground rent for £350, or thereabouts, to turn it into a freehold. At the time we bought the freehold, I had a client friend to whom I did a great service by saving him £25,000, which he had imprudently allowed as a mortgage to somebody who bought his hotel and was likely to abscond. He asked me how he could repay me and I told him to give me the money to buy the freehold, which he did.

We moved into 48 two months before the Second World War began. The mortgage was frozen when war was declared, but on this pay and subsequently in the army and their pay you can guess what a job it was for Eve to keep things going. If it hadn't been for the sewing work which she did later on in the war, we would have been in an even worse state. Which is the appropriate moment to say what a marvellous cook, dressmaker and practical lady she was, a lovely mother and lover.

Mrs. Joan P. Dobson (née Moody) is now living at Folkestone, but was brought up in London.

Did one grow up in the Thirties? Or did it take a World War in the following decade to achieve that?

I feel that my generation, boys and girls, were quite naive during the growing-up period. Our little lives were completely wrapped up in our immediate surroundings. When the Thirties began I was at school and life was entirely school, friends, Guides and Guide camps. By the beginning of the next decade I had been to university, been married for eighteen months, was expecting our first baby, and we were already plunged into a six year war.

The word 'teenager' had not been coined in the Thirties, and adolescence may have been a fact but did not crop up in daily conversation. We of an earlier generation were regarded as school children until the age of eighteen, and students only if we went on to further education at College or University. The normal school leaving age was fourteen, but if we went on to take Matric and Higher School Certificate (equivalent to the modern 'A' level) we wore school uniform until the age of eighteen.

I felt rather remote from my family at that time - Father, Mother, my brother, who was the oldest, then me, followed by two sisters. Their lives seemed not to be connected to mine. My friends at school and Guides and later the group known as Bobs, came to mean much more to me. My mother, though a caring and loving parent, was engrossed in her garden to which she gave constant and ferocious attention, producing luscious fruit and nourishing vegetables.

My father was Hon. Secretary of a gentlemen's club in the West End of London, near the Athenaeum and St. James. Twice a year we all went off together, Father complete with cheque book, to the Kensington sales. It was mostly to Daniel Neal's for shoes and clothes; our feet were measured in x-ray machines to be sure we had the right size. I remember having a navy-blue blazer bought for me at a Harrod's sale, which I loathed. My mother said that it was much better quality than the regulation school blazer, but it had SQUARE corners instead of ROUND. I felt completely humiliated.

When I was sixteen a great change came over my life. My father's club, the 'Baldwin' was becoming an unviable concern. This was a great shock to him as he had managed the day to day running of it since the end of the First World War, when he had been in the Royal Flying Corps. We had all benefitted from the club, as each year, during the season, several members would send us from Scotland or Yorkshire part of their 'bag' in the form of pheasant, partridge or sometimes salmon. I also remember my father coming home with a large yellow tin labelled 'Marmite'. A member, concerned with the new product, wanted the family's opinion, and it met with our approval: I have been an addict ever since.

Due to the financial decline of the club, the committee, headed by Lord Bligh and Viscount Doneraile, decided to make the club over to my father to see if he could turn it into a going concern. This meant that my father had to live at the club in order to be there all the time, as there were resident members, some of them friends of the Royal Family. The domestic staff had to be reduced to save money, which meant that my mother also had to live at the club as a kind of housekeeper. My sisters were too young to be left and went with them. Mother was extremely reluctant to part with her home (and garden!) so the house remained with me in situ and my brother. An aunt lived next door and provided us with an evening meal, but other than that it was all up to me, and I did not feel capable as I had never been domesticated.

My brother never seemed to be there and I spent many a lonely evening in company with my homework (at least three hours per night). It was at this time that I came very much to rely on my friends and particularly the Solkhon family and Bobs. Bob meetings gave me an ethereal, walking-on-air feeling, an ability to express emotions which I found too difficult with my own family. I think I would have been embarrassed to have told them all that being a Bob meant to me -- freedom and the joy of life.

Mummy Solkhon was a substitute mother, as I saw my own only about once a week. My friendship with that family was mainly with Jessie (Jane Madders), Jack (John) and Biddy. Grace was away in Bristol most of the Thirties. They were a very close family, with similar emotions and experiences to mine. I remember a lovely family camp in Sussex, in sight of Chanctonbury, and Bob carol singing with mince pies and other Christmas fare.

After a time it was obvious that it was costing too much to try to run the club and it finally folded. My family returned home, but not for long. In my final few months of school, whilst I was preparing for 'A' levels, they considered the possibility of taking up farming. These ideas came to fruition by the time I had arrived at Goldsmiths College to train for teaching.

Meanwhile, my father had taken over a small dairy farm in Kent. Thinking back, it was a crazy thing for him to do. A life-long black jacket and striped trousers existence exchanged for a country life, including driving a horse-drawn milk chariot on a village milk round! The horse was also required to draw a hand-guided small plough for the trifling amount of arable land attached to the small holding. Often horse and plough had to be lured ahead by another member of the family holding a slice of bread and jam (for horse, not ploughman!). The whole affair was a dead loss, particularly as in that first year there was a glut of all fruits: they could not even be given away! My parents returned to the family home somewhat disillusioned.

Mrs. Alison Yeaman Hudson, another member of a large family, is now living in Nottingham, but she was brought up in Galashiels.

Galashiels is a medium sized town on the Scottish Borders. In the Thirties the main industry was all about wool from the fleeces to become best quality tweeds.

Our family at that time consisted of Father, Mother, three girls and one boy, ages from fifteen to two years old. I was the second daughter and ten in 1930. My father was well known and was on several committees in town, such as Church and hospital.

Unemployment was still rife in those days, but my father had a good position as clerk to a building company, and my mother actually owned our house, so we were always well fed and clothed. Granny lived with us and she was a well known and respected midwife.

Although I was shy I joined a dance troupe and became the singer. I was too plump to dance on stage! I had some lovely times singing at charity concerts and village hall events round the district.

Towards the middle of 1939 the family moved to Edinburgh to live, when Father changed his job. War was nearly upon us. I stayed with an aunt and uncle until I joined the family in November that year. Many young men went to war; too many did not return, which saddens me to this day.

Mr. George Topping, also from a large family, was born in Lanarkshire, the most thickly populated area in Scotland.

We were a typical working class family, the daughters either bringing up younger brothers and sisters, or going into domestic service in Glasgow or Edinburgh, at about £8 to £10 a year, plus keep. However, during the Thirties there was a great desire to better themselves and take advantage of bursaries to enable students to follow higher education in Colleges and Universities.

The larger families were poorly dressed, boys in standard jersey, with collar of the same material, trousers, stockings and boots; girls with a pinafore dress, straight hair tied with a ribbon, though a few with longer hair had plaits down the back. They often had 'hand-me-downs'. The many cooperative stores sold more then, and many had dressmaking units.

Life in Shotts during the Thirties was rather mundane -- girls liked nursing, some home making. Shop assistants needed no formal education; but conductresses galore had nearly £3 a week against 25 shillings to 30 shillings in a shop. By the time I was called up I had 30 shillings a week, paid monthly, and if lucky an extra 2/6d for an all night removal of a 'lunatic' to the asylum, as I worked in Council Chambers.

Wishaw and Motherwell combined was a Scottish burgh (population 70,000) before the regional set-up; now Strathclyde covers the whole area of Glasgow, and stretching as far as Islay and Tiree!

There were sixteen collieries in seven square miles in our area, many connected up underground, and Co-op stores allowed credit, payable quarterly. Most purchases were recorded in a pass book, all numbers by 'share'. In our block of four houses, 7, 9, 11, 13 Bowhousebog, Shotts, the men were all employed in what we now call a psychiatric hospital (then a lunatic asylum) and rents were deducted before pay was received, on a monthly basis.

Spread through the other houses they came from Outer and Inner Hebrides, Stornoway, Harris, North Uist, Argyll (Lochgilphead), Shetland, Inverness, Oban, Fort William, all drawn south to a steadier job, mainly from farming and crofting. Many Irish crossed over for heavy labouring jobs on roads, steelworks and blast furnaces. In Shotts (21 miles to Glasgow, 25 to Edinburgh) the Shotts Iron Co. Ltd., founded 1801, which closed in 1951, employed hundreds in their collieries. Coal wagons had SHOTTS on the outside.

Council houses cost approximately 5 shillings per week rent in 1921 onwards, but by the Thirties had risen to 6 shillings or more. My dad bought a two bedroom detached cottage with a large garden in 1930 for £100. The 'feu duty' (ground rent) was 15 shillings a year.

In the Thirties the pig iron was carted to Leith Docks, Edinburgh, on solid tyred motors (e.g. Dennis, Albion, Beardmore), which hitherto had been taken the 25 miles by horse-and-cart.

Mr. Don Clark now enjoys retirement in Cornwall, but his childhood was spent among the mining community in Wales.

I was seven years old in 1930 and grew up with two older brothers and a twin brother; later my parents adopted a 'sister'.

We lived in a small coal mining village, Cwmcarn, in South Wales. My father was a pit winder so he worked above ground. Our home was a small bungalow on the hill side and we looked across the valley to the coal pit. In those days everything was black; now it is transformed into a scenic area.

7

The mines were still struggling to make ends meet after the 1926 strike and we were very poor, but as everyone else was poor it didn't worry us as children. We all had to help with the household chores -- fetching coal, feeding the chicken, etc., and then we were turned out of the house either to go to school or to play. In fine weather we played in the woods or the stream, and in wet weather under the bridge that we called Ramplin.

My mother cooked our simple meals (on Sundays salt cod or salt bacon cut off a flitch which hung on a wall). We kept chickens so had eggs and chicken to eat. The baker delivered bread and buns by horse and cart, and my father grew potatoes and some green vegetables.

Mother looked after us when we were ill, but our family life was with brothers. We were not allowed to go to the pit and from where my father worked he could see if we tried to sneak up. The only time I ever went to the pit was if my father worked on a Sunday shift and I had to take his dinner to him in a basin covered with a cloth.

Many of the miners were still unemployed and so did not get their coal allowance. In the winter we children would watch out for 'copper' Roberley, while the men would steal coal from the coal train, hide it in the woods and then collect it when the coast was clear. We set up a system of signalling with mirrors. This was an exciting pastime!

The pocket money we earned as young children was 1d, which was spent on broken toffee in a paper cone. We didn't have -- or need - toys and the lack of them made us enterprising. It was a happy childhood (except for school) and we had a lot of freedom in spite of the strict discipline of my father. When my parents adopted a sister we found her an intrusion, although she did take over some of the household chores.

As young children we all wore handed-down navy blue suits made of cheap material, which we called 'Bradish' because bradish was used to felt roofs! We wore hob-nailed boots, and Father cobbled them for us. The Church helped to clothe the poor.

Mrs. Lilian Smith was born in Enfield, Middlesex and had an older brother and younger sister. Her family was one of those struggling against poverty.

I was six years old in 1930. Dad worked in the local brickfields, as did most of my uncles; this was seasonal work and most winters were hard moneywise. We had to rely on the pawnbrokers and Dad's gold watch and chain on more than one occasion. The pawnbroker's shop was owned by two elderly spinster sisters, who wore pince-nez and had odd pens -- three nibs so that they could write three tickets at once.

We were never lonely as children as both parents were from large families: aunts, uncles and cousins lived nearby.

Doris Burrows, one of four children, is now living in a bungalow at Hayling Island, enjoying the luxuries of modern conveniences, yet she looks back with pleasure to life in the Thirties.

How different life was in those bygone days; a four storey Victorian house in Tooting, London, where I was born. The house had a flight of stone steps, kept white by using hearthstone -- a weekly chore carried out by my brother, two sisters and myself. There were two attics at the top of the house and a basement below ground level, usually let out to tenants to help towards the £1 a week rent my father paid.

In the dining room there was a beautiful, heavy oak table which had four carved ornate legs, one for each of us children to sit under and polish, to see who could make their leg the shiniest. A crafty plan of our dad's! The floors were covered with linoleum; polishing this was also turned into a game. We would sit on an old velvet cushion, hugging a broom, then take it in turns to push the broom, with the weight of the body on the cushion, back and forth. Or sometimes one of us would rest our head on the cushion and the other children used the legs as a handle. Another of Dad's bright ideas. Work made fun and the result - a gleaming floor.

School was just around the comer and, being a very inquisitive child, I loved school and wanted to know about everything. For a halfpenny we could have one-third of a pint of milk, but sometimes I 'lost' my money: I stopped at the corner shop and bought a bag of broken chocolate toffee. The lady broke the slab with a hammer, weighed it and put it in a cone-shaped bag. I kept it hidden in my desk. I still love chocolate toffee, but it's not quite the same.

Our parents were hard working but not wealthy: work in those days was not very remunerative, so for we four children pocket money was practically non-existent. However, where there's a will there's a way, so we never threw away jam jars but washed them carefully, polished them and then took them back to the grocer's. We were rewarded with a halfpenny for each 1lb jar and a whole penny for a 2lb one. Yes, we did have lots of bread and jam, and syrup - no return on syrup tins, so instead we punctured two holes in the bottom of the tin, threaded enough string through to reach our hands, and so made ourselves excellent small stilts. Our mother was Scottish, so nothing was ever wasted

-- a very good habit which has served me well throughout my life.

As we had no bathroom or running hot water, on Friday nights in winter we filled up a two-handled zinc bath with water and took it in turns to have a bath in front of the fire. On rare occasions we were given 2d and told to go to the bath house, which was situated on an island in the middle of the road. There we gave the attendant the money and waited our turn. We were then ushered into a cubicle housing an enormous bath which had a large mixer tap. The water was controlled from outside: I was always scared it might be too hot! We were allowed just enough and the temperature was usually right.

On a Saturday night, just before the shops closed -- not too early -- I would be sent to the butcher's to buy our week-end joint. It usually went at a rock bottom price at that time of day, but I had to speak up quickly as the meat was auctioned. With no refrigerators many foods would not keep over the week-end. There was no glass window at the butcher's, instead shutters came down so it was more like buying off a market stall.

Frugality was the name of the game and I recall on many occasions getting up very early, especially on a Friday morning, well before school opened, wearing the longest coat in the house to cover my school uniform, in case I was spotted by any of my class mates. I looked both ways before I went scurrying into the corner home-made baker's shop, then I asked very sheepishly if they had any stale bread. It was only yesterday's! I must have looked hungry as I came out with a bag nearly as big as myself full of different shaped loaves. I also asked for two pennyworth of stale cakes and received a big bag full. I rewarded myself for this chore with the pick of the cakes and ate it with gusto on the way home. Not a sign of a school pal! I expect they were still under the covers!

Broken biscuits were also on the menu, especially at week-ends after pay day. Who cared if they were broken! If we took a basin the dairy gave us a big bowl of cracked eggs for 2d.

At the greengrocer's we bought 'compo' - a selection of bruised fruit for next to nothing, and for 2d a bag of potherbs comprising an onion, swede, turnip and carrots. With six pennyworth of scrag of mutton this all went to make a nourishing stew. Vinegar was supplied from a barrel with a tap: we took our own bottles. Shopping today is not nearly as interesting! In those days you had to use your own initiative. It was a very good training in how to become a thrifty housewife and mother in later life.

Above: The Solkhon Home.

Biddy & Jack indoors.   *Rita, Audrey & Biddy in the garden.*

Having been born in South-West London and spent her early years there, Biddy Clark now lives in Cornwall.

I was the youngest of five children: we grew up in a large London house. My father was strict, but kind, and determined to give all his children a good education. We always had books, and he would insist that we 'look it up in the encyclopedia' if we had any questions. My mother had come from a large family and loved to have our friends in the home. We had a large playroom with a wind-up gramophone and we made up dances to the scratchy records we played over and over again.

11

Mondays were memorable as wash days: the chaos in the scullery -- the copper alight, mangle put ready, big galvanised baths on the floor full of sheets. The copper-domed 'dolly' was used to squidge the sheets clean. It was bubble and squeak day, with meat left over from the Sunday joint.

We had a long garden and after our two hours' homework was done we played there if it was fine. My father bought a 'cumback' -- a new game with a tennis ball on elastic which you hit with a bat. In the summer holidays my friend and I camped at the end of the garden, buying and cooking our own food on a fire. When war broke out we were devastated when everyone was asked to 'dig for victory', and my father dug up the lawn to plant potatoes. He also had an allotment.

The Revd. Alan M. Sax experienced the persecution of the Jews at first hand during the Thirties.

I am of Jewish origin and my sister and I were brought up to think that all Gentiles were Christians. My grandparents had escaped to England from the anti-Jewish pogroms in Russia and Poland. We lived in the East End of London and had personal experience of persecution through the British Union of Fascists led by Sir Oswald Mosely.

My mother had left school at a very early age to care for her family. She could neither read nor write, but she was able to calculate figures in her head quicker than some could do with pen and paper.

Mrs. Juliana Ray lived with her Jewish family in Hungary until 1957, when she and her husband and mother, after the invasion of her country by the Russians in 1956, were able to escape to England.

My mother (Shari mama) was born in 1881 during the peaceful period of the Austro-Hungarian Empire under the rule of Franz Joseph: she was brought up in comfort and prosperity in the midst of a loving, closely knit Jewish family. Then, the First World War changed this cosy family picture, and there was only a temporary improvement during the Twenties and Thirties. My father, Armin, was awarded a medal for his outstanding conduct during the war. He survived, and was able to start a timber business to support his family. My brother Bandi was born in 1912 and a younger brother, Sanyika in 1916, but sadly I never saw him as he died of the virulent Spanish flu.

I was born in 1923, and my early days were very happy ones. Shari Mama had a lovely soft voice and my abiding memory is of her singing tunes from operettas by Strauss, Lehar and Kalman, as well as Hungarian folk songs. In our lounge we had a gramophone with a large horn sticking out from it. The Charleston craze had reached Hungary and often, when I was supposed to be asleep in bed late at night, I heard faint music, so one night I went downstairs and peeped through the keyhole of the door. The furniture had been heaped into the middle of the room, with the carpet rolled up, and my parents and their friends were jumping around the edges of the room. Their feet were twisting to wild music blaring out from the gramophone. I was stunned! Fancy grown-ups behaving like that. When I complained about it to my brother, he just shrugged his shoulders and said they needed their amusements too!

I used to have my evening meal earlier than my parents and when I was in bed Shari Mama would either tell me a story or read to me from a Hungarian or German book. She usually stopped at an exciting point in a chapter, so that I would want to complete the story myself, which I did. My father usually returned from his Club whilst I was reading and he brought me a bar of chocolate, which I enjoyed eating whilst I read.

Being the daughter of a Scottish minister, Mrs. Jessie A. Lintern, now living in Essex, had a number of different homes during her childhood: she also had to cope with the untimely death of her mother when she was just thirteen.

After six years' ministry in a Lanarkshire village, my father was appointed to a United Free Church in Closeburn, Dumfriesshire, to which we moved in the summer of 1930. Our new manse was at Park, one of five hamlets a couple of miles or so from the main village. It was a very pleasant house, with running water in the bathroom and kitchen, though the tank had to be filled by pumping several hundred strokes of a pump in the latter -- a tiring exercise after a bath had been run or a lavatory flushed! Behind the house was a wash house, a coal house, a pigsty, a stable and a byre, plus accommodation for a pony-trap. Only the first two were in use, and I had access to the others with my seven year old brother, playing there on wet days at hopscotch (known as 'peevers'), skipping, marbles, houses, shops or schools.

The lower windows on the South side of the manse had been concreted in to avoid the glass tax of an earlier era, and we used these for tennis practice or, with stumps chalked at an appropriate height, for games of cricket, especially when our cousins came to stay on holiday. The garden was long and narrow, with an orchard at the end, ideal for hide-and-seek, and providing a corner where we could build a fire on which to roast potatoes, cook sausages, or stew fruit.

What had once been a linen cupboard was given to me as my study, the shelves housing my library, the wide window ledge acting as my desk while, as a carpet, I had a lovely Inca blanket -- a gift from our missionary uncle on one of his visits. A large porch abutted the protruding South wing and, where its roof met the house wall, I contrived a secret den in the angle. Armed with cushions and my Inca blanket I used the upstairs landing window as my exit and spent many happy hours there, reading to my heart's content every book on which I could lay my hands.

As a family we greatly enjoyed picnicking, especially when various relatives were holidaying with us at the Manse. From a farmer of the congregation we had unlimited access to fields, woods and a rushing hill stream, where we learned to swim in a deep pool, daring each other to be the first to leap into its chilly water. We collected twigs and dried gorse for the fire, supervised with enthusiasm by my father, thoroughly enjoying what he called a REAL picnic! On the way home we filled our baskets with big juicy raspberries which grew along the road sides there. Later there would be brambles to pick and crab apples to collect so, with fruit from our orchard, our larder was always well stocked with home-made jams and jellies. At the beginning of November it was with great pride that my best friend and I sallied forth with our tray of scarlet poppies and our 'Poppy Day' collecting tin, calling in at farms and cottages over a five mile route. There was always a delicious smell of fresh baking when a door opened, and we were never sent on our way without some tasty morsel. Occasionally we caught up with a farmer's cart and gratefully accepted the cheerful offer of a lift back to Park. How happy, carefree and safe were those days of the Thirties!

One afternoon, my Mama, brother and I were invited to have tea with a very old lady called Miss Shackerley. She was born in 1830, and at the age of seven had travelled with her parents to London to see the celebrations for the young Queen Victoria's Coronation. She had a small but most beautiful home, and I was torn between listening to the interesting conversation and looking with wondering eyes at all the gleaming antique furniture, the lovely china and glass, and the paintings and photographs. Afternoon tea was served by an elderly maid in true Victorian style: I shall never forget taking part in this ritual of a bygone age.

In the spring of 1932 Mama told me that we would be having a new baby in the family about the time of my own birthday in June, and that, as the 'Big Sister', I would be given charge of the new arrival. I was delighted at the prospect, hoping it would be a sister, but sadly neither Mama nor the baby survived the birth. Mama had started a Sunday School Kindergarten the previous year, and after her death I was allowed to take it over. This, in a way, was the start of my training towards my future career.

Apart from Halloween and Christmas parties, the most exciting event in the Sunday School year was the Picnic, which involved a trip by charabanc to the sands of the Solway Firth -- for most of the children their only visit to the sea-side, I can still hear the shrieks they made as my father suddenly appeared, clad in bathing trunks, and ran down into the incoming tide. "Look!! Look!! The minister's Soomin'", they shouted in glee as they leapt about on the sand, seeing he was the only grown-up in the water. Having been brought up with his brothers and sisters in Girvan, he was no mean swimmer.

During the following year I spent some leisure time in the pleasant home of a member of the congregation, who became my father's wife in 1934. It was then that my brother and I learned that we were moving away from Closeburn to a new charge at Colmonell in Ayrshire. We both felt very much at home there in that district of Carrick, with its winding river, moorland hills and comfortable landscape where the folk were friendly and hospitable. It was not until many years later, when researching my paternal ancestry, that I discovered that Carrick was indeed our native land, where our forebears had toiled for generations since the 15th Century, and had served the Kirk faithfully there until agriculture was no longer an economical prospect. In 1940, Father and Mother left Colmonell to take up a new post in Renfrewshire, and my days in Ayrshire came to an end for that decade.

Ian MacLachlan is now living in Glencruitten, Oban, and was born and bred in that area of Scotland.

We were a very united, happy family - a real clan! My Granny lived to be ninety-four. In her later years her memory failed and she would wander down the village, into her former home, and sit by the fire, quite unconcerned. Then someone would take her back home, where she lived happily with her daughter and two sons. No Granny farms in those days!

We all spoke Gaelic; English was only spoken when non-Gaels were present, but we could not read the Gaelic in our household. My father's English improved as more English was spoken. He would say he "put the cart before the horse", e.g. "It's fine the day".

Mrs. Joan MacLachlan, now living in Oban, describes the difficulties faced by a widow trying to bring up a family on a small pension in Nottingham during the Thirties.

My father died in 1929, aged forty-two, when I was thirteen. As we entered the Thirties my mother had a Police pension of 10 shillings, plus 5 shillings each for my younger brother Raymond and me. My older brother Bernard took a post as a psychiatric nurse, living in, and received 25 shillings weekly: he gave my mother 14 shillings for rent and 6 shillings for coal, keeping 5 shillings for himself. He earned a little extra by playing the violin in the hospital band for the patients' dances.

He helped us long after he married in 1936. When I went for a College interview in London he paid for a new coat for me - a grey trench coat, which cost 8/11d by mail order. When I was sixteen the Police pension stopped. My mother heard of a local fund to help the needy. She explained her case to a Doctor who was in charge of the fund and was told, "Mrs. Chambers, you must cut your coat according to your cloth." She never forgot that rebuke, but we struggled on and I stayed at school.

In spite of this, I was never conscious of any class distinction. My mother cleaned two mornings a week for better off neighbours, and earned half-a-crown (2/6d) a time. Sometimes we got the pickings from the rich man's table, but we never felt inferior.

My mother managed to keep on my piano lessons, so we had family sing-songs. My brother brought home hospital friends, one of whom was a good pianist. We never had a radio but went to a neighbour's to listen in; we were with her when Edward VIII made his abdication speech -- very moving.

Mr. Barclay Hankin's father died when he was young, but through the perseverance of his mother he was able to go to Christ's Hospital, and is now a Donation Governor of that school.

I was four when my father died. My mother had no money and no job. In those days many intelligent women had no special training, but she could cook and keep house. She obtained a job as housekeeper at a little Kindergarten School in Wandsworth. Her salary was £50 per annum, but she could live in and I could be educated and accommodated free. The headmistress was a Miss Collard, Froebal trained, strict but very forward looking. Meals were with her and one other mistress. It was jam or butter, never both! We were near the prison and used to see prisoners on outdoor working parties, with broad arrows on their prison clothes. Miss Collard was very kind and took us for picnics in her Trojan car. This make produced a peculiar popping sound and had a starting lever inside the car, so that women could avoid having to crank it with a handle outside: there was no self starter. We were very happy there.

When I was about seven, my mother began to seek a presentation for me to Christ's Hospital. Unless you were of high academic standard or qualified for one of the other entry methods, a presentation was the best way in, but it was not easy to obtain. Mother wrote to numerous Donation Governors. Some replied saying they already had someone in mind: some did not reply at all. If an address was conceivably within walking range (and we walked long distances in those days), we would deliver the letter to save the stamp! Entry to the school for presentees was then at nine years. By the time I was over eight my mother was getting desperate, so naturally let her friends know the position. One such was a Mrs. Saunders, whose husband was a Fellow of the London Zoo. On a Sunday the zoo was open only to Fellows and their guests, and we were occasionally invited to lunch on my mother's day off in the 'Fellows' enclosure, followed by special visits to elephants, lions, giraffes, snakes and, best of all, the Chimpanzees Tea Party! Mrs. Saunders was a guest one day at a Ladies' lunch given in London by a Mrs. Bridgewater. To her great embarrassment a row broke out between two other guests. Mrs. Saunders considered how to calm things down. She had met my mother a few days before, so managed to change the subject to Christ's Hospital and my mother's need to get me accepted. When the guests were leaving, the hostess approached my mother's friend and said, "I have been thinking. I believe it is just possible that my husband might have a presentation in his desk. I will ask him!"

A week later, my mother and I were invited to tea to meet Mr. Bridgewater, who awarded me the presentation. Sadly he died before I entered the school, so he was unable to follow my progress. My mother paid no fees at all for nine years of my education at this famous public school. Many years later, I became a Donation Governor myself and have had the privilege of awarding a number of presentations. I invariably try to seek out a deserving widow of limited means.

Divorce and separation were must less common in the Thirties, when there was no free legal aid available, that it is now in the Nineties, yet unfortunately some children suffered the distress of a split up between their parents and Mrs. Hazel Rolf was one of these.

In 1930 we were living at Rosehill, 81 Hamilton Road, Reading. The detached double-fronted house had a large garden. There were four big rooms and a scullery downstairs, and one of these on the North side was fitted with shelves for storing fruit from the twenty fruit trees. Upstairs there were four spacious bedrooms and a bathroom round a large landing. There was no wash basin in the bathroom but we had a china basin on a table for washing. All this was for a rent of a £1 a week, plus 11/- rates, but of course there were no modern conveniences, only gas lights and a black coal range in the kitchen.

The front garden had a large conker tree and a privet hedge. We soon made a hole in it so that we could push through and save a few yards walking to the back gates. 'Rosehill' was an apt name for the house, for round the back lawn were many rose trees between the fruit trees, with masses of daffodils and jonquils underneath. We often took bunches of them and bags of fruit when we went visiting.

Dad was going out a lot in the evenings, giving football lectures, and sometimes staying away all night. Mum found he was staying at Hungerford with a school mistress' family and soon visited them: they were surprised to learn he was married. The woman was sent away to her sister's and later wrote Mum a letter of apology. In 1931 Dad moved us to a rented house at Burghfield Common, called 'Hillside', on Clay Hill. There were only a few houses and nearby was a market garden with fruit bushes and about 500 chickens and greenhouses for tomatoes. It was delightful there in the summer, especially for us children, as there were all the woods and Common to play in. We went swimming in the pond on the Common when Mum had time to take us; for her it was hard work, with only a pump for water just inside the back door, no drainage, and the toilet in a shed in the garden. There was also a rainwater tank let into the ground for all washing purposes -- we let down a bucket on a rope. The actual well was never dry, even when those in the village were. The house was detached, with four rooms downstairs and three up. At the back was the kitchen with a stone sink -- no pipes -- a black coal range, a single oil gas stove, and also another room with a coal range. Some days, when the wind was in the wrong direction neither stove was hot enough for cooking, and saucepans were put on the open fire, thus become very black. It was depressing in winter, especially when rain drummed down on the corrugated iron roof of the back porch, and it was hard to keep warm. There was a large garden, about three quarters of an acre, enriched when Dad emptied the sewage bucket. It was enclosed by a high privet hedge.

The next year (1933) things were again unsettled with our parents. In the summer I remember the family came by car to take me out for the day, Whit Monday, at Hertford. We had a picnic

and the parents hardly spoke. Mum was pregnant and not enjoying the hot weather. The summer was very hot but Mum
sometimes managed to take us to the pond. Often she had her
sewing machine in the garden and made baby clothes. Of course
we were not told of the coming baby, but it was obvious. A row
broke out when it was time for me to return to Christ's Hospital
at the end of September. Mum must have said she could not take
me up to London by train and persuaded Dad to hire a local driver
to take us.

Dad enjoyed living in the country, but he had the car and drove
to work in Reading every day, only coming home when it suited
him. Sometimes we went in the car on Saturdays to shop, other
times we used a local private bus, 6d return from the main road.

My brother Alan was born on 6 November at the house. Mum
wrote to tell me and said the evening before she had walked up
the road to watch the Guy Fawkes day fireworks. When the birth
was imminent Dad went to fetch the doctor (no phone) from Mortimer three miles away but had a puncture and had to change a
tyre. So Alan was born with the help of the local midwife before
the doctor arrived.

When I reached Reading for the Christmas holidays I walked
round by Dad's office in Valpy Street and saw the car outside. I
thought of waiting for him to take me home at dinner time, but as
it was only about 10 am decided to go by bus instead. My mum
met me off the bus and spent the ten minute walk home telling
me that Dad had left home and was living with a young woman.
This news was relegated to the background when I saw the new
baby -- a fair headed chap with nicely rounded limbs. We had a
folding Tansad pram for him and took it on the train many times.
We went to 11 Eastworth Road, Chertsey, where I was born, for
Christmas and excuses were made to friends as to why Dad had
not come. I heard that he left home when Alan was just ten days
old, the first day that Mum was able to come downstairs.

Soon after this our landlord said he wanted the house for his
daughter, so we had to move. My older sister, Vera, was working
at a privately owned library in Reading and the owner offered
Mum the job of managing the branch at the Cemetery Junction
and, in lieu of rent, occupying the house, the front of which was
the library. I was at Christ's Hospital during the move but my
grandmother came and helped. I heard our piano would not go
through the front door so the upstairs sitting room window had
to be removed and the piano hauled up that way. It was quite a
roomy house. There was a garden at the back, but Mum had no
time to cultivate it, with Alan still a baby and the library open

from 9 am to 7 pm, including Saturdays, but Wednesday was half day closing.

First she employed Mrs. Aldridge, a retired children's nurse, to live in, but soon tired of waiting on her. Then we had a fourteen year old girl, Barbara Kent, daily. She used to steal our sweets.

It was lovely having all the library books to read in the holidays, sometimes far into the night. The customers paid 2d per book per week. It was handy for the shops and I would be sent out to buy cakes for staff tea -- fancy cakes at 7 for 6d.

At this time Mum arranged a legal separation: Dad never asked for a divorce. She was to receive £3.3s per week, the 3 shillings being for my fares and pocket money at CH and to keep me in the holidays.

We were only at the library for a few months, as Vera decided to change jobs and work for another library. Mum's employer gave her notice to move out. I remember her going to look at houses to rent. I wanted a modern house, but Mum had heard about boarding students at 2 guineas a week, more than for other lodgers, so she needed a four bedroom house to take the five of us and four students. So we settled for 345 Upper Redlands Road, near the Convent. The rent was 17/6d per week and the rates then 5 shillings; there was no electricity, but a coal range in the kitchen and a black gas stove in the scullery.

Again I was at CH during the move but Grandma Lowther helped. Our furniture was old and insufficient, but Mrs. Love arranged for Mum to buy a three piece suite on hire purchase – difficult for a woman to do on her own in those days. Reading University sent three students, after checking the rooms, but unfortunately they were all Jews and needed their strict diet. They used the front sitting room and two bedrooms. We had no wash basins in the bathroom, so Mum took them up jugs of hot water every morning to use on the wash-stands. Bath water was heated by the kitchen range, so it was alight winter and summer, and Mum cooked on it too. Most of the rooms were large and with coal fires downstairs needed a lot of cleaning, and the three steps in the hall meant that meals had to be carried on trays. Stretched to provide for seven people, our bedding was rather sparse, so in winter we had coats on our beds, including Mum's fur coat she had bought in better times.

The students wanted to use electric razors and the lady living next door at No.32 put a wire through under the roof and through our ceiling: she charged Mum 1 shilling a week.

We'd lived there about a year when the man at 32, a Merchant Seaman, gassed himself. Vera, Pete and I persuaded Mum to move there, as it had electricity and gas. We moved during my

Easter holidays, so Pete and I lifted the smaller things over the garden wall at the back. Heavy things we had to carry down our path and up the other one, over tricky steps. We were pleased to have electricity and there was an electric cooking stove in the kitchen, but Mum couldn't get used to it except for making toast under the grill. One day when the top plate was hot she put a loaded tray on to it and the tray cloth and tray were burnt. So we arranged for the Electricity Company to take the stove away. They came at mid-day. When Mum went to take the cold joint out of the oven, where it was put to keep away from flies, we realised that that had gone too. So we had bread and cheese for dinner, as the Company was closed until 2 pm, when I went to fetch the meat.

Our kitchen living room was rather dark, as the window over-looked a sideway with a high wall between the two houses. There was a large wooden dresser with open shelves at the top and cupboards below, so with dust from the boiler which had to be lit every day, the dresser needed dusting every day and scrubbing once a week.

Mum lived there from 1935 until 1971 and it was hard work, with two coal fires and the boiler to light every day while the students were there, and no vacuum cleaner until after the war. The students had four meals a day with a three course lunch and dinner. The Jewish students had their own cutlery, dishes and pans. It was hard work with Alan only a toddler, but tradesmen delivered frequently: milk and bread daily: fish, meat and green-grocery twice weekly, and grocery weekly. There was no money for holidays, and even when the students were away we were busy doing extra cleaning and washing curtains. Without their money we had very little for food or extras and I came in for all the ironing!

Mrs. Virginia Youdale is almost a League of Nations in herself! Sadly her father died of TB when she was quite young, and then one of her five children a little boy of six was drowned, and her only daughter killed in a car crash in England whilst studying nursing at Stoke Manderville.

I was born in France, as was my second sister, when my parents were living in Le Havre near my grandparents. Between the wars life was cheaper in France and we were able to live there comfortably on my grandmother's annuity. Her son, my father, was seriously ill with T.B. Incidentally, my maternal grandmother was 100 per cent Swedish and my grandfather of Swiss origin. My father was born in Dublin, his family having gone to Ireland during the 17th Century; one of his predecessors was Lord Mayor of Dublin in 1840 and 1844. In fact, I found myself stateless when trying to renew my passport in 1948 as my father, who died in 1938 had not opted for either Irish or British nationality under the Aliens Act! Having spent all the war in England I was allowed to be considered a British subject, and it wasn't until an officious French official at Geneva airport quibbled about my status -- not a citizen with right of abode in the UK -- that many months' later, with the requirement of my husband's parents' birth and mar-riage certificates, etc. (he was born in Monaco in Buckingham Palace!) that I became British.

The years we spent in the small village of Cambo-les-Bains just before the war were for me some of the happiest of my life. We didn't realise, as children, the difficulties of our parents, though we knew my father was very ill -- most of the time in the Sanato-rium (Cambo was famous for its TB sanatoriums). Our long summer holidays – 14 July to 1 October -- were spent in Biarritz with friends: I suppose we paid for our board. We were packed off there when my father was so ill and died: he was then living at home. We also spent part of our holidays in Le Havre where my aunt and uncle and three cousins lived in a great big house, not far from the beach in Ste Adresse. We always travelled by train overnight. I went there from Christ's Hospital in 1938, then as war seemed imminent my mother packed us all back to London to my maternal grandparents: we arrived on the Saturday to hear the first siren on Sunday, 3 September 1939.

Everyone was so friendly to the 'petites and anglaises' (the lit-tle English children) in Cambo -- we were the only foreigners except for the refugees from the Spanish Civil War, who could get across the frontier (the Basque speciality is smuggling across the border!). They lived in a large house outside the village, which one night took fire. Exceptionally cold weather froze all the pipes and the firemen were unable to put it out. I always remember this: these poor refugees had to start all over again. We had snow that winter and we were the only children who had ever seen it before!

Mrs. Nina Armour has very happy memories of the village in Germany where she spent most of the early years of her life, before her parents were divorced.

If anyone mentions 'Wickersdorf' to me, it conjures up memories of an idyllic spot where I spent my early childhood from the age of two until I came to boarding school at Christ's Hospital, Hert-ford, when I was ten years old.

ntions 'Wickersdorf' to me, it conjures up memories of an idyllic spot where I spent my early childhood from the age of two until I came to boarding school at Christ's Hospital, Hertford, when I was ten years old.

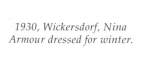

1930, Wickersdorf, Nina Armour dressed for winter.

In later years my father once said to me, "You will always re-member Wickersdorf as something special, because it is the first place you can remember". And so it was. My first feelings of consciousness were experienced here, in this remote Thuringian village bordering on Bavaria. For many years it was hidden away behind the iron curtain in East Germany but then, as now again, simply part of Germany.

Wickersdorf was a small village where hard working peasants earned a meagre living from a few strips of ground between the village and the forests all around. A beautiful land with hills and valleys, meadows and streams. The forests were mainly spruce, but oak, ash, beech and birch could also be found.

I had come here at the age of two when my father was offered a teaching post at the boarding school, which had become quite well known and where, in fact, my father had been sent as a boy from Russia. It was a school on the lines of Bedales, Dartington and Gordonstoun and was known as the 'Freie Schulgemeinde Wickersdorf'.

The village people benefitted from the presence of so many educated men and women, who were the staff of the school. For instance, there was a thriving chess club, whose members met at

'Kammers', the village pub. Many of the men of the village played chess and the women would come along and bring their knitting and listen to the lively conversation that took place there. After the war, when the Communists took over the school, all this stopped and the village was the poorer for it.

From my point of view, it was just a lovely place -- my parents were there and were together and I was happy because there were so many friendly people, children and grown-ups, to make a fuss of me. I soon had some little German friends and was talking German like a native, and English too, of course. My mother insisted on our speaking English at home so that I would speak my own language properly. My father, although he spoke good English, always had a slight if rather attractive accent, but he spoke perfect Russian and German. My mother, whose parents were both English, had been born and brought up in Russia, so my parents often spoke Russian to each other.

My mother taught me to read and write English, and a German friend at the school gave me similar lessons in German. But at the age of seven I went to the village school, where all ages, from six to fourteen, were taught in the same room, a row for each age group. The schoolmaster was the father of my special friend, Ursula. She and I were in the same age group and were usually top of the class - one could say 'row'.

Joining the school in the middle of the year, and not at the usual age of six, meant that I missed out on the traditional practice of presenting the new pupil with a 'Zuckertute' (sugar bag), which was an enormous cone-shaped bag made with brightly decorated card and paper, filled with all sorts of goodies. Photos would be taken of the new children clutching their cones, as big as themselves.

While I was at this school Hitler had come to power, and things were gradually beginning to change. I remember marching with the rest of the school down to the valley, where a swimming pool had been built by the joint efforts of three villages. As we marched we sang songs associated with the Nazis. They were very tuneful and we all sang with gusto.

I remember a bright summer morning in the playground when suddenly planes appeared (unusual for those days). There were three planes, with double wings, like our training planes. Suddenly there was a terrific bang and explosion, and a shower of golden fragments rained down against the deep blue sky. Three ex-pupils of the big school, who were training not very far away for Hitler's 'Luftwaffe', had decided to impress their former school chums. Two of them had crashed into each other; one was killed, the other landed in a field, narrowly missing my friend's mother who was working there. After this experience the mere sound of a plane terrified me and it was a long time before I got over it. Probably, just as I did, there was another sound to make me fearful, the drone of German bombers over London, but that was several years on.

When I was nine, my father decided that I should join the big school, in the first class. The usual age for this was ten and it was not a good idea, as I was not academically ready for it. I was out my depth and felt lost and miserable. Also there were no other girls in my class. Hitler wanted the school to be for boys only; the few girls allowed were daughters of members of staff. There were no girl boarders.

Mrs. Audrey Butler, now living in Cornwall, has had an unusual but very interesting life. An only child, she was born in Yorkshire, then married a true Romany and thereafter lived in a horse-drawn caravan. They had a child and a book *Born On The Straw* has been written about their life.

I was born in a rather isolated Yorkshire village. We weren't rich, but neither were we poor. My father had his own business -- he was a wheelwright. Sometimes my mother took me to see him working. I remember still the smell of clean new wood and sawdust, and the hissing cloud of steam as the metal rims, red hot from the forge, were plunged into water. The fellies (or felloes) were sections of the whole rim of a wooden wheel, on to which a metal tyre was shrunk.

I was an only child and there were not many children of my own age to play with. But I never felt lonely, as my parents were country lovers and at weekends we went by bus to explore new haunts high in the Pennines, going out for the whole day and taking picnic meals and flasks. We were animal lovers so for years we were accompanied by two dogs, who were part of the family, and very often also by one of my boy cousins who lived two miles away. My auntie Lily and her husband, uncle Fred, had eight boys, as they were desperately anxious to have a little girl. But they never did.

We were usually armed with empty baskets to gather whatever was available in country bounty, according to the season: elderflowers for wine and champagne, elderberries for wine, blackberries for pies, bilberries for tarts and pies; incomparable in flavour and delicious made into jam. Picking bilberries was a task for the women and children, for the men found them too fiddly to pick.

Before 5 November we had great fun collecting old clothes to make the guy and saving pennies to buy fireworks and cinder toffee - a bonfire night treat.

In winter time each Friday evening a man came round the villages shouting: "Peas all 'ot!" and we used to go out with a basin or jug into which he would ladle peas (the mushy peas of Yorkshire, the dried peas having first been soaked and then simmered until tender, with some ham bones to give a delicious flavour).

My mother baked all our own bread, but my auntie Lily with her very large family bought hers direct from a bakery. If I was visiting her I went along with one or two of my cousins to collect the loaves. So many were needed we took one or two spotlessly white pillow cases to carry them in.

Our nearest village was Longwood, at the top of a steep and stony lane, known as Ballroyd. The little shop there was kept by Mr. Helliwell and his sister, Miss Helliwell. They were both fascinating, for Mr. Helliwell was totally blind and always carried a stick: Miss Helliwell was a midget. We children always hoped Mr. Helliwell would give us the wrong change - too much, of course, but he never did! Miss Helliwell was even more fascinating: she was no more than 3 feet tall and was very beautiful, with a fresh skin, rosy cheeks, a soft, pleasing voice, long wavy brown hair and very pretty white teeth.

My mother cooked in the side oven and over the fire. At the other side of the fireplace was a boiler, which heated water. In the hearth was a can which held about two pints, called a lading can (I suppose it should have been a ladling can!).

On Sunday mornings we went with my father to see a friend of his who had a huge allotment. We bought our vegetables from him and he always picked them fresh. The great charm for me was the unusual pet he had -- a very old, very large tortoise. It was so huge I could have ridden on its back, but though I loved it and talked to it and fetched it fresh greenery, I drew the line at riding on its back!

Molly Campbell, an only child, spent her early years in London but is now living on Dartmoor.

I lived with my parents in a large old house. None of the doors or windows fitted properly and the house was full of draughts. My mother employed a 'woman to do the rough', but I also had my Saturday jobs. They were to clean the front door brass and also the seventeen heavy brass stair rods; in addition I cleaned the steps up to the front door with white hearthstone, and the step by the gate with grey hearthstone, first washing off the footprints from the previous week. An icy job in winter! Also I used to roll my father's cigarettes in a Rizla machine -- the cigarette papers came in a little book, the glued edge ready for a quick lick when rolled. Then there was another fag ready on the pile.

Sometimes I helped with the ironing. This was done with a flat iron heated on the gas, but in 1932 the Electricity Board offered free cookers to any householder willing to change from gas to electricity. This offer was accepted by my parents and a gleaming new cooker made its appearance. However, we thought the first roast cooked in this oven quite tasteless compared with those previously cooked by gas. We also changed to an electric iron.

Mr. Dennis Thompson recalls the early Thirties.

In the Thirties I lived with my parents in a ground floor rented flat at Chiswick, West London. I was at school until 1936, when I went out into the big wide world to earn my living.

Life in all the aspects I recall seemed to be quite peaceful and smooth-flowing. No doubt that is how our elders wanted it after the horrors of the First World War, then the depression and General Strike of 1926, and the slow recovery from that.

My father worked at Southall: this meant his travelling by the District Railway to Ealing, and thence by tram to Southall. The total travelling time was about one hour each way and this he had done for fourteen years, so in 1936 we decided to move to Southall. My father bought a nearly new three bedroom semi-detached house for £750 by means of a local authority mortgage at £9 per month -- the interest rate, I think, was two and a half per cent. We little knew at that time that it was to be a fortuitous move, as it meant we were ten miles or so further away from London -- and the bombs that were to come!

Mrs. Pauline Thompson lived in the mining village of South Heindley during the Thirties.

In 1930 when I was six my parents moved to an old farm house in a village in West Yorkshire. They required a larger house because, apart from myself, sister and brother, we had my maternal grandfather living with us. It was almost the norm in those days for families to have elderly relatives living with them. My mother was always busy; washing was done in a tub with a *posser (also known as a peggy stick) and rubbing board. Bath time was in a large tin bath in front of the fire in the living room, water being heated from the copper in the kitchen.

My father worked in the mining industry. He was a winding engineman, operating large steam engines which raised and lowered cages of men or coal up and down the pit shaft. He had to walk the five miles to work in snow or icy conditions, or ride his bicycle when the weather was fine.

I often wondered as I grew older how Mother managed to feed us so well on three pounds per week -- less when the pit was not on full time work.

Life was a routine: Monday was wash day, Friday was black-lead day for the old fashioned fire range. Then as soon as we were off to school Mother would begin her baking for the weekend and the week to follow -- bread, cakes, pastries and pies. Coming home from school we could smell the newly baked bread before we opened the front door. It was a real treat to sample a piece of warm oven cake (like a bap) with butter and treacle. All cooking/baking was by coal-fired oven. Winter evenings, lit by paraffin lamps in this particular house, were spent round the fire, talking, reading or knitting or doing needlework. We would play dominoes, snakes and ladders, draughts or do a jigsaw puzzle.

Christmas time was always a happy family affair, with a decorated tree and paper decorations. Our Christmas stockings contained an apple, orange, sweets, nuts and a cracker; other gifts would be left at the foot of our beds -- books, paints, games, a knitted doll, and sometimes new winter clothing such as a knitted jumper, gymslip, stockings and shoes.

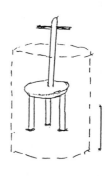

A Posser

The posser went inside a container like a metal dustbin, with the clothes floating in the water. When the posser was turned by hand it was similar to the agitation of a modern washing machine -- but very tiring work.

Mrs. Ruth Meyer's mother was English and her father a Scot, so although she was born in Northumberland where her mother's parents lived in 1924, they returned just two weeks later to join her father. He was employed on the Earl of Moray's estate as a painter. There was quite a contrast in their social backgrounds! She now lives at Chelmsford.

We all lived on the estate until I was eight; my sister Doris was four years older than myself. Our house faced into a square and adjoined a bothy for the unmarried estate workmen. On the second side was the chauffeur's house, while the third and fourth sides were comprised of the stables and garages, where the cabs and traps to take out the Earl and his Lady, were kept. When we met her we had to curtsey.

Their castle was only a three minute walk from our house and some of my earliest memories are of going down to the laundry with Mam to watch the maids washing the linen. I can remember the ladies' maid, Miss Miller, and the housekeeper, Mrs. Reid -- a small old lady who wore a long black cloak and a black bonnet tied under her chin. One day I went to Perth with them and Mam and Doris, in a horse-drawn trap. There were no other children on our part of the estate, but the gardener and his family lived further down beside the kitchen gardens.

At the back of the garages were the joiners' shop and the shed, where Dad kept his paints and all the tools of his trade. Nearly every day found me at the joinery watching with fascination as the lengths of wood were cut and trimmed for use on the estate.

The Earl sold Kinfauns in 1932 and we moved to Doune Lodge, another of his properties. Our house this time stood literally in the middle of fields and was one of two, the other being occupied by a carter and his wife and son, who bore the noble name of David Livingstone. An iron fence ran right round the houses on three sides, enclosing the gardens and protecting them from the Highland cattle, with their huge curling horns, which grazed in the fields and roamed at large. They often congregated at the little wicket gate through which we had to pass. They stubbornly stood there and had to be pushed out of the road before we could reach the path that led down to the gate into the steading (farm buildings), and so through to the main road.

Kinfauns Castle.

This house was an improvement on our previous one and had an upstairs (something new to us). There were two bedrooms with coombed (sloping) ceilings and our bed was tucked under one sloping wall. There was a small fire-place with a black grate and at night in the winter our little oil lamp stood burning on it.

Very occasionally if it was very cold or if we were ill, Dad lit the fire. Then it was lovely and cosy lying in bed with the firelight playing on the walls and the embers falling on to the hearth below. Our feet were warmed by a hot brick wrapped in newspaper, and when we had sore throats Mam left a butter ball rolled in sugar on a chair by the bed. Before going to sleep we scratched each other's back and Doris regularly told me a story which I loved to hear over and over again about 'the poor lady who lived in a vinegar bottle'.

Ruth Meyer with 'Granfie'.

Behind the house and separated by a dry stone wall was the back road, very rough and stony, leading up to the outlying farms and into the hills and lonely, deep Loch Mahiack. At the back of the house were glorious woods, full of the deep mysteries which most of them hold, and a bracken covered brae which in spring put forth such an immense carpet of bluebells that even the more sedate grown-ups couldn't resist picking them. To the right and left were the fields bordered by trees and the pheasantry, where the pheasants were reared and fed by the young gamekeeper. The 'big house', as the estate workers called the Earl's home, was a lovely white edifice standing in parkland, with behind it the famous Japanese gardens. Bonnie Prince Charlie is reputed to have stayed there and to have 'pree'd the mou' (kissed the mouth) of a certain lady.

Ruth Meyer's mother outside their old home.

There were two sinks in the kitchen, one deep and brown for the laundry and the other a shallow one for ordinary domestic use. In the corner stood the old fashioned boiler, and on top of the copper lid, for safety, was the spirit stove lit by methylated spirit, which was a temperamental thing and hissed and spluttered and roared away, but Mam used it a lot for cooking when there was not enough room on the fire. We bathed in a galvanised bath in front of the fire.

Outside, was the dry closet. Later, a flush one was built on to the side of the kitchen and oh, the thrill of pulling the chain and watching the water come gushing out. On the North wall between the houses hung the meat safe, which we shared with our neighbour as well.

In front of our house was perhaps the loveliest view of all, built as it was on a slope and so commanding a great stretch of countryside. In the foreground at the bottom of the field was the steading, consisting of the sawmill next to the curling pond, on which we used to slide in winter. Also there were the joiners' shop and Dad's paint shop, plus the factor's office and many other outbuildings and hemmels (farm buildings). There was a cobbled archway topped by a steeple and clock, which chimed every quarter of an hour. In the middle distance we could see Gartincaber tower, said to mark the centre of Scotland.

Mr. William Findlay, now living at Bishopbriggs, Glasgow, describes his earliest recollections of his family home.

The house was typical of the village of Auchinairn in which we lived. Later I learned that it had an interesting history. It was built by a man called Wark, an Iron Master in the early nineteenth century. The land, plus the right to quarry for the stone with which to build the house, cost him £140. Later he sold the house to William James Findlay (my grandfather) for £150. The house provided three homes, two upstairs and one downstairs, plus a small shop. We lived in one of the upstairs flats and, in theory, collected a very small rent for the other premises. By that time, however, the property was in very poor condition, not through neglect but due to decay. Although property owners, there was no question of my family being anything other than working class. All the income from such property was, invariably, spent on maintenance.

Access to the two upstairs flats was by means of a communal outside stairway. There was no electricity in the house, neither was there a toilet or water supply. The occupants had to draw water from a well in the garden, then transport it in buckets to a large sink which stood at the top of the staircase. Hard work, especially for mothers of young children. Our garden, like most others in the village was well kept, and produced both flowers and vegetables.

There was a municiple golf course at the rear of the house. Golf was popular in the district and in other districts near Glasgow. While Glasgow was only five miles away, it seemed much further in those days of limited transport.

Mr. Roland Thomas is now living in Dawlish, Devon, but was brought up on a Welsh farm.

During the Thirties farming in Wales relied on horse power and human power, and it was only towards the end of the Second World War that we saw the coming of tractors.

The farm animals provided much needed manure for the fields, and muck handling and spreading by hand were very much part of farm life -- as was the accompanying smell! At harvest time everyone jomed in. When the horse-drawn reaper had cut the corn, the children joined the adults in tying and stacking the sheaves ready to be loaded later on to the waggons and made into a stack. It was fun for the youngsters, helping to pitchfork the corn higher and higher on to the stack, or standing on top to help receive it.

Sheep shearing was another busy time: they looked so white and thin once they had lost their long woollen coats. There was no motor transport to take them to market, and the shepherd and his dog, with other helpers, would have to take them on foot. Fortunately, there was not much traffic on the roads in those days!

We had our celebrations, too: weddings, funerals, and shows. On Sundays we would put on our best clothes, the ladies always wearing hats and gloves, and take part dutifully, though sometimes reluctantly, in the services at church or chapel.

I have tried to portray the kind of life we had on a primitive Welsh farm in the Thirties -- which is well within the living memory of many. The changes in our way of living, communication, travel and especially the world of finance, has been immense over the last fifty to sixty years.

My world in those days was devoid of such matters as Eastenders, the stock market, Maastricht - instead, it was a simple life involving my immediate family and community. In those days one was more acquainted with chapter 13 of Corinthians (Paul's wonderful description of love) than the finance pages of the Times.

However, those were the days of my youth. I doubt if the folk of our age felt the same about life in those days: social services and pensions and other benefits were not as widespread as they are today. Sixty years ago the old people still used to talk about the workhouse and all its horrors. How lucky most of us are today.

Mr. George J. R. Tod, CBE, now lives in North Berwick, but spent much of his life in the Middle East.

My father was a Scot. He had gone to Mesopotamia after the South African war and was the Manager of the affairs of Lynch Brothers, which included river transport between Baghdad and Basrah and on the Karun, based on Ahwas. My mother was Italian; she had met my father in 1907 while she was accompanying her brother, who was a doctor in the service of the Turkish Government. His remit had been to check up on the quarantine arrangements, including those for leprosy, and they had come from Hodeida and the Yemen. They were married in the British Consulate General in Baghdad in 1909.

Mr. Donald Brian Vowles, BSc, is now living at Newport but spent his early years in the mining village of Aberfan.

I was born in Aberfan, in the borough of Merthyr Tydfil, Glamorgan, about twenty miles north of Cardiff, in June 1930. At that time my parents lived in Moy Road with my mother's father and some other relatives. My father was one of thirteen children and my mother one of seven; there were three in my family, my elder brother who died in a road accident before I was born, and a sister two years younger than myself.

Not long after my birth we moved to another terrace house in Aberfan, which my parents bought with the financial help of her father. Although houses were cheap, it was unusual for people to buy their own house in the Thirties; they generally lived in rented accommodation as they had a dread of getting into debt. Some people could not even afford to rent and so went into lodgings. These were usually young married couples, but I do remember an older man, his wife and their son in his late teens boarding with us for a while.

We had a small living room, a small parlour and a small kitchen; upstairs there were two small bedrooms and a larger one. The wc was a small building in the garden. It was not until much later in the Forties than an extension was made to form a bathroom and toilet attached to the house. Because of the inconvenience of an outside toilet, it was usual for a chamber pot to be kept under the bed; this was especially useful on a cold and windy night!

My father was a coal miner before the First World War, when he was only a youth. In the valleys of South Wales coal mining and steel smelting were the major industrial occupations for men. There was very little work for women and girls: the latter tended to stay at home to help their mothers with the household chores. Some young girls went into service with more wealthy people. My mother's youngest sister went into service in Bournemouth. It was there she met her future husband and spent the rest of her life in that area.

My father told me that during the First World War the losses were so great that although mining was a reserved occupation, every house with more than one able-bodied man had to supply one male to become a soldier. Normally this was the oldest son in the family, but after a family conference it was decided that my father should enlist instead of his older brother, also a miner, because he was more street-wise and better able to look after himself. After the war my father went back to the mines; he married my mother in 1921 and my brother was born later the same year.

Due to the depression in the Thirties, my father was unemployed for the greater part of the decade. Towards the end of the Thirties he got work as a linesman for Cardiff Corporation Waterworks, to the great relief of himself and the family.

During these hard times my parents did their best to provide for my sister and myself. The dole that my father received was a pittance, but Mother was very innovative and shopped around for the best buys in food and clothes. I never remember being hungry, thanks to her careful management. I ate a lot of bread and jam - strawberry I liked best - but our main diet consisted of soups and nourishing stews. My special favourite was a dark brown fruit cake mother made, which I called crunch, because of the texture of the cake.

My father spent much of his time on our allotment, about ten minutes walk away. When I grew older I helped him there and my sister helped my mother with the housework. Being a housewife in the Thirties was more than a full-time occupation! The women spent much of their time shopping for the best bargains, and they had none of the labour saving devices that make life so much easier for them today. Notwithstanding the poverty of the times, the wives took great pride in their work and many homes were spotless. Mother black-leaded the fire grate and polished the brass and steel fenders (the metal guards in front of the open fire that prevented burning coals from falling onto the floor). She scrubbed the front doorstep so fiercely that quite a lot of it was worn away!

Washing and ironing were very time consuming and it was strenuous work. Mother used a scrubbing board, a bar of soap and a large bowl of water. Ironing clothes was a very primitive affair. The iron was placed on a metal shelf, which rested on the open fire supported by two metal hobs on either side. When the iron was judged to be at the correct temperature, it was carefully used to ensure that none of the dust dirtied the clothes. Some women were so impoverished that they took in other people's washing to earn an extra penny or two.

I don't remember seeing any gas stoves in the Thirties: cooking was done on top of the fire or, if you were fortunate enough to have one, in the iron oven adjacent to the fire. Usually the kettle was boiled on the hob, but if you were in a hurry for a cup of tea it was often placed on top of the fire itself. Many accidents were caused by the kettle of boiling water falling off the coals onto the floor.

In large families clothes were handed down from older brothers and sisters to younger ones. As there was only my sister and myself, Mother had to economise by darning our socks and knitting pullovers for us. An aunt, who was a very good dressmaker, made dresses for my sister and trousers for me. Some of the clothes we had grown out of were sold to a second hand shop if they were in reasonable condition.

One of my uncles was very practical with most things. He had an anvil on which he repaired our shoes, and he also did any plumbing and painting needed inside and outside the house. He was very artistic. His own house had a porch, on the walls of which he painted country scenes.

During the holidays, if we were away from home for a day or two, staying with relatives, this uncle would do some necessary jobs, as he liked to see the look of surprise and delight on our faces when we returned home. We showed our appreciation and gratitude by giving my uncle some produce from our allotment. In general, when money was short, people bartered their services for goods instead of money changing hands. They did not use banks as nowadays; workmen were paid in cash, not by cheque, and they seldom had enough money to put in a bank!

Many families had allotments which they rented from the local council: the unemployed not only worked there, but the allotments provided a social meeting place. The men sat down and chatted outside the sheds they had built to store their gardening tools. My father's allotment made a great contribution to our domestic circumstances. He had quite a large plot and we had many small fruit trees and bushes bordering it. During the late summer and autumn months we picked blackcurrants, redcurrants, loganberries, gooseberries, strawberries, raspberries and other soft fruit. My father also grew all kinds of vegetables and fruit in season. Any surplus I sold to neighbours or, when there was a glut, to shops as well. Mother made jams with the fruit and also used special preserving jars, so that we were partially self-sufficient in fruit and vegetables throughout the winter months.

We had a plentiful supply of potatoes but we did not grow many in our allotment. My father rented from a nearby farmer a long strip of ground on which we planted potatoes. When we harvested them we had a game to see who would be nearest in estimating the number of potatoes under each plant.

Life was quite tough for Mrs. Elsie M. Dickinson when she lived in Yorkshire in the Thirties.

My earliest recollections are of living with my paternal grandparents until the age of three, when we moved into the neighbouring semi which my parents rented. In 1930 I was four years old; the only plumbing was one cold water tap in the kitchen over a small stone sink, with a wooden draining board. As Southport was a hard water area, there was a pump for soft water on the left-hand side. A cast-iron gas cooker was the only appliance my mother possessed. Outside, across a yard and beyond the wash-house, was our toilet -- a bit nippy on a frosty morning!

My father had gone into partnership with a friend in the plumbing business. He worked long hours. I clearly remember the red dawn skies when he took me on the crossbar of his bike to his tiny shop, from where he took orders in the affluent district opposite Hesketh Park. I spent much of my time in the cellar drawing on a blackboard, which Dad had fixed up for me. He drew teddy bears, so I became quite good at drawing bears my-self.

I remember we had an old tiled fireplace with a small fire to keep us warm in winter, and a kettle on a very sooty hob to enable us to boil water to make tea.

Should a customer arrive to place an order, he or she would tread on a bell near the door, whereupon a face would appear through the trap door in the floor, as one of us ran up the wooden stairs. Other days I was taken by Dad to my maternal grandparents' house, where I could play in the garden or help my grandad in his greenhouse.

Mr. Brai Harper was fortunate that his father's employment took him to the South coast of England when he was ten years old.

In 1930, when my father was promoted by his firm to be Sales Manager for Kent and Sussex, we moved from Wimbledon down to Bexhill-on-Sea. It was the start of the happiest and most fulfilling boyhood that anyone could have wished.

We moved into a new house on a low cliff, overlooking the sea, in what was probably regarded as the nouveau-riche part of town, a newly developing area with a scattering of largish houses in every architectural style, from mock Tudor to Spanish hacienda. They all had mod-cons. We had a balcony, four bedrooms (each with wash basin), central heating, large garage and a large car, with a live-in maid. Many of these things, in 1930, were regarded as posh.

I was the middle one of three brothers, and I was ten. My father was a quiet, gentle man, and I cannot remember ever seeing him angry. He was devoted to his work and good at it, hence the promotion. Our newly blossoming affluence did not affect him, but my mother (God bless her soul) was very conscious of it. We boys were constantly told about 'Keeping up appearances' and what 'People in our position' should not be seen doing. Of Yorkshire stock, she was blunt, down-to-earth and full of energy. She loved housework, and everything was spotless and well organised. She knitted, sewed, and made curtains, loose covers and rugs. She made toffee and coconut-ice, ginger beer, chutney and jams. Her pantry was like a little grocer's shop, with rows of 'sweetie' jars full of sugar, flour, rice, etc. On the floor was a large earthenware jar full of preserved eggs.

We had every meal as a family, with startlingly white table-cloths and serviettes, and Dad carving the joint. Tea was possibly the main event during the week and was what, in Scotland is called 'high tea'. In winter, we had a hot dish, plus crumpets or toasted teacakes, bread and butter, jam and cake. In summer there were salads and jellies, strawberries and cream. I made the latter on a cream machine -- pints of it.

2. SCHOOL

One of the most important pieces of legislation affecting the education of children during the Thirties was that introduced by the Labour Party in 1930, to raise the school leaving age to fifteen. This was originally proposed in 1927 by the Hadow Report on Education but it was rejected by the Lords in 1931. It was intended that every child should have primary education up to the age of eleven, and secondary from eleven to fifteen. The School-leaving Age Act was finally passed in 1936, but it included provisions for local authorities to grant exceptions to children who could enter beneficial employment, or whose parents were so poor that they needed the help of their wages. Accommodation would have to be provided in secondary schools for the additional pupils; accordingly voluntary schools were to be offered grants between 50 and 75 per cent of the necessary cost of enlarging their buildings. The Bill was not to be implemented until 1939 -- then the Second World War caused it to be delayed yet again, until the Butler Act of 1944.

The Hadow Report also recommended the establishment of nursery schools; there were already some private ones, but poor families that most needed them could not afford the fees. So some authorities attached nurseries to girls' secondary schools, with the intention of training older girls in mothercraft.

The 10% cut in teachers' salaries, introduced during the economy campaign, was finally restored in 1935, and the building of new schools also commenced late in the Thirties. However, by 1938 63.5% of all children over eleven were in reorganised modern schools. In 1930 17.8% of children aged 14 to 17 were in secondary schools.

Another important innovation in the Thirties was the introduction by the BBC of broadcasts to schools, with special talks by experts to supplement the ordinary curriculum. Education authorities supported this project by giving grants for the purchase of receivers, licences and BBC pamphlets. Educational films were also shown at local cinemas, where the schools were admitted for morning showings. These were much looked forward to by the children.

Many more girls' boarding schools were opened between the wars and became more fashionable. Mostly they followed the traditions of the boys' boarding schools, with spartan accommodation and the popularity of sports.

Mr. Eddie Boyle is now living at Wishaw, Lanarkshire: he gives some poignant descriptions of Scottish schools there during the Thirties.

Borrowing the words of Charles Dickens, we might claim that the Thirties were the worst of times and the best of times for growing up.

The worst of times, because of the depression which had followed on the Wall Street crash of 1929 and led to record unemployment and widespread poverty. Children came to school hungry, barefooted, clad in rags held together by safety pins. Underfed, many were unable to survive childish complaints like measles, mumps and chicken pox, while those stricken by diphtheria, scarlet fever and dysentery were invariably doomed. It was not uncommon for my class to be led to the home of a dead classmate to recite the De Profundus and other prayers for the repose of his or her soul. We did not enquire of what our chums had died, but we did realise that they always seemed to live in the mean streets of the town. Even those whose fathers were working were not all that well fed or dressed: a male trained teacher with a university degree started at £200 per annum and with an annual increase of £10 took eighteen years to reach his maximum. The average worker would take home £2. 10 shillings a week and there were no family allowances.

The unemployed and their families were subjected to all kinds of investigation, especially by the iniquitous Means Test. There was government research to find if a child could be sustained on one shilling a week -- one shilling in those days could buy a packet of 20 cigarettes, 12 boxes of matches or 28 doughnuts; and there was inquisition of older members of the family to ascertain if they were really trying to find work and if they justly qualified for the weekly shilling.

If homes were drab, schools were even drabber -- barrack buildings jostling with grimy tenements, playgrounds that never seemed free of mud, and some of them were located on the flat roofs of schools. Classrooms were cramped, with fifty pupils on the roll. Tiered floors allowed children to see and be seen, and walls were painted in alluring shades of muddy brown and bilious green. On the walls were the two to twelve times tables, and world map with the glorious British Empire set out in bright red. Teachers were not too unkind to their charges but it never crossed their erudite minds that the weans might enjoy a Christmas party or a trip to the seaside or the pantomime.

Scotland, 80% Presbyterian, was a most unusual country in those early Thirties. Catholic schools were wholly maintained by the local education authority and had been so since the Education Act of 1918, when the authority bought the buildings and took over maintenance and teachers' salaries. The church was given the right to teach religion for an hour daily, the half hour before and after lunch, and priests the right to visit the local school: this was probably built next to the church before 1918.

Pupils in High School had to present themselves in class on a certain Saturday morning to sit the prospective Teachers Examination. All pupils were subject to an annual religious exam and the results published for every school in the country. During the scholastic year, Catholic schools closed on Holy-days of Obligation and made up attendance by having a shorter summer holiday than their pals in the non-denominational schools.

It cannot be claimed with certainty that Scotland was unique in that all children were entitled to free education: primary, secondary and advanced, but it is a tribute to the Scots' traditional regard for learning.

Nowhere is this better shown than in the sons and daughters of the working class and of the unemployed who went to university in large numbers. These were sustained by discretionary grants from local authorities and from the Carnegie Bursary, which was awarded to everyone born in Scotland. Nor did they have to worry about prescribed books, for there were free Carnegie libraries in every decent sized town, and Glasgow undergraduates could visit the Mitchell, the largest reference library in Europe. The Thirties saw the first of working class doctors, lawyers and graduate trained teachers: all males had to have a degree and training to teach, even in Primary School.

Audrey Butler had mixed experiences of school.

I began school at Longwood Church of England School, and I loved it. The boys had one play yard and the girls the adjoining one. The boys used to climb the wall, hanging over and squirting us with water pistols, or using catapults to bombard us with acorns. I was happy there when I first went, but when I was eight I had a different teacher, the Headmaster, Mr. Hemingway. He was a sadist. He flogged the poor boys, those with ragged jackets and holes in their shoes, for the slightest excuse. The well-dressed boys escaped punishment. One day he had beaten a poor boy in front of us all until the boy's loud cries subsided into a pitiful moan. I could stand it no longer. I burst out weeping and

41

dashed out of school and back home. When I got there and my mother had comforted me, she told me some exciting news -- we were going to live in a different house, in Paddock a suburb of Huddersfield, and I would be going to a new school. Shortly after we moved from Ball Royd to Church Street, Paddock. Great excitement, for it had electricity, and also a gas stove. But I never forgot Ball Royd and the happy times of the Thirties.

From 1924 until 1930 Mr. Roland Thomas attended school at Llansilin in Wales.

Life was quite different in the Thirties compared to today. Most of the seventy children attending Llansilin School came from homes which had no electricity, no gas, no telephones, no motor cars, no radios, no bathroom, no indoor toilets, no indoor taps and, most definitely, no television. My home, the (old) Fron, was such a place.

We all came to school on foot. I cannot recall any pupil coming on a bicycle or pony. Some children had quite a distance to walk and public pathways across fields were much used -- particularly Cae Llan, where there was a well trodden track from near Peniarth Cottage. Boys seldom wore shoes or light boots; footwear was always 'heavy boots', which had strong leather tops and tick soles which were heavily studded.

The school in those days had no catering facilities. We brought sandwiches for lunchtime. I can recall that mine were mainly jam, bacon, and sometimes sugar sandwiches. All our food in those days was 'organic' because farmers used no artificial fertilizers or chemicals. No hot drinks were available, even in winter, so we had to be content with going to the old fountain and drinking water direct from the tap. Once the school was emptied and locked throughout the lunchtime period and we all had to go outside to eat our sandwiches. The old cloakrooms were open when the weather was very cold or wet.

On arrival at school it was customary to sing a hymn to the tune called 'The Old Hundredth' (Yr. Hen Ganfed). Then followed the marking of the register. School attendance was very important and book prizes were awarded to those who had good attendances. I remember receiving such a prize in 1927 -- it was 'Alice in Wonderland', which I still have.

In those days we had much interest in collecting cigarette cards, always aiming of course for a set of fifty. I vividly recall collecting Players 'Do you know?' cards between 1926 and 1928. Card No.28 was very difficult to get (every set had some rare numbers). However, one of the Wernddu boys became the proud finder of No.28, which I needed for my set. I gave him 2 shillings for this card (the value of four pints of beer in those days!).

Playing bowls, a hoop with a stick or hook, was a popular pastime. Very often we crashed our hoops against a wall and fractured them: the remedy was to go to Wernffrwd Smithy to get Dan Williams to do the repairs. Marbles were occasionally the fashion, but this game did not take on very well as we had no suitable surfaces on which to play. In autumn a game of conkers was played; a good conker tree was difficult to find locally.

There was no central heating system in the school; each of the three classrooms had an open fire and it was the duty of the strongest boys to fill buckets of coal from the cellar and carry them to the classrooms.

John Thomas, the Headmaster, acquired a crystal wireless set in about 1926 and I remember a group of us being invited to his home at Aelybryn to listen to a musical programme. The set had no loud speaker, but in order to boost the sound from the earphones he placed them on a large plate, which seemed very effective.

The school curriculum was concentrated on the three R's - reading, writing and arithmetic. Being a Church of England school, religious tuition was also important. Very little attention was paid to the use of the Welsh language in those days, in spite of the fact that about 75% of the children came from Welsh speaking homes. However, the cause of Wales was well represented in the top classroom, where there hung a large portrait of Sir O. M. Edwards, the great Welsh writer and teacher. He was the Chief Inspector of Welsh schools from 1907 until 1920.

Singing lessons were given about twice a week and John Thomas impressed on us how very important correct breathing was for good singing. The Curwen Modulator was often in use and John Thomas used his cane to point to the tonic soh-fah scale.

It was a treat to be taken to Cae Llan for a game of football occasionally. Strangely enough I cannot every remember playing cricket there.

The cane was in use daily. Minor offenses such as speaking in class were punished by two cuts with the cane, more serious offenses such as being late in arriving for school resulted in four cuts. The really serious crime such as throwing a stone through a window, called for six cuts -- three on the right hand and three of the left. Whenever I was caned at school I never admitted this to my parents, because they would immediately agree with the teacher's action.

Fighting among the boys was quite common and always created interest, with plenty of spectators. In the top class there was a pecking order and the school champion in my days was nearly always one of the Jones' from Wernddu.

Compared to today, school life in those days was quite primitive and rough, but nevertheless purposeful. A good foundation of education was laid down and I look back with pride at the accomplishment and dedication of the late John Thomas and his supporting staff during my period at Llansilin School.

School was not a happy experience for Don Clark.

I was ill as a child and so missed much schooling. My first memories were of being paraded with my brother as twins, followed by being bullied by other boys and being humiliated and caned by the masters! The discipline was very strict and I had a hard time because I was backward at reading, spelling and arithmetic. I longed to join the woodwork class, but because I was poor at the three R's I was not allowed to do the one thing I felt I would be good at. Instead, I helped my father with carpentry work.

There was no sex education. We were not interested in girls -- not even in our adopted sister. A very macho society! My first date was at the age of eighteen, and that was quite usual. Girls were terrified of the consequences of becoming pregnant.

At this time hundreds of people were dying of TB, and when it was discovered that I had TB and pleurisy I wasn't allowed to go to school even when I recovered, and I was thankful.

So I was able to enjoy our Welsh games and outings. As young children all our games were played outside. In fine weather we would dam up the stream and swim or catch fish. We found old sacks, opened up the bottoms and put fine mesh in. Upstream we drove the fish out of their crevices with sticks. If we caught any we cooked them over a bonfire. All our 'toys' we made ourselves: kites and 'batcatty' sticks. For the bat we used a piece of broom handle: the 'catty' was a 12 inch thick stick pointed at each end. The game was to throw catty into the air and hit it with the bat then race round a circle before you were caught. Rather like rounders. Whistles were made from hollowing out sycamore branches and cutting holes. We kicked anything around as a football and rolled up magazines as a rugby ball!

We made sledges in the winter and went bird-nesting in the summer. The challenge was to get crows' eggs from the highest tree. We had to walk everywhere as we had no money, but one year I managed to construct a bicycle out of odd parts I found. I let the rest of the gang take turns on it.

In wet weather we played under the bridge -- cigarette card games and marbles, jacks or knuckle dibs, and whips and tops.

Once a year we walked over the mountains to the fair at Riska. My uncle fought in the boxing booth to make extra money, and we tried to win a coconut or a prize of a big fairground dog made of chalk.

Mrs. Kathleen Stirzaker shares her school experiences.

In 1930 I was just nine years old and I attended the local Church of England School in Exeter. When we were eleven we had to take an examination to see whether we were good enough to go to the Secondary Modern School. I did not pass. I can't remember having any traumas about exams, as children seem to have today.

We had lots of subjects to learn: scripture -- always the first lesson of the day. We always started arithmetic with ten mental arithmetic questions each morning. I found writing English very difficult, as I know now that I had a Devonshire accent (which I have since lost). There was also nature study (botany), reading, for which I am most grateful, drawing (art), sewing and knitting.

Our last three terms at school we did laundry for the first term, cookery the next, and a full week at housewifery the third term. We had to attend another school one day a week for this. We took a few of our own articles to wash, and ingredients for cookery. We could either take our own or buy whatever we made.

At housewifery we were shown how to bath a baby. Their baby was a large doll. We were also shown how to clean a house.

Elsie Dickinson found work was much more difficult in her second primary school at Southport, Yorkshire.

When I was five I began my school life at Holy Trinity Infants' School, near Dad's shop, but if I had to walk from home it was over a mile.

I still remember the smooth, shiny, wooden coloured shapes that we played with in the reception class to make patterns. These were kept in boxes and passed along our straight rows of desks, later to be replaced and returned. I'm afraid a lot of time was wasted playing games with counters when I should have been working. I hadn't learnt a great deal , as I discovered when we moved to a larger house to accommodate my grandparents, on my grandfather's retirement, and I had to change schools. I was well behind the other seven year olds.

They worked you harder at St. Philips. We sat in rows and work was formal. Only the boys were allowed to draw and paint, which I loved; girls had to do needlework. P.E. took place in the playground on fine days. Toilets were at the far end of the playground – a great discouragement in winter. Girls and boys played in separate areas. During playtime we drank Horlicks at 1d per day: on hot days fresh lemon juice was made by the senior girls.

Once each year we had an outing. We could pay 6d a week towards this until the 14 shillings was paid. For this princely sum we had a day out by rail; one year to London, another to Windsor, and another to Edinburgh. I was able to go on all three trips. This price included a hot roast beef lunch, and on our return a lovely tea in white china cups with pink roses on them. At Windsor we had a canal trip to Maidenhead; in London a bus tour to the Tower of London and St. Paul's Cathedral, when I well remember climbing up to the whispering gallery. In Edinburgh we visited the castle, Holyrood Palace and the zoo. The sun always seemed to shine in those days.

At the age of nine I was promoted into the next year's class so that I would be in the correct age group to take the scholarship exam at eleven. This I sat and passed. I only moved to the local High School for Girls. When the Second World War began we shared our school with evacuees from nearby Bootle, so we spent our afternoons knitting balaclavas and socks etc. for the troops. We also had air-raid drills into shelters put up in our playground. I remember learning *Green Grow The Rushes O* with our history teacher: it seemed all wrong that she should know any songs.

Mrs. Biddy Clark lived in Wandsworth, London, during the Thirties. She found that being the youngest in a large family produced its own problems at school.

I was nine years old in 1930 and I attended Swaffield School. Each morning the assembly began with a hymn and a talk by the headmistress and every week we had a moral saying which we repeated each morning: 'If at first you don't succeed, try, try, try again.' 'Do as you would be done by', and so on. I was learning to play the violin and each Wednesday morning our little group had to play the music for the classes to march to assembly.

Assemblies were very important. On Empire Day we had a huge map hung on the wall with the Empire coloured in red (there was plenty of it in those days!) and we saluted the Union Jack.

Also on a Wednesday pupils of our class each had to take a sheet of newspaper to school as we had a 'swimming' lesson in the hall. I remember the difficulty of doing the breast stroke without bumping my nose on the floor!

Discipline was strict and our punishments were a hundred lines or to sit behind after school for half-an-hour with hands on our heads.

Our uniform was a navy blue box pleated tunic, with girdle, a white blouse and black lyle stockings. In needlework lessons we made navy blue knickers. As we sewed we took it in turns to sit in front of the class and read a book aloud -- usually a classic, Dickens, Stevenson or Bronte.

I remember having my photograph taken outside school in my uniform: the payment was ten jam jars!

We learned poetry and put actions to the words so that we looked like a ballet class. I still remember the actions that go with:

> 'Slowly, silently now the moon
> Walks the night in her silver shoon'.

My main memory of school at that age was of the extreme pressure to pass the Junior County Scholarship examination at the age of eleven. I was the youngest of the family and my three sisters and brother had all passed and gone to public or grammar schools, and I dreaded failing. In spite of this I enjoyed school life and did pass the scholarship examination.

Anna Cunningham has mixed memories of her school days.

I went to a primary school (public school in the Scottish sense) close to where I lived. I remember my first day at school in 1932 when I was enchanted to see the piles of books and had no thought for my tearful mother, being completely unaware of her absence when she slipped quietly away. I suffered from the handicap that my aunt had been headmistress of this school and much was expected of me.

My early years in the infant and first primary classes were happy, but it was a different matter when I reached the sub-qualifying class. This had a male teacher who used the horrifying enforcement of a strap for every mistake in dictation. Apparently I used to beg my mother every week to reassure me that I would not be strapped -- and then accuse her of breaking faith when my spelling let me down. I was terrified of this teacher and went through a year of misery in his class. We did not wear uniform, just skirts and jumpers in winter and dresses in summer.

In 1936, my last year in this school, I took part in a competition to see who should become Temperance King and Queen of Port Glasgow. This entailed memorising and reciting a speech on the evils of strong drink. At that time I was having elocution lessons, which gave me a head start over the other competitors, and I was chosen to represent Chapelton School. I then competed against

47

others from various schools and churches and, once again, was successful. In the national competition held at St. Andrew's Hall, Glasgow, my King and I were not successful, but as we were the youngest competitors we received a great ovation.

Mrs Anna Cunningham-1936. Middle row, fifth from right. Chapleton School, Port, Glasgow.

Ruth Meyer and her sister had to walk the two miles to school and back when they lived on the Earl of Moray's estate.

At the bottom of the road in front of the castle we met up with the gardener's children; then we all walked down the long drive to the East lodge gates and into the main road. There were four lodges on the estate, North, South, East and West. A short walk along the main road brought us to the rough stony path which led up through a small glen, bounded on one side by a steep ravine at the head of which was a large pond, deep and dark. The glen came out on to a narrow road opposite Kinfaune Church, then a short walk past some cottages and we were at the school.

By the time we arrived there were quite a few added to our number. Four miles daily we had to walk in every kind of weather. The school was very small, consisting mainly of children from outlying farms and houses. Every dinner time there was hot, peppery soup, dished out in the kitchen of the headmaster's house, which stood next to the playground. The bones for the soup were brought out each day on the Perth to Dundee bus, and we children collected them as the conductor threw them off at the entrance to the glen.

Later on we left that school and started at the Moray School in Perth, which meant travelling by bus, catching it on the main road at the South lodge. At dinner time we caught a bus back to the lodge and in a shed loaned to us by Mrs. Haliburton, the wife of one of the workers, we sat and ate the cooked dinners which Mam had carried all the way down from home for us, in a basin wrapped in a cloth. I hated that school and was glad when we had to move from the estate, so that I could leave it.

So the day came when we said goodbye to the swing on which we had had such fun, adults, children and visitors alike; goodbye to the huge fallen beech tree, on whose smooth trunk we played and rode astride; to the bank behind the midden where we each had a 'shop' and made hats from laurel leaves, which we'd 'buy' from each other, and where in spring a profusion of snowdrops grew. No more going up to the top of the road to collect the milk can, which was left for us on the gate-post. However, there was one consolation for us, as nearly all the other workers were also moved with us. So Kinfauns was sold and we flitted to Doune Lodge, another of the Earl's properties some thirty or forty miles away.

Our new school was fairly small. The headmaster, Mr. Miller, had a funny habit of licking one finger and shrugging his shoulders at the same time. He would stand in the playground or in the classroom and shout at the boys, "I'll cuff your lugs you infernal nuisances". Still, he wasn't a bad master really. Once a week the girls were initiated into the gentle art of cooking by our visiting cookery teacher, Miss Sprunt. We were told to bring an old cup without a handle or cracked, no matter, and we were taught how to make an apple dumpling or Eve's pudding; then we put the mixture into the cups, covered with greaseproof paper, and gingerly placed them in the big fish-kettle bubbling with boiling water on top of the range. After the cookery lesson we had to wash the dirty tea-cloths and dusters in the deep, brown sinks, standing on the wooden duckboards on the cement floor. The school dentist also utilised this room on his regular visits.

While the girls were learning home-making, the boys were in the headmaster's garden being taught the rudiments of gardening. Miss Sinclair was the infant teacher and could be heard away down the street instilling the alphabet into them by putting it in singing. The one that sticks most in my memory is 'T for Tapping Tommy', over and over again in a sing-song voice.

As I was eight when I started that school I missed having her. There was a teacher, Miss Millicent MacNaughton, small, fat and very fearsome! She'd rap our knuckles with the ruler, and often boys got the strap which she wielded with ferocity. Once I was the recipient of it! She used to pull my hair, which was long and curled because Mam put it into rag dumplings every night. At times she pulled my ears, too. Once, when I was standing up reading a sentence which included 'the policeman shouted loudly', she told me to repeat 'shouted loudly'. I understood her to mean that I should say it louder, so I spoke louder. Again she told me to 'shout it loudly', as I thought, and so it went on. Apparently it was my diction which left a lot to be desired: it had nothing to do with shouting it louder. She frightened us all, but at Christmas she became more human and then there would be decorations strung up round the room.

Then, last of all, we landed in the headmaster's class, and we'd hear again how he was going to cuff the boys' lugs. I hated that class as I couldn't do mental arithmetic and dreaded being picked out to answer. At playtime, if we were lucky enough to have a penny or a halfpenny to spend, we'd run down to Jeanie Brock's shop and hum and haw over what to buy; a sweetie potato or dolly mixtures, toffee or liquorice?

On the whole it was a happy little school, and at the end of the summer term, before the holidays, there was the prize-giving and a concert given by the children for our parents and anyone else who wished to go.

Mrs. Kittie Webster, who now lives in Surrey, is one of the few in the Thirties who had the privilege of completing her education with a grand tour of Europe.

I sailed with my mother in SS Baltic, one of the White Star Liners, from the States to Europe, leaving my stepfather behind. We had a friend on the ship who was the Chief Engineer. Later in November 1930 we took off for the South of France and spent four months in Nice, which was very pleasant. It was a busy time there -- before the advent of package holidays, people went to the south of France to avoid the northern winter and then they usually returned home again in the spring. Instead we went on to Rome and were there for Easter.

We stayed in Rome for three-and-a-half months and during that time I sang in the choir at the British Embassy Church. We were very friendly with a priest in the English College, and through his influence we had an invitation to have a semi-private audience with the Pope. That was Pius XI. Before he entered the Vatican he was a well known mountaineer and wrote a number of books on mountaineering. In those days when a Cardinal was made Pope he became a 'prisoner of the Vatican'. Once in the Vatican he did not come out again. However, about that time Pius XI and Mussolini arranged a treaty which allowed the Pope to travel, but he himself never left the Vatican except to go to St. Peter's and also to St. John's, one of the other cathedrals. Then with the war the following Pope did not travel either. It was only after the Second World War that the Popes suddenly developed wings and flew around all over the place.

This invitation to the Vatican created quite a stir in the square where we were living. It was delivered personally by a man in a horse and carriage with the Vatican arms, who drove up and knocked at the door, creating no end of a disturbance, and we had our invitation, which we duly accepted. It was very elaborate and I wish I could have kept it. Then came the day when we went to the Vatican. First of all we were met by the guard in their brilliant uniforms. They looked at the card and waved us on; then we went up some marble steps and met another lot of guards with plumes: presumably they were higher ranking. They, too, waved us on. We went up through corridors and great rooms in the Vatican. We were walking on our own but the guards waves us on, and periodically when we got to a door someone looked at our ticket. Eventually we came to quite a small room, with a little throne. There were about a dozen of us. There was one family, a man and his wife and a little girl, all in white, presumably she had just taken her first communion and was about seven or eight. We had to be in long black dresses with long sleeves and a black veil. Apart from that small family the others were Nuns. I had brought a number of rosaries and crucifixes for my Catholic friends and held them in my hand. Eventually the Pope came in. He was a very small man, all in white with a little white cap, and red slippers that squeaked every time he moved. When he came into the room we all knelt down and he came and blessed us. When he saw the rosaries etc. in my hand he put his hand on my hand to bless them. He spoke to each of us and then sat on his little throne and spoke a few words in Italian. We were the only English people. Then we were duly escorted out. It was quite something in those days.

A few weeks later we had another invitation: this time to a pilgrim mass at St. Peters. That came from the Dean of Vatican city, and we went to that. Again we had an invitation and as we went down the aisle we were sent towards the front. My mother whispered to me "It's like friend, go up higher". Everyone was standing except for two rows in the front. Again we were among the Nuns and had seats in the front, right opposite the high altar with St. Peter's grave beneath it. There were eighty thousand people in St. Peter's that morning. There were just those two rows of seats at the front: all the rest were standing, and those against the walls were holding the flags of the nations they had come from. Presently the Pope was brought in on a chair on a platform, carried by some of his guards. Everybody went wild.

They shouted "Papa, Pope, Father" in various languages and hats were thrown in the air. As I said, we were right opposite the high altar. Throughout the high mass he changed his garments several times, and the priests put on this and took off that. We tried to look as though we belonged and watched what the Nuns were doing, as we did not know the high mass, which was in Latin in those days. Then there came a point when there was absolute silence: I think it was a tribute to St. Peter. Up in the high dome of the cathedral there were men with silver trumpets and they played. It was the most beautiful sound I have ever heard. It was a marvellous occasion- very moving.

That was 1931 and on 1st May all the policemen in Rome changed into white uniforms. It had got very very hot and most people went to the hills. There were a lot of British people living there and in the South of France, mostly retired people or single ladies on small incomes. They could live in style they would not have been able to afford at home. We left Rome then and went to Paris, where we stayed for two months: we didn't get any invitations anywhere but it was a very interesting time. We were there for the annual celebration of the fall of the Bastille, with fireworks and great excitement.

At the beginning of August we came to England and we stayed for some time in Canterbury, where we knew the red Dean: Dr. Hewlitt Johnson. We were there when he had Mahatma Ghandi as a guest and he stayed at the Deanery. He came to the cathedral and he looked so odd. Dr. Hewlitt Johnson was a majestic figure, all in red, and beside him walked this skinny man in a white sarong and sandals. He was always attended by Miss Slade, a disciple of his: they both stayed at the Deanery. We later returned to the States.

As well as formal schooling, George Tod enjoyed that wider education which comes from travelling and meeting people of other nations.

I went to the French Nun's school in Baghdad, and as Italian was often used at home these two languages came to me before English, although a smattering of the latter was inevitable. For us children it was great fun to travel up and down the river on the flat-bottom paddle steamers, particularly the Laqlaq, which plied between Baghdad and Basrah. We also had our own pony and a dog, Maxi, which we all spoiled.

When it was time for me to have more formal education, I was sent to live with my Italian maternal grandmother (Nonna) and my aunt Sylvia (known as Ziella because she was so small) in Bologna, where I attended first the Dorothean Nuns (Madre Sacchi was the saintly Mother Superior) and later the Italian State School, 'De Amicis'.

However, my father wanted me to have a Scottish education and the time came for me to go to school at the Edinburgh Academy. I was thirteen when he took me to stay with his brother, who was running the paper mill in Lasswade. Uncle John's party trick was to put a pencil through the inner part of the cartilage of his nose, where he had a hole by which the Boers had held him prisoner of war, like a bull. His sense of humour was nil and his arrogance overflowed the bounds of modesty: totally different from Ziella.

He ran a very disciplined house; up at 7.30 am, breakfast 8.00, off to school at 8.30, back at 5.30 pm for high tea, prep. at 6.30, glass of milk and biscuits at 8.30, and bed at 9.00 pm. These times exact and to the minute. The whole household seemed to be devoid of any form of love or affection. I was shattered!

Everything was different; the light switches, the door knobs, the sash windows, the language with its unpredictable spelling, even the numbers were written differently. The first time in class when I was asked to read a piece of Latin prose there was a near riot; the boys fell about with laughter, and I can see now the old master mopping his eyes with a large white silk handkerchief, at the same time trying to regain order and saying: "We laugh, but Tod's pronunciation is much more likely to be nearer the true one than ours".

I had to learn fast and spent a very unhappy time, unable to understand what was being said. Nor was I able to express myself for fear of error and consequent ridicule or fear of offending. Holidays were still spent in Italy, either in the Dolomites or in Viserba. As time went on I found my feet in school: having fenced in Italy, I was soon in the school team. I took up shooting, became captain of the VIII and got a bronze at the 'Spencer Mellish' at Bisley for UK schoolboys at 500 yards. Also I was in the athletics team as a half-miler. But I never felt at home: indeed I had no home.

Later my parents came to London and I spent my holidays with them.

Unfortunately Clapham County Secondary School, Broomwood Road, is no longer in existence, but it has a very active Old Girls Association, Quondam, and Mrs. Joan A. Sharp, MBE, (nee Clark) is a member who has happy memories of her schooldays there.

In the Thirties, Clapham County School was held in high esteem not only by the education authorities but also by its neighbours.

So it was with great pleasure and excitement that I learned I had been accepted there: the pride I felt when I first put on the uniform knew no bounds!

There were some five hundred girls at the school and we all assembled in the Hall, together with staff, on the first morning of the school year. After prayers we learned which forms we were to be in. This in itself was a feat of memory by Miss Jones, the Headmistress, who read our full names from a list which gave only the surnames. The Christian names she knew by heart.

It was a very well equipped school, with three large science laboratories on the top floor: chemistry, exuding the inevitable rotten egg smells, physics and biology. I remember, too, the rabbit having been skinned, pinned out on a board with various parts of its anatomy duly coloured and ready for the students to draw. The large art room was on the same floor. Here during one term, each of us had to design a square to be incorporated into a bedspread. The following term we worked it out on linen and finally all the squares were joined together to make a very satisfactory bedspread, which was purchased by one of the girls.

Also on the top floor were the needlework and music rooms. In the latter we had singing lessons and among the most interesting of these was when Miss Thomas decided to produce *Il Trovatore*. Those of us who took part in it thoroughly enjoyed the experience, especially when we performed it to the whole school.

Another activity I well remember was a competition when each form had to choose a play and act a scene from it. There was an outside adjudicator who, after choosing the winner, explained in detail by acting where the losers had gone wrong.

On the first floor as well as the Hall there were class rooms and the geography room, firmly run by Mrs. Linton, and also the library, a beautiful room used only by senior girls. It was a joy to do research work there.

The ground floor had the domestic science kitchen, where Miss Gell held sway, and adjoining the school's kitchen, where lunches were cooked. For a hot meal of two courses we paid 1/8d for two, 3 shillings for four, or 3/6d for five days. Then there was a large gymnasium with wall bars on one side, two hanging booms, a horse, a box, ropes hanging from the ceiling and spring boards and mats. Oh what joy, if we were very lucky, to be awarded a green gym stripe at the end of the year.

We were also fortunate to have hard and grassed tennis courts in the complex as well as a netball court, but we had to go to Wandsworth Common to play hockey.

In the spring of 1937 a small group of us was taken to Paris for a week by Miss Asquith and, I think, Miss Bridge. This was the first time the school had undertaken a trip abroad.

Apart from these activities, there was some very hard work done by pupils and staff, as the results proved. It was a strict regime led by Miss Jones, for whom we always had a great deal of respect and affection, as we had for all the staff.

Looking back, I realise how lucky we were to be educated in such a healthy and happy atmosphere, by women of such a high standard.

Mrs. Ivy Green (Crittenden) is now living at Merrow, Guildford, but spent her early years in south-west London. She is another who appreciated the excellent education she received at her secondary school.

I was a member of the 'Lavender Hill Mob', and my father had a job in London at the princely wage of two guineas a week. My playthings were fivestones, hoops, tops, skipping ropes or dolls, also hopscotch on the pavement. The beginning of the Thirties saw me at Elementary school studying hard for the Junior County Scholarship at the age of eleven. Thanks to a dedicated teacher, I passed this formidable examination which, to a great extent, shaped the future of my academic life.

In 1932 I started at Clapham County Secondary School. The uniform comprised a square-necked tunic (with an awkward pocket hanging from waist to hem), navy blazer, panama hat (velour for winter), black woollen knickers, beige stockings and cream blouse and, in my case, a liberty bodice! I had half-an-hour's walk to school, crossing Clapham Common in all weathers. On arrival we put on house-shoes -- a strap shoe costing 1/11¾d a pair, which we wore indoors all day.

On entering the hall for assembly, I was struck by the spaciousness, and by the beautiful gallery supported by angels. I was moved by the simplicity of the daily service over which Miss Jones, our Headmistress, and her Deputy (both gowned) presided, and which culminated in the rousing strains of *Scipio* on the piano as we filed out.

Everything was so different from the Elementary School, and there were so many mistresses to get to know, but we quickly adapted to this new life as we had a stable, basic curriculum, carefully planned and regulated. I started learning German and was put in touch with a German girl as a penfriend. I still write to her after sixty years although I have only met her twice!

We were made aware of 'those less fortunate than ourselves' and were encouraged to join the Working Party, making articles of clothing etc. for the poorer children of Battersea. These items were put on display in the hall before being collected by the

Mayor. We also helped the families of the Wrexham Colliery disaster and of those lost in the Airship R101.

Prize giving was a very special occasion and was attended by the local M.P. or other dignitary. A tiered structure (known as the 'cakestand') was erected in front of the window, where pupils sat in lofty state, the hall being reserved for parents and visitors. The choir sang, speeches were made and prizes presented; but throughout the whole ceremony ran an atmosphere of loyalty to the school. This sense of loyalty has remained with many ex-scholars up to this day. We deeply respected our Headmistress and her staff, tinged also with affection, knowing that they were dedicated to giving us the best education possible. There was discipline, certainly, and punishment was meted out when necessary. Sometimes we felt that prefects were high-handed in making us use the stairs on the correct side, but we benefitted from the orderly fashion in which we were taught to conduct ourselves and to show consideration for other people.

Cookery lessons were fun, and rice puddings, soused herrings, soups, pies and cakes were dutifully eaten and praised by parents.

Scripture lessons instilled in us a deep sense of religion, an understanding of the Bible and the poetry of its language. We had periods of meditation to consider the meaning of difficult passages, and I feel that in these lessons the seeds of christianity were sown in many of us.

We were fortunate in our beautiful, well-stocked library, where we could study quietly and undisturbed: we were encouraged to enjoy reading and explore new subjects.

Homework was rather onerous and took up a lot of time. My family had no radio, television, or even a telephone, so there were no distractions, but the work laid down sometimes seemed to be excessive. When we had free time, my friends and I walked unmolested through the parks and commons of south-west London, and sometimes round central London itself, enjoying our growing independence.

Sport was important at C.C.S.S. and we played netball, tennis and hockey. Once, whilst I was keeping goal on Clapham Common, King George V and Queen Mary drove past and they waved to us as they went by. Sports days were great occasions and we learned the meaning of team spirit, as well as the pleasure of personal achievement. During break time we often played on the '5/10' tennis practice boards - large boards on legs with net pockets aligned to the flight of a ball across a tennis net, a ball in a numbered pocket scored 5 (reasonable) or 10 (good). If it was wet we stayed in the hall and danced -- Palais Glide, Lambeth Walk, etc.

As we progressed through the school, we prepared to take the General Schools examination, which was a high standard: matriculation level meant a very good pass indeed. It was hard work but we were used to working to attain a good measure of academic proficiency.

Ivy Green's photo of Miss Clay (English mistress at CCSS 1936) The 5/10 tennis board in background.

Occasionally we went on educational outings; one sombre visit was to the local cinema to see the funeral of King George V on screen.

Our annual school service at St. Luke's Church was a moving and unforgettable event, with its atmosphere of sincere devotion. We all gathered as one family with one common loyalty -- *The School.* I always associate the hymn 'I bind unto myself today' with this occasion.

At the end of the Thirties, armed with good matriculation results and a rather limited knowledge of shorthand and typing, I began looking for work. In the face of considerable competition, I was engaged by the Grand Union Canal Company at 25 shillings a week. The background which I had acquired - even the Latin and Greek - stood me in good stead and I progressed upwards in the firm for twenty years.

I look back on the excellent grounding we received in education and conduct. Although perhaps we did not realise it, we were moulded into caring, reliable, responsible citizens, willing to work and to give loyalty to our employer. In 1939, however, we were called upon to give our loyalty to our country, which many of us gave willingly.

Rev. Wendy Berridge, who now lives in Sydenham, London, also enjoyed the very happy days she spent at Clapham County Secondary School. This equipped her for work at the Foreign Office as translator and interpreter from 1940-1959.

I attended Bonneville Road School until 1928, when I won one of the Junior County scholarships awarded by the London County Council and went to Clapham County School. I stayed there until 1935. There was strong pressure from an aunt, who had been to Clapham High School with Phillipa Fawcett, for me to go there rather than to the County. Snob value, I suspect! However my father, a schoolmaster, had heard good reports of the County school, so there I went. I am very grateful that this choice was made, as I owe a great deal to the time I spent there. Miss Ethel Jones was the headmistress, and she exercised a firm, but kind control over the six hundred girls and about twenty-five staff. She was about 5ft nothing, but disciplined quietly with a look.

The atmosphere at the school was excellent. We were a mixed bunch from the middle-class homes of the West side of Clapham Common, to girls from quite poor parts of Battersea, but there was a good team spirit, not only at games but throughout the life of the school.

Each day began with a brief school assembly, conducted by Miss Jones: just a hymn, a Bible reading and prayer, seemed to set the tone for the day. The school had a good academic record at that time. An earlier pupil, Elsie Tostevin, had come first in the Civil Service examination, and she was held up as a shining example. Certainly, the Honours Boards were already well-covered when I arrived.

The premises were good for their day, and the main hall with its balcony and finely moulded ceiling of really fine architecture. Form rooms were light and airy. We had a well-equipped gymnasium, which doubled as a dining-room for those doomed to school dinner! There was also a good library off the main hall, furnished tastefully by parents and the Quondam (Old Girls') Club during my time. The cloak rooms were not quite so good and smelled of plimsolls, naturally sweat and, on a rainy day, damp clothes. We each had to have a pair of indoor shoes, into which we changed each day on arrival, with a suitably marked bag in which to keep them. Everything had to be marked with Cash's name tapes.

There was a fair amount of ground round the school, where we played tennis and netball. For hockey we had to go to Clapham Common, at the top of Broomwood Road. We were very competitive against other local schools, and usually won our tennis matches and most of the netball ones. Hockey wasn't so good. We persuaded Miss Jones that we only lost a tennis match in my last year because we were wearing dresses and the opposing teams shorts! I believe they were introduced the following year.

We all had standard uniforms. Hats had to be worn coming to and from school. I hated wearing a hat at any time, but there were penalties for not doing so. When I became a prefect I had to conform! We went to school from 9.00 to 12.30 and from 1.30 to 3.30. I think on the whole we worked hard at lessons. Life was disciplined.

I remember some of the staff better than others. We had Miss Purver in Lower 2.A2, a rather prim, strict lady who wore her hair in coils and earphones, and taught French. We all started with French, but I don't think I learned much from her. However, in Upper 2.A2 we had Miss Bridge, who was livelier. Each year we had a Mademoiselle from France and a Fraulein from Germany to help us with accents and conversation.

Other staff come to mind. Miss Corbett (botany) and Mrs. Linton (geography); the latter had a quick temper and although very short was like a little turkey-cock when roused. We had a rather boring history teacher (who had better be nameless) and later Miss Merrifield, a stimulating and interesting personality, who made history come alive. My great bugbear was maths, although my father taught this subject and could not understand my difficulties. Miss Landon, the maths mistress, was rather fierce and to her, I suppose, I appeared a bit dim. Miss Rotheram was much more sympathetic!

Music and drama played quite a part in the life of the school and under the leadership of Miss Morgan-Smith we had a good choir and also a verse-speaking choir. I was school pianist when in the Sixth form. I found the elocution lessons useful in my later ministry. Folk can hear what I say even though they may not agree with it! We performed 'Toad of Toad Hall' while I was at Clapham, and the staff did 'Arms and the Man'. Miss Freeth, the English teacher was a great producer.

Left: Arms and the Man 1938. Miss Collen as Raina's father [Ivy Green's photo]
Right: Miss Evans as Raina and Mrs Williams as her mother

Miss Barnard taught Latin, but discipline for her was not easy and sometimes small disturbances broke out, in which paper pellets featured. Another, Miss Cullen, the chemistry mistress, gave us a lecture on behaviour in 4.A2 (she was our form mistress). At the end she said 'Here endeth the first lesson' -- and she had no further problems.

There was great excitement when Lady Helen Asquith was appointed to the staff to teach classics. Many girls had a 'pash' on her. She was a delightful person and didn't use her title. She taught well, too, and later became an Inspector of Schools. I liked Latin and we had Miss Evans for that as well as Miss Asquith. Because my French was better than my Latin, the moment of choice came in 4.A2, when School Certificate and Matric loomed on the horizon. So although I would like to have taken Greek, it had to be German, as the lessons clashed. I owe a great deal to Miss Dallas, the German teacher, who was very fierce and reduced some to tears, but she did drive home the German grammar, and successive Frauleins gave us good accents.

We also had an exchange visit to Berlin in 1934: I was there when Hindenburg died and Hitler had his first Volksabstimmung (Vote). Two of us also had Travelling Scholarships in 1935. I went to Munich and Aachen for three months before entering Bedford College (then only for women), London University, to read Modern Languages. This was all quite advanced for girls in the Thirties.

I owe a great deal to Clapham staff and pupils. I was an only child and was encouraged to invite friends home.

Molly Campbell was fortunate to win a scholarship to a grammar school when she was eleven.

In 1931 I passed the scholarship examination and went to Finchley County School. My parents paid three guineas per term. This school had been co-ed but in the year of my entry it was decided to turn it into a girls' school. However, by the following year the policy had been changed back and again boys were admitted. So the two forms in my intake year had only girls until the 5th year, when a solitary boy, Eric, joined us because he had failed Matriculation. He was unmercifully teased.

Memories of school are dominated by the horror of the first days -- the piles of books to be taken home and covered with brown paper, the mysteries of algebra and geometry, chemistry and physics: the complete bemusement at Shakespeare's '*The Tempest*' and French. Then there was the agony of having to change rooms for each lesson and getting lost in what seemed miles of corridors. Later, of course, things fell into place, but discomfort remains the overall feeling.

Our uniform consisted of navy gym-slips and square necked blouses, black woollen stockings and black lace-up shoes. Later the uniform changed and we had proper blouses and ties. Coloured sashes denoted the House: green for North, yellow for West and red for South. East was missing as East of the school were open fields called The Roughs. We had maroon, black and grey striped blazers and pink gingham dresses for summer, with lisle stockings. And of course panama hats and gloves. Woe betide any unfortunate girl found outside the school without the hat and gloves!

Cookery and needlework were taught by Miss Sturgeon. To demonstrate our ability at run-and-fell seams, the first garments chosen were to be cotton print knickers. Unfortunately, I managed to finish the garment with one leg the right side of the material and the other leg the wrong side. It was hardly worth threading the elastic in! Miss Sturgeon was not remembered for her sense of humour! However, she did read to us during needlework from '*Anne of green Gables*' for some light relief.

In the year prior to School Certificate we had to attend in the Headmaster's study an event called 'The Inquisition'. A few girls waited in the corridor in trembling trepidation for their summons to the Presence. In my case I was totally demoralised as it became clear that I was a completely worthless girl with the minimum of brains, and one by one my subject options were discarded until I was left with the bare minimum of five demanded by the Matriculation Board.

Leaving school at the time seemed to be the happiest day of my life, but perhaps it is in retrospect that the worst aspects are uppermost. On the positive side we did not have to contend with drugs and it was safe to walk the streets. Discipline was fairly applied and our fears were trivial compared to now.

Joan Dobson (née Moody) shares her memories of school days.

As a Thirties' schoolgirl, I went off in the moming to the Elliot School in regulation uniform, which was navy-blue overcoat, pleated navy gym-slip (worn 4" above the knee and always under threat of measurement on arriving at school), and white blouse with school tie. Undemeath in winter we wore itchy woolly vests, with sleeves, navy woollen knickers and long, long black woollen stockings, so long that my vest had to be tucked into stocking tops. The more daring among us retained our stockings with black elastic garters, but the rest had just graduated from childhood liberty bodices to brief suspender belts. Mothers said that garters were bad for the circulation. The outfit was completed in winter with a brimmed black velour hat, with school band and badge. School rules decreed that hat brims should be turned up at the back and down at the front. Such was conformity! In summer panama hat and blazer replaced the velour and overcoat.

I changed to Putney County School after Matric, but uniform and rules were very similar, except for berets in the winter and gloves all the year round. In my final year at school we, the prefects, who sat with staff and a representative from each form in the Senate (quite democratic for those authoritarian times!) managed to persuade the Head that gloves with blazers were quite ridiculous, and this rule was abandoned. Sixth formers were allowed to wear a white blouse and navy skirt as a concession to our advancing years.

Anyone discovered eating in the street was considered quite beyond the pale and subject to punishment. Each morning buns were sold in the gym where a notice was always found, which either read 'No break outside, indoor shoes to be worn,' or 'Break outside, change to galoshes'. The buns were probably a penny (1d) or, if Chelsea buns, then tuppence (2d) A penny in those times has no equivalent now as it would be worth nothing. A large loaf was 2d and a pint of milk 1d. You could buy an apple or an orange for a penny.

Mrs. Margaret Elizabeth Vanderkar (Peggy Edney) was born in Wandsworth, London, in 1919, but is now living at Horley, Surrey.

I started school at Winchester House Preparatory School and when I was eleven won a Rothschild's entrance scholarship to the City of London School for Girls. This meant a ride on a number 26 tram, which I hated, from Battersea Town Hall to Blackfriars, and took about 45 minutes. On the homeward journey, I did homework and wrote lines, if necessary. One day, to avoid being late for school, I took a flying leap as the tram was moving. The weight of my case dragged me backwards and I was pulled along by the tram. My knee was bleeding but I did not dare go home and face Mother's wrath, so was bandaged up when I arrived, shaking, at school. Quite an experience!

At school I met a Muriel de Hamel, who was slightly older than myself. She lived at Wandsworth and was a Guide. It was through her that I met the Solkhon Brigade, Connie Grant and the Lovegroves, who ran the 5th Wandsworth Guide Company. This introduced me to a good time in my life. Mummy Solkhon, with all her loving care, drew my mother into her circle of friends and their activities. I remember a lunch invitation for my mother which had on it: 'And Mrs. Bruce will sing'. Biddy and I, for some unknown reason dissolved into unholy glee and this became a saying among us. Sometimes I got off the tram at Vauxhall to meet Jessie (Jane Madders) and walked with her to her transport to the Addey and Stanhope School, where she was teaching, then resumed my journey or even walked from there to Blackfriars. One day I nearly missed a School Certificate examination because I had been to St. Paul's Cathedral. I rushed into the room all hot and bothered.

We had drawing lessons on a ship on the river Thames, and for netball we had to go to Lincolns Inn Fields -- one of the disadvantages of being at a school in the city of London.

On Speech Day the Lord Mayor, his Corporation and the School Governors arrived in all their glory. The Lord Mayor was very popular because he gave us a day's holiday to celebrate. We all had to wear white dresses, with black shoes and stockings, and wore red and white carnations, the City of London colours. I was in the choir. The school song began with 'Sisters, companions, with voices in unison, hopeful and gay with the vigour of youth'. Afterwards there was the great treat of a cream cake in a Lyons Corner House in celebration of Speech Day. I actually received a prize: Edward Wilson in the Antarctic, beautifully bound with the City of London coat of arms on the cover. To be at school in the heart of the City gave us a great feeling of being real 'citizens', the name given to CLS boys and girls.

63

I remember queuing for hours on the way home from school for the Lying in State of King George V: very impressive. We were told not to go anywhere near the hunger marchers from Wales, but one day I ssaw a whole gang of the m as I was coming home drom school. They were not at all fierce or frightening looking -- rather subdued, grey and spiriless. I was sorry for them, not afraid.

Jessie took dancing classes in the evenings, which many of us enjoyed. On the way home we ate 2d of chip and crackling: the one with the most money paid!

Brai Harper enjoyed school whilst he was living at Bexhill-on-Sea during the Thirties.

My older brother and I went to the County grammar School, on a hill at the back of the town. It was fee-paying (£25 a term), so only the 'nice' boys went there. The others went to the Council Elementary School which, of course, was at the bottom of the hill. We had some scholarship boys, but I never knew who they were.

We cycled to school and usually went home for lunch. If we stayed for school dinner it cost 9d, which is equivalent to about 8p today. The emphasis was on academic achievement, not sport. There was no gymnasium and no P.E. master. We played games on one-half day per week and, although I loved getting muddy and breathless on the soccer field, I hated cricket and used to get the job of long stop, so that I could sit on the roller and read my Modern Boy or Eagle comic. On very hot days, the headmaster would announce that we were all to assemble at Howe's Bathing Station, on the seafront, at 2pm, which was fine. I went home for lunch, then changed and paddled to Howe's in our canoe.

I remember that Trafalgar Day and Remembrances Day were special at school. We all assembled in the hall for the two-minute silence, and in those days everything stopped, even the trains. On St. George's day we went to school in our young movement uniforms -- Scouts, Guides or St. John Ambulance: it was a great day for a bit of showing off. What a shame that our pride in all these occasions has disappeared.

Miss Margaret Willis is now living in Chiswick but spent her early life with her parents and brothers and sisters in Cologne, the capital of the Rhineland.

I was a teenager in the Thirties. The Weimar Republic (1918-1933) gave scholarships to pupils from the age of eleven for education at the fee paying Grammar Schools, I enjoyed one of these from eleven to eighteen.

One form had been together for a number of years and the time had come for some to leave, so we who were going on to A Level studies decided to give them a really good send off. Six of us planned to rehearse and perform a classical German comedy. It was great fun. Looking back on it after so many years I am surprised to find that four of the six involved in this performance were Jewish or half Jewish. There was Eva, the best at French, Mirjam, top in Latin, Ruth, a born actress and myself heading the form in Maths and Physics and Chemistry. We represented 25 per cent of the form. I mention this only to show that there was some truth in the Nazi accusation that Jews being only 3 per cent of the German population filled the professions; but we felt thoroughly integrated in German society and culture. The performance took place in the grand ancestral hall of a medieval castle (Freusburg, turned into a youth hostel) during a five day walking and youth hostelling tour of the Westerweld.

While we were studying busily and happily for our A level exam (Abitur) for another three years, the storm clouds began to gather in the political arena. Hitler made a bid for the premiership and was finally voted in on 31st January 1933. This was a turning point in our lives. I had read his book, Mein Kampf: the whole book can be summed up in that one sentence: 'Fighting the Jew I am doing God's work'. It stood out for me in flaming letters.

Soon after Hitler's arrival there were rallies held in Cologne by leading Nazis in order to explain to the people what the Nazi ideology was: the supremacy of the Aryan race, the duty to keep German blood pure, a preservation of national characteristics, and the value of folklore and work. I went to the one held by Alfred Rosenberg. The people were spellbound, almost mesmerised. Independent judgement had ceased. They rose en masse to give the Hitler salute. I myself not doing so beat a hasty retreat for fear of being lynched by the fanatics. Freedom of conscience, of speech and action, freedom of independent thought had gone out of the window.

At school we took our examinations. For months we had planned and saved up money for a wonderful farewell party, but when it came to it, in March 1933, nobody had a mind to celebrate. We gave the money to charity and dispersed, never to meet as a form again.

Mrs. Jessie Lintern enjoyed her school days and made the most of them.

I had passed the eleven-plus exam in Lanarkshire at the age of ten in 1929, so there was no problem for me when we moved to Closeburn the following year. Wallace Hall Academy was a find red sandstone building, founded by two local brothers who had emigrated to America. There was a primary school close by, which my brother could attend, and a large rectory in use for boarders: it also provided lunches for day pupils at a minimal cost. There were fine gardens and greenhouses, where I was to learn much about plant fertilisation and development. The Rector was Dr. Menzies, a benign and scholarly gentleman, who might greet us in Latin, Greek or Hebrew, according to where his thoughts were at that moment! Not long after my arrival, he stopped me in the school hall to enquire whether I was enjoying my new school and whether I was interested in any other subjects. I said that I would very much like to learn French. Next morning the Doctor appeared in our classroom to ask if anyone else would like to study French. That was the start of a French class for about eight pupils, taken by the Rector himself.

Our walk from Park was about two miles, and in winter the road was liable to flood, either from rainstorms or from snow melting on the hills. This was no excuse for missing lessons! A road worker was stationed at each flooded spot, ready to carry us through dry shod. If the floods had not subsided by the time we were on our homeward way, our St. Christopher was ready and waiting to deliver us on the other side!

When Mama died, the church was filled with beautiful flowers from the school garden and brought to us in Park. Our botany lessons often took place in a greenhouse, where we were instructed on the effects on plants of water, heat, shade and various fertilisers -- a wonderful way of teaching and learning. After Dr. Menzies retired, the new Headmaster put greater emphasis on agricultural and veterinary subjects, and it became quite common for us to be given a sheep's eye to dissect, or to find a cow's complete skeleton laid out to dry in the playground (having first been boiled in our domestic science boilers!) ready for a class to master the names of the bones and the reconstruction of the animal's frame. This was not quite my bent and, after much pleading from me, my father contacted the Director of Education in Dumfries, who eventually gave permission for me to transfer to Dumfries Academy, where I spent four-and-a-half very happy and rewarding terms. I was heartbroken at having to leave, especially as I was due to enter for the J. M. Barrie Shakespeare Prize that term, and hoped later to gain a bursary for entry to Glasgow University.

My next seat of learning was Girvan High School, a twelve mile journey from Colmonell along the coast road, first in an ancient taxi and then a rickety bus, up and down the winding road high above the rocks and down to shore level where, with an incoming tide, the boys delighted in winding down the windows. This meant that we girls received an icy cascade, much to our fury and that of the owner driver who, as well as delivering us to our destination, collected shopping instructions and made deliveries on behalf of sundry farmers and housewives along the way.

My grandparents had brought up their family in Girvan and my father and his brothers had attended school there. My father was left-handed, and developed a severe stammer through ill treatment by a master determined to force him to use his right hand. His copperplate writing was a joy to behold throughout the rest of his life, but at what an emotional cost! His experience was a lesson to me each time I entered a classroom during teaching practice days! I was somewhat taken aback on starting High School to discover that the Head of the Maths Department had begun his teaching career there as a young graduate and had taught one of my uncles. His comment to me became, "Och, you're no' like your uncle, lassie. He was good at mathematics!" However when the Higher Certificate results came out his remark was, "Is this as much of a surprise to you as it is to me?" I must owe a great deal to his teaching skills and experience! On my being awarded the Dux Gold Medal he wryly stated, "Your uncle James should have had that. He missed it by one mark!"

As the only girl among a dozen boys, I greatly enjoyed being in the sixth form that final year: head girl, school librarian, school magazine editor, chairman of the debating society – I found school life challenging and rewarding. I had taken most of my Higher Certificate exams the previous year so, with only Latin and German to come, I had ample time both for studying and for school responsibilities. As editor, I heard the radio announcement of the passing of King George V. During his visit in the Twenties to the Sick Children's Hospital in Edinburgh, where I was a patient at the time, the King stopped by my bed, smiling and saying, "You must be a farmer's daughter because of your lovely rosy cheeks." I quickly informed him that my father was a minister, though we did live next door to a farm! A huge trolley of toys then came to a halt at the foot of my cot, and His Majesty said, "I expect you'd like a doll as a present". He seemed quite surprised to hear me say, "I'd rather have a book, please". This encounter was the basis of the article I wrote that evening for the magazine, as the voice of the announcer was heard to say: "The King's life is moving peacefully towards its close".

As chairman of the debating society I attended my first and only Burns' Supper where, with knife in hand, I delivered the traditional 'Address to a Haggis'. It was also the first and one of the very few occasions in my life when I have sampled that so-called delicacy!

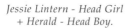
Jessie Lintern - Head Girl
+ Herald - Head Boy.

In 1937 Coronation year coincided with my final year at school. Girvan Town Council decided to celebrate the former by inaugurating a ceremony, the crowning of the Carrick Queen. Being Head Girl of the High School I was given this honour and escorted by herald, pages and maids-in-waiting, perched regally on an immaculately decorated horse-drawn coal lorry. We processed through the town en route from Council Chamber to the Green, where I was duly crowned by the Provost's wife, using a replica of the royal regalia provided by a national newspaper! My fourteen year old brother was at great pains to assure his schoolmates and other interested parties that his sister's 'launching' had not been the outcome of a beauty competition!

A country clergyman's stipend in those days was far from generous, and my father had been persuaded not to apply for an Open Bursary entry form, so I had to forego all thoughts of University: I enroled at a Teacher Training College instead.

Anna Cunningham remembers with pleasure her years at High School.

I moved on to Port Glasgow High School in the autumn of 1938. This was quite a distance from my home and involved a fifteen minute walk. As I went home for a midday meal, this meant a very rushed dinner break. It was a co-educational school, but I think the classes were divided by gender. I took Latin, French, mathematics, science, art, music, English, history, geography, physical education and bible studies. I remember very well my Latin teacher, Miss J. P. Milne, who offered sixpence to anyone who could recite the Pater Noster correctly, and I duly managed this. Having a good memory, I seem to have sailed my way through these first years of secondary school, except for art at which I was abysmal, and was told by my teacher that all I was fit for was hanging out my washing on the line! Even today that remark rankles!

Our mathematics teacher was a fierce gentleman who not only tried to explain the mysteries of his subject but also took us for Bible studies. He had a bee in his bonnet about death and resurrection, and would go round the class asking questions to which we knew we had to give the correct answer, such as, "Gurrl, where do you go when you die?" Answer: "Your grave, sir." "What happens then?" Answer: "You stay there till the day of resurrection."

As I look back I can see that we had some very good teachers who struggled with unpromising material, coming from what today would be described as 'disadvantaged' backgrounds.

Our sports were hockey, netball and tennis. I was commandeered to play rousing marches on an ancient piano for the pupils to march in and out of school, which gave me certain privileges and perhaps explained why I was not given lines for tardiness, as long as I was not late on my day for playing the piano.

My first years in high school happened at the beginning of the Second World War and our lessons were regularly interrupted by practices for air raids and, occasionally, the real thing. Tests were abandoned because of an air raid the night before, which had entailed hours spent in a shelter. I was very interested in what was happening on the war front and recorded in my diary the events of the Finnish-Russian campaign and of the ship movements at the Tail of the Bank, where the Clyde widens into an estuary and does a sharp 90 degree turn southwards.

The Thirties were for me a happy time, growing up in a secure and loving family, sliding effortlessly through school and enjoying myself as a child should, with games and friends.

Andrew J. Blair who now lives in Romsey describes school life at Greenock, where he was born, in the Thirties.

I was born in 1916 in Greenock, south shore of the Clyde at 'The Tail o' the Bank', where it stops being a river and becomes a firth. With the neighbouring towns of Gourock and Port Glasgow, with both of which Greenock marches, the total population is about 90,000. I was born into reasonably comfortable circumstances, as my father was a local newspaper proprietor. By 1930 the town was badly hit by the slump and the family had slid into genteel poverty. I left in 1938 for Dunfermline, a smaller town in Fife.

I was fortunate in that I attended the 'best' (the only fee-paying) school in the town. I think the fees were £2 to £4 a term. Pupils of both sexes were taken at age five through to the age of fourteen or, for those who wanted and could afford to go on, to University entrance.

We had a wide choice of subjects - I remember Latin, Greek, French, Spanish, German and I think Italian. To the age of eleven I was in the top 15% but as the genteel poverty took hold my achievement dropped lamentably. I did, however, achieve a rather basic Day School Leaving Certificate (Higher) in a variety of subjects at the age of fourteen.

Jobs in the depths of the slump were very scarce and at that age the only possibility was message boy (in English, errand boy). So I spent another year at school in the hopes that I might then be old enough to get a job with more future. Vividly I remember sundry adults advising me to 'try to get one with a pension'. A pension! And me not yet sixteen! In 1932 the lot of anyone retiring without an occupational pension was bleak.

George Topping had the advantage of going to a high school, but fitting him out with the appropriate clothing caused problems.

I was an only son, a big boy, hard to clothe, took size 10 shoes when I was twelve, was fitted out with an odd pair of heavy, thick cloth *long* trousers and an odd jacket, and new shoes from the Co-op etc. to go to Wishaw High School in August 1931. All boys normally wore *short* trousers in those days up to about the age of fifteen or so, but I was nearly 6 feet tall.

I was a pupil at Wishaw High secondary school from 1931 to 1937, when I obtained five Highers (A levels) and many Lowers, including maths and science with an extra language, French. We had a periodic French master or mistress, who arranged for many of us, especially in years 4, 5 and 6 to have a French correspondent. Mine was a pretty girl from Auch, in Gers (South) near the Pyrenees. We were in touch again in 1949 after the war, by which time she was a teacher and married to a teacher.

Village life for most of us was such that money was tight. The poorer families could get a free bus/train pass to school in 1931 onwards, as I knew.

My dad earned about £3 per week then, when working. When unemployed he got 24 shillings per week for the three of us at the Labour Exchange. Thus I had a free train pass, Shotts-Wishaw via Holytown, on the old LMS railway until 1934, when we moved over to the frequent bus service (Shotts-Glasgow, via Wishaw, Motherwell, Hamilton, Uddingston and Glasgow). At that time, the fare to Wishaw (adult) was 6d single and 10d return. It is now 95p single!

The general idea of the cleverer students was to go to university if possible, and in my 1937 class of sixteen the split was: four doctors, two for minister, two for local/central government, one vet, four teachers and two girls (farmers' daughters) to agricultural college, and one to engineering.

In spite of financial handicaps, Joan MacLachlan had an excellent education.

Before my father died I had won a scholarship to a small, very select secondary school and had the finest education I could wish. I loved school and still have many of my old school friends. Uniform was a problem as money was short, but my aunt got a wonderful gym slip at a village jumble sale. It belonged to the Squire's daughter and was dark green. We had it dyed navy blue and it was beautiful. It saw me through school, college and into teaching, until shorts became fashionable.

School outings were a problem, too. I could never go to school camps, but often the Head paid for me to go on a day trip, such as to Bournville. I had good exam results and my name went on the school honours board. I was a very popular form captain, and was a record money-earner when we had school efforts to raise money.

A friend and I were accepted as student teachers. We were based at our old junior school and spent two days a week at a training centre, learning handicrafts and elocution. We were paid 15 shillings a week -- a fortune, as my mother's pension never increased beyond the 10 shillings originally awarded.

Meantime my brother Raymond also won a scholarship and went to an excellent boys' school: no co-education for us!

Mr. Barclay Hankin describes the boarding school he was privileged to attend during the Thirties.

Christ's Hospital was founded by Edward VI in London in 1552 'to provide an education for poor and needy children of both sexes'. The boys moved to a 1,200 acre site near Horsham in 1902, obtained from the Aylesbury Dairy for £53,000. Hindsight has shown it to have been a very wise decision. The sale of the small London site eventually paid for the new land and the cost of a very significant part of the fine new buildings. The Railway authorities collaborated with a C. H. station and agreed special rate tickets for boys, staff and parents.

Christ's Hospital Dining Hall.

There were sixteen houses (including two for the Prep) and a total of roughly 800 boys. In addition, there was a huge dining hall, so that all the boys could eat centrally, a fine chapel seating the whole school, Big School (for speeches, school entertainments, prize giving, etc.), the quad, classrooms, science schools, library, manual school, music and art schools, and houses for married masters. The designs arose from a competition mentioned even as late as 1911 in the Encyclopedia Britannica as an example of excellent and up-to-date school architecture. The buildings were surrounded by extensive green fields for playing rugger, cricket, and so on, and a number of fives courts, a gym and swimming baths.

Children presented to the school by a Donation Governor entered the preparatory section at the age of about nine or nine and a half. The Prep taught us how to dress in the attractive Tudor uniform of shirt, white bands (fixed with difficulty with a safety pin), knee breeches, yellow stockings, black shoes and the distinctive coat almost to the ankles, with seven 'silver' buttons and a leather girdle. Very senior boys, aged say seventeen to eighteen and a half, were called grecians, and they had fourteen buttons and velvet cuffs. All this uniform was supplied at no cost to our parents, and we were proud to wear it. In those days we wore it to go home at the end of term and occasionally a kind city gentleman, on seeing it, would make a short conversation and give us a half a crown (2/6d)!

A week after arrival at Horsham new boys were marched to the Music School to be subjected to what was, for some, a terrifying experience. We were to be tested for the school choir by the Director of music, Mr. Wilkinson. We had to climb on to the stage alone, and sing 'God Save the King'. I knew I could not sing and could have saved him the trouble! After no more than two lines at most, Mr. Wilkinson said 'That's enough, Hankin, thank you'! That, effectively, was the end of any musical career I might have had, but I found plenty of other very interesting activities. Those who were more musically inclined entered a feast of experience, for C.H. has always been and remains a school interested in music of all kinds. On Sundays we had an official letter-writing hour, during which there was strict silence.

In the Prep we learnt rugger, played cricket, went to the gym where sympathetic ex-army PT Sergeants taught us to vault horses, hang on parallel bars and so on. In and around the house we collected stamps or butterflies, played conkers and a variety of indoor games. These included noughts and crosses, draughts, 'L'Attaque' (a military board game based on the French army in the First World War), 'Battleships' (a pencil and paper game possibly invented in the school), and the favourite board game 'Dover Patrol', featuring the British versus German navies. I also did fretwork, encouraged by a kindly master. We got used to sleeping in dormitories for twenty-five and, very occasionally, we were ill. Each Matron looked after two houses and supervised maids, who polished floors with Ronuk and mended and stored our clean clothes. If we were off colour we received a dose of Gregory powder, which did the trick but tasted like brick dust! Far more palatable was Cod Liver Oil and Malt, which most enjoyed. I did a little sleepwalking and banged my head on a radiator. This produced three days in the Infirmary (known as the Sicker) to be under observation. I was fine and soon grew out of it. I think this was my only visit there in nine years.

On reaching the Upper school we were assigned to a house of fifty boys, where we would normally remain until sixteen or eighteen plus, according to academic progress. L. C. C. (London County Council) scholarship boys went straight into the Upper and were all clever and probably destined for University scholarships. Fierce competition across all London State schools had creamed off the brightest. Life in an Upper house was regimented and routine, but we were progressing and accepted it all. There were six monitors (i.e. prefects) per house, including one or two grecians. We looked up to all these in awe. Monitors were allowed swabs (fags) and they surveyed the new arrivals with interest to find a suitable candidate. I swabbed for a considerate senior called Weatherston. I had to make his bed, clean his shoes as well as my own, run errands and make, light and clear out his fire in his study. We did not mind doing this; it was part of our duties and, provided the monitor was kind and respected, we gained something in a form of reflected glory. We also knew that one day, perhaps, we might aspire to being a monitor or grecian and receive the same privileges.

The senior monitor was the house captain and to us he was a god. All monitors could allocate punishments, including occasional beatings and, more commonly, 'runs' (round a mile path) or 'changes', carried out in our spare time. Both involved changing into sports kit and back again. They marched us up to Hall for all meals and monitors supervised everything. The house in those days was a 'family' of fifty boys of ages eleven to eighteen and a half. The monitors set an example and trained the juniors in matters of dress, behaviour and discipline, thus helping the house master to control the house, keep it tidy, etc. A good house captain was worth his weight in gold to the house master.

Every day had its routine. We woke to a school bell at 7am, washed in the 'lav. ends' adjoining the twenty-five bed dormitory, and folded our sheets and blankets in military fashion. The mattress had to be arched to air it while we were at breakfast, which consisted of porridge on certain days when there was no main course, followed by a small pat of butter, Prewett's wholemeal bread and tea (with coffee on Sundays). On other days we had corned beef, rissoles, smoked haddock, a hard boiled egg, etc., fixed on a no choice basis for certain days of the week. Occasionally there was a spoonful of marmalade and from time to time a small delicious piece of dripping was supplied in lieu of butter, which we spread on bread with salt. Tea came in large aluminium cans known as 'kiff' cans and was served into china bowls called 'kiff bowls', which were like large sugar basins with the school crest, and you learnt to hold them with one hand. After breakfast we made our beds carefully, to the satisfaction of monitors and matron. A long wooden pole was supplied to 'pole' the beds to smooth the blanket and make a neat crease at the bolster. Spare items were kept in a 'settle', an iron box with an oak lid brought from the London school, beside each bed.

A little later we were marched to Chapel for a short service, which took place each morning before school (on Sundays there were two longer services). We walked up to the first of the morning lessons soon after. There was a break at about 10.15am when we returned to our houses and quickly changed into PT kit and had ten minutes PT on the asphalt outside, in all weathers except rain, under a monitor. Then we changed back again and had a glass of milk and a wheatmeal biscuit before the second two lessons. At 12.15 we were free in our houses until lunch, and we would play asphalt cricket or read the papers in the day room (mostly the cricket scores), play chess or table tennis or browse in the Strand magazine or the Illustrated London News. We formed up outside for lunch parade when we heard the band reaching the Quad. Just before 1pm the whole school marched formally into lunch each day, with the band on weekdays striking up rousing tunes like '*Colonel Bogey*' or '*Sussex by the Sea*'. In wet weather the band was cancelled and we marched to hall in 'the tube', an underground passage thoughtfully provided by the Architects to connect all the houses. Pipes and services were also carried in this tube, which smelt of coke but was warm and comforting. Wet games clothes were dried there in heated rooms under each house.

Lunch in hall for eight hundred boys was an impressive sight. There were long oak tables and forms lined up together to produce seating for each house, with a master sitting at the head. Prior to lunch the tables had been laid by boys performing their 'trades', allocated at the start of each term according to seniority. Junior boys got the less congenial trades like clearing up the dirty plates and putting leftovers into waste pans, which eventually went to the school pig farm. Older boys laid the knives and forks, or glasses, and a fairly senior boy filled the glasses with water from a water can. The hall itself was magnificent and eight hundred hungry boys made much noise! A master earned extra money by acting as hall warden to maintain discipline. He had a raised desk and an auctioneer's gavel to produce silence for grace, said by a different grecian each day from the pulpit. A further knock by the hall warden to start our meal produced pandemonium. Other trades collected clean plates and were served the main course by kitchen staff and vegetables by house monitors, who had to learn to judge the quantities or they would run out! Plates were distributed to members of the house in seniority order, with small boys being served last. There were some well liked meals like cottage pie and treacle pudding with the favourite being 'Soup and Duff' on Wednesdays. The soup was a tasty thick pea/lentil soup with stock and small pieces of left over corned beef added. It gave us the most appetizing meal of the week. Duff could be date duff, or currant duff, equally welcomed despite the fact that Wednesday was a half holiday with cricket or rugger to be played soon after! I think the worst meal for me was 'cold gag' i.e. cold overcooked beef of uncertain colour. Another was boiled beef and carrots. This was hot and watery, of peculiar colour and taste, possibly produced by steam cookery in the kitchens. Several puddings did not appeal, such as dried apricots which had been soaked overnight, which tasted of aluminium! The taste could be disguised a little with custard. Another was tapioca or semolina, known no doubt to all school children of the period.

We were always hungry, but made the best of it, comforted perhaps by statements from Dr. Friend our Medical Officer, who had worked out all the calories! If anything was over the seniors had first option to it. Around the walls were huge oil paintings, one extending most of the length of the hall, and portraits of the Treasurers and Head Masters. The boys cleared the tables, but washing up was done by the kitchen staff.

Afternoon activities depended on the day of the week, the time of year, and the weather. Normally there would be games followed by lessons. Sometimes in wet weather there was a house run of two or three miles to keep boys exercised and occupied. Tea was the last of our three meals at 6pm and did not consist of very much - butter, jam and unlimited bread was the norm, which could be supplemented by your own jam, treacle or marmite. Occasionally there might be a piece of cheese or cake. On the occasion of our Headmaster's wedding (H. L. O. Flecker, brother of James Elroy who wrote Hassan), we were treated to a very memorable and welcome extra boiled egg! One boy I knew had an ingenious way of supplementing his food at tea. He would bring with him a tin of baked beans and heat them by putting the tin unopened in a kiff can full of hot tea. This did not improve the taste of the tea! Boys could supplement their food in the house with cakes sent from home and visits to the Tuck shop, where Mars Bars were 2d (and larger then!). Evenings were occupied by homework in the day room, or various other entertainment on certain half holidays. Prayers were read before bed by the House Captain. In our case this was good practice for him for Ross Hook later became a Bishop! We were quite tired by the time we got into bed. In winter it could be cold in the dormitory for there was very little heating for twenty-five boys. If necessary we warmed ourselves in bed by rubbing our legs up and down to produce friction, and by adding the school coat on top. The bed had boards and no springs, but with a good horsehair mattress. We soon got used to this. We had hot communal baths after games, and a private hot bath once a week.

Rev. T.R. Hine-Haycock,
vicar of Christ Church, Newgate Street.

No account of life at C. H. would be complete without mention of two major events of the year. St. Matthew's Day is in September, and to ensure the annual renewal of links of the school with the Lord Mayor, the City Companies, and the City of London, a sizeable proportion of the school travelled to London. A service was held at Christ Church, Newgate Street, adjoining the old site. (This Wren church was destroyed by a bomb in the Second World War). We marched to the Mansion House for tea with the Lord Mayor, headed by our band, and were entertained in the Egyptian Hall. After that we all shook hands with the Lord Mayor. Those who went received from his newly minted coins... mid-school boys 1 shilling, monitors 2/6d and grecians a guinea. In the summer term, the Lord Mayor and all his retinue paid us a return visit on Speech Day. There was a chapel service and a ceremonial march past with the salute taken by the Lord Mayor. We had a cold lunch in our houses, while the Lord Mayor, the Treasurer, Head Master, Clerk Almoners, Governors and their guests had a special lunch in the dining hall. After lunch we all assembled in Big School to hear the senior grecian give his twenty-five minute oration, which he had to learn by heart, followed by a shorter speech from the Lord Mayor and a concert from the school orchestra, the choir and band members. After speeches, boys would traditionally meet their Governors by the statue of Edward VI, and sometimes be given half a crown or five shillings! If we were fortunate, an Almoner or Governor might invite us into the guests' tea, where there was a huge spread of delicious sandwiches, biscuits and cakes! The visitors had all had a good lunch, so we certainly made the most of what was left.

I shall be forever grateful for the academic work which enabled me to get my Matriculation and to reach Inter BSc level before I left school at eighteen and a half. I have found the detailed instruction in geometry, mathematics, applied mathematics and physics especially useful and, although I did not shine greatly at French, I obtained a good start and found it very helpful indeed in North Africa in the Second World War.

I invariably looked forward to visits to the Manual School (now called craft, design and technology). As a young boy I was taught to forge sturdy pokers, shovels and tongs, which were passed with pride to embellish the firesides of my relations! We went on to other metalwork and woodwork and, as a more senior boy, I opted for engineering drawing where Mr. Usherwood and later Mr. Averill introduced us to wide engineering principles, forming an excellent grounding. I often refer back to things I learnt there, in spite of having later obtained an Engineering degree.

My deep interest in design in all its forms started at C.H. in the Manual school and I still derive huge pleasure from making anything, especially in wood.

I joined one of the four Scout troops, under George Newberry, and that too laid deep and valuable foundations. I was lucky to be one of fifteen scouts who were supplied by C. H. to represent the UK at a Norwegian Jamboree. Lord Wakefield gave money for a superb new Scout H.Q., which was opened in person by Lord Baden-Powell. He inspected us and shook hands with every scout.

The school OTC led to Certificate A, valued later by military selection boards. The Signals section under Bill Kirby taught me in incomparable fashion about flag waving, morse code, clove hitches, cable laying, road crossings, telephones, earth pins and much else besides! All this unwittingly gave me a flying start for war service later in Royal Signals, and also provided me with a wise and trusted friend for life. I much enjoyed most games especially keeping wicket for my house on hot summer afternoons. I was very lucky to have David Roberts and Gordon Van Praagh as house masters in my last two years.

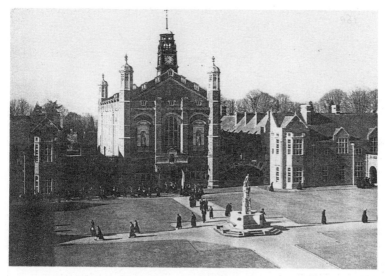

Christ's Hospital Quad, with Edward VI statue in centre.

I recall the visit of H.R.H. The Prince of Wales to open the new science building. He came by aeroplane, which was quite something in those days, and landed in a field belonging to the school. Above all, I relish the joy, excitement and pride in becoming an Engineering Grecian, getting my fourteen buttons and velvet cuffs, and one of the two house studies. This meant a coal fire in winter and the ability to do my school work in peace and quiet. I also remember with gratitude a distinguished Almoner, Sir Reginald Spence, himself an Old Blue from the London school, who invited me and other boys from C. H. to stay in great luxury at his beautiful cottage in Sussex. He once honoured me by taking tea in my school study and was helpful in numerous ways.

It was not all work and no play. There were numerous interhouse competitions which led to intense interest and healthy rivalry. We produced our own house plays and were entertained by the best orchestras, visiting players of high quality, and had numerous lectures, talks and sermons from distinguished visitors. We were certainly not pampered at all and the life made us struggle to survive. My own belief is that Old Blues of that generation developed as a result a strong instinct of what was good and what was right from the school traditions and from excellent and dedicated masters, and an exceptionally deep determination to overcome obstacles in the face of difficulties.

Barclay Hankin, left of the masters.

Mrs. Lis Solkhon (née Bettina Hutchings) has had a very interesting career, including nursing, singing and broadcasting professionally, promoting the Brighton Youth Orchestra, being a Councillor at Brighton and a co-partner of 'Face the Media'; she would agree that she owed much to her excellent education.

I was very fortunate to gain admission to Christ's Hospital in 1930 at the age of nine because, for me, it represented an ordered existence, something which had been missing from my life until then.

I had spent a number of years in what was known in those days as a 'Home School', where you were often sent if your parents were in the forces abroad or in some other profession where you were unable to go home during the holidays. When I was there we had a wide spread of ages, all being taught in one classroom, and of course there was no opportunity for organised games. I had no idea that other children went to schools with large classes, played in the playground or took part in team games.

So for me Christ's Hospital was a revelation -- but also a shock in many ways. I had never worn uniform and, as I was at that time very small for my age, I found the heavy serge tunics, long black woollen stockings and solid underwear quite difficult to get in and out of. We each had a 'school mother' and mine helped

80

me to come to terms with the regimented life needed to manage a house (or Ward, as they were known) of some thirty-six girls, ranging in age from nine to eighteen years. There were eight Wards and I was in Ward Three, but for someone like me who had lived a very independent life, as much the youngest child around, it was all very strange. We had to do everything for ourselves, including darning our clothes, which were supplied by the school. We did 'running around', a version of physical jerks, every morning out-of-doors before breakfast no matter what the weather, and our meals were taken in Hall. It was a lovely building with an organ which was also used for things like Speech Day, when we were visited by the Lord Mayor of London and the Sheriffs, the school Governors and other dignitaries, to the strains of 'The Entry of the Queen of Sheba' played by one of the organ students.

One of the first duties laid upon our infant shoulders as new girls was to learn the Carmen, the school song which was in Latin. We were set a date by which we must be able to perform it faultlessly before our peers, and woe betide any unfortunate who let her school mother down by breaking down during the performance.

Happily for me the school had a good reputation for music, as I was an irrepressible singer and soon got in the choir, which gave me a foundation in choral singing which has stood me in good stead all my life. We attended chapel every day, and twice on Sundays (three times if you were confirmed) and sang many different settings of the services, most of which I could probably sing from memory even now.

Work was demanding, but once I settled down that didn't worry me too much. I had some very odd gaps in my knowledge, but in some spheres I was ahead of the field. We had exams every year and reports every term, and we were fiercely competitive, both individually and at Ward level, no bad thing when you remember that we were in a depression then and we all had to make our way in the world when we left.

Most girls had visits from their parents at least once a term, though we were actually allowed out three times a term. I did not have one visit from my adoptive parents during my whole time at the school, and weekends became times of great loneliness, much of it spent reading. But then I discovered team games!

I had never played any team games in my life, but I found that if you got into one of the school teams you visited other schools, and you also became something of a heroine as you missed prep to do cricket practice in the summer, or paraded around the school with the visiting team for netball, hockey or swimming.

You also had team teas, which were luxurious by the general standard of food! So I buckled down and got into the cricket team, the netball team and the swimming team, and from then on I enjoyed life on a different plane. We wore the coveted school crest on our blazers, only allowed to those who made the first teams, and generally basked in the approval, and sometimes envy, of our peers. All very Angela Brazil!

There were some rules that we would regard as odd these days. For example, we were not allowed to see any daily papers, except the Children's Newspaper, until we were in the Upper Fifth, when we were allowed to read them in the library. There was no radio except in the Ward Mistress' private sitting room, and visits to the cinema or theatre unimaginable treats to be granted as educational adjuncts only. We never saw a man except the Steward, the laundry boy, the chaplain and the doctor, and consequently when the Senior Grecians (the senior boys from our twin foundation at Horsham) came for Speech Day they were the object of yearning for many a young maiden. Spotty they might be, but they were unattainable gods to all but the senior Monitresses.

The staff were all single and when one of them had the temerity to get engaged and then married we could not understand how any man could fancy anyone so old! She must have been all of thirty! Many of the staff must have been in their twenties and thirties, but to us they were as old as Methusalah! When we left and returned for Old Girls' Day we were surprised to find that they were real human beings in spite of being teachers!

Some of the experiences we were exposed to were very forward looking for the times. There was a flat in the domestic science building and towards the end of our time in the domestic sixth (as opposed to the classics sixth or the science sixth) two of us would live in the flat for a fortnight, with our own budget for food, etc. We were excused school duties except for chapel, and at the end of the time we cooked and served a formal five course meal to the Head Mistress and the domestic science mistress. It was excellent training. We were advised to take physics and chemistry for Matriculation, and with no boys around to intimidate us in the laboratories we often did well in the exam.

The school encouraged every one to do the best she could with whatever gifts she had been given. Scholarship girls were looked up to at Christ's Hospital, unlike some outside schools where scholarships were seen as evidence that your parents couldn't pay for your schooling and you were looked down on.

I was very happy during my time at school at Christ's Hospital, partly I suspect because I was not happy at home. I was the one who cried at the *end* of term! Girls who had a happy family life found life there very regimented, but for me it was a haven of security. I knew what was expected of me and I knew that if I delivered all would be well. My early life had made me very independent and in many ways I paid for that because I found myself up against authority. I was often in trouble, but at least it was trouble I had brought on myself.

One of the things which had a great influence on me was the result of the termly interviews conducted by Miss Craig, the Headmistress. We were summoned one by one to the Ward Mistress' study and taken through our term's record. For me this was usually fairly hard going and words such as 'could do better', 'does not fulfil her potential' were often part of my interview. But however much I had been castigated for my sins, Miss Craig always found some positive note on which to send me away, and it is a practice I have never forgotten.

When Nina Armour's mother brought her to England from Germany the problem of her education had to be faced.

After two months, my mother brought me to England and I went to the Erith County School for about two terms. Although I was still unaware of this, my parents were about to divorce and my mother intended coming back to England where we had relatives. An aunt who was a widow and had a son at Christ's Hospital, Horsham, persuaded her to try to get me into the girls' school at Hertford. Mother wrote countless letters to Governors of the school, to try to get a presentation for me, but only one of these had not so far chosen a presentee. Because of the difficulty of getting money out of Nazi Germany and the growing Hitler menace there this governor, Mr. John Harrison, after first seeing us at his office in the city of London, decided to give me a presentation to Christ's Hospital.

I missed the official entrance examination at Great Tower Street, because I had chickenpox, and Miss Craig, the Headmistress, kindly invited us to Hertford to have a special test there. I sat with Miss Craig in her study, while my mother waited in her sitting room. I was good at the arithmetic, but not so good at spelling! But I passed and on the way home my mother bought me a box of Black Magic chocolates to celebrate. I was to start school at Hertford in September 1936.

We returned to Wickersdorf for the summer holidays, and it had been arranged that an aunt would come out to us for her holiday and she would then bring me back to start school. However, it was not to be! A few days before we were to leave, I went down with scarlet fever and was in a children's hospital in Jena, where the Zeiss lenses were made, for six weeks. I finally reached

England with another aunt after Christmas, in time to begin school in January 1937.

The January intake at Christ's Hospital, Hertford, was never very large, most starting at the beginning of the school year in September. That year there were four of us. Miss Craig took us in a group from her house and dropped us off one at a time at the different Houses, and then I was left in the kind hands of Miss Druitt in Sixes.

I remember the open door into the day room, with a tidy row of chairs standing on each side of some long tables. A group of girls was sitting there, chatting probably curious about the new arrival: my general impression was of kindness and helpfulness. It was the custom for a new girl to have a senior girl to be her 'school mother'. Mine, unfortunately, was late in coming back to school because of measles, so various other seniors looked after me at first. I was kitted out with school clothes -- black woollen stockings and all!

I can remember being asked countless times what my name was, and rather wished it was a bit less unusual (Gerhardi). The teachers were very kind and encouraging too, and I soon settled down to a completely different life in England.

One of my early memories of life at C. H. was of my first Ascension Day picnic in a Hertfordshire bluebell wood. I had never seen bluebells, as they don't seem to be a feature of the German countryside, and I shall never forget my first sight of a sea of blue under the new green foliage of beeches and hazels on a day in late May. I'm sure that bluebells now flower a month earlier than they did then, but the joy at the sight of them is still the same, and as then, magical.

Christ's Hospital Speech Day 1938.
Monitresses in coat frocks with detachable silk collar.
Miss Craig   Duke of   Duchess of
Headmistress   Gloucester   Gloucester

84

Virginia Youdale compares her small village school in France to a boarding school in England.

I went to the one-room village school in Cambo-les-Bains. We had a fabulous teacher, Mlle Carricabura. She would not leave the village because of her old mother, in spite of being offered jobs anywhere she wanted. She was severe, but just. I can remember recreations when we had been punished and we had to walk round and round the playground, or write out fifteen verbs in all the tenses! But she managed that class with ages ranging from six to fourteen. I jumped a couple of sections. We had holiday work for a month in the summer, and how I hated it; but my mother stood firmly over me and I won a beautiful cartable for the best holiday 'cahier' (exercise book)! We could walk to and from school, which we did four times a day. We envied the children who brought their lunch, as they lived too far to go home, and could heat their 'gamelles' (tin containers of food) over the stove in the classroom.

Thanks to the Institute of Journalists, who advertised two places at Christ's Hospital, Hertford, England, my father got two of his three daughters accepted for presentations, as he knew he was dying.

It was quite a culture shock, especially as I was very much ahead in schooling, thanks to my marvellous French teacher. The worst shock was having to wear stockings and suspender belts and living in red-brick houses! Our hair either had to be cut short, or plaited -- one plait only, and when someone in Ward 4 (house) was ticked off for wearing two plaits, she turned up with four!

There was no sex education, though biology lessons gave us the bare bones. During the war years these were interrupted by the boys from Battersea Grammar School, who had been evacuated to Hertford. They used the physics and chemistry labs and had to walk through ours. There was much giggling and blushing!

We were not allowed our own books but could read anything from the school library. I got caught reading 'All this and heaven too', and had it confiscated. So of course in the holidays I finished it, but never understood the ban. Magazines were forbidden, but I was allowed to keep on with my French one until the subscription expired.

We occasionally had films in the hall at school. The only one I can remember (as I never understood it and was frightened by it) was 'The Passing of the Third Floor Back'! Music was a great joy, although it was not as well taught in my time as later. Singing in the chapel choir was wonderful. I never minded all the chapel services and now am grateful that I know my bible and psalms so well. Religion became a habit which was transformed into some-

85

thing really meaningful many years later. But the grounding was there.

I loved all the games, especially the summer ones - rounders, cricket, tennis, and swimming, even though they were obligatory. It must have been terrible for those who hated them. Only during the summer term, on Ascension Day, did we have an outing, when we went for a picnic somewhere nearby where we could let our hair down and have a good time. Apart from that, we never went out except on terrible walks like crocodiles. Ghastly! Seniors had special privileges and could ask permission for three friends to go into town or for a walk, but never alone.

The train journey from Liverpool Street Station to Hertford East was horrible! So dismal and so slow. Just before the war, at the end of the summer term 1939, I was authorised, exceptionally, to leave one day early to go to France to join my mother, and I travelled up by myself to Liverpool Street Station. In the carriage a man kept looking at my suitcase and at me, then he said, "Is that your case?" When I said it was he replied, "Oh, I thought it might have been an IRA bomb!"

The onset of the Second World War was the most frightening experience. My mother was already nervous, and that first siren really upset me. My heart still does funny things when I hear the local ones once a month!

Mrs. Hazel Rolf lived in Reading and so was eligible for one of the West Gift scholarships to Christ's Hospital.

My brother Pete and I spent three happy years in Alfred Sutton Junior School, Reading, and my older sister Vera attended the Central school. There were fifty-two pupils in my class, and it was a treat to have central heating in the school. We sat two children to a desk, and these were arranged in tiers with the floor at different levels. Girls were on one side of the room, boys on the other. We were not allowed to talk, of course. Each day began with assembly in the hall, around which the classrooms were placed. Everyone went home to dinner from 12 to 2pm. Miss Chatterway, the Headmistress, was very awe-inspiring, and always wore a long blue dress with a beautiful brooch at the neck. It was she who suggested I should take the Christ's Hospital Examination, and was very pleased when I passed. We also had several passes for Kendrick and Reading that year, so to celebrate the school put on a concert. I was in two items, one a play about seasons and I was summer, dressed in bright yellow muslim. For the song *'Soldier, soldier, won't you marry me?'* I was the biggest of about five girls dressed in white muslin in 'Empire' style, with high waists. We had to trip round the stage singing and presenting the soldier with the appropriate garment. Officials from the

Education Office were present. Then in 1931 I went to Christ's Hospital.

At the end of my first year there I was in the Infirmary with quinsy (no antibiotics then) and Dad and Mum came to fetch me home by car. I was put on a mattress in the back of the car. I was very tired and soon in bed. Luckily my throat swelling had burst the previous day and I was able to eat slushy food. The doctor came from Mortimer and told Mum to feed me up with chicken. He said in my hearing 'Tell her it's mutton'. When my dinner was ready I just could not eat it. I never ate chicken until the Second World War.

In July 1938 I left C. H. in a suit borrowed from aunt Nip; I had to leave behind the uniform that was provided there.

Edward (Ted) Chaplin, who now lives in East Sussex, was a very gifted youngster, passing the equivalent of today's G.C.S.E. with very good grades when he was only fourteen – two years younger that most of his peers. So it was very unfortunate that circumstances in India made it impossible for him to pursue his ambition of going to Cambridge University.

I was born in Calcutta in 1917, where my father was a partner in a firm of publishers which operated in India's principal cities. A brother four years older, and a sister four years younger were also born there. We were sent to boarding schools in England, as were nearly all the children of the British serving in the Forces, Civil Service, commerce or elsewhere. Usually, this was when children were seven or eight years old, but because I had been operated on for diphtheria and was ailing, I was sent care of the ship's captain to join my brother, and I entered Colston's School, Bristol, in 1927. This school was founded by Edward Colston, Bristol's greatest philanthropist, 'as a Hospital for the clothing and education of a hundred poor boys'. Colston endowed the school with a trust fund in the name of The Society of Merchant Adventurers of Bristol, of which he was a member; the Society continues to act as the school's estate governors.

Colston was a governor of Christ's Hospital, London, and the boys of his school wore the same blue robes, wide leather belts, breeches, yellow stockings and shoes with large buckles. When we entered, this clothing was no longer worn, and the school had moved from the forty roomed mansion in central Bristol, where Queen Elizabeth I had held court in 1574, to the former palace of the Bishop of Gloucester and Bristol at Stapleton, Bristol.

Here, the numbers had increased from the original 100 to 175 pupils, all boarders between the ages of ten and eighteen, and remained at this level during my seven years at the school. Of the 175 pupils in my time, 76 were Foundation Scholars, chosen by examinations from boys attending either state or independent schools in the city of Bristol or the counties of Gloucester, Somerset and Wiltshire. The scholars received total remission of tuition and boarding fees, which made the scholarships attractive, and competition was keen. The fees for paying pupils were low, which also made the school attractive to parents who were not well off.

In 1930 the school was, as it remains, an independent boarding school run on typical public school lines but, as the Headmaster was not a member of the Headmasters' Conference, it was not rated as a public school. In social and business contacts in my early adult life, this was a handicap. Snobbery was prevalent and ex-public school men looked down their noses when I told them I had been at Colston's: "Where's that?" they would say.

The headmaster, Canon A. R. Millbourn, MA, 'Joey' to the boys, had an imposing presence with a deep resounding voice. He was a scholar at Christ's Hospital and also of Oxford University, taking a First in Classics. He was responsible for getting the chapel, swimming pool and a new pavilion built. He was a good linguist, familiar with seven languages. I recall he taught us Greek in the sixth form for a couple of terms when I was in it, but Greek was not on the curriculum, which in later years I much regretted; nor were German, Spanish and biology. Latin was taught throughout the school and all the Fifth form took it at the School Certificate Examination, because it was a compulsory subject for entry to Oxford and Cambridge.

Some of the masters had fought in the First World War, which had ended nine years earlier. The second master had been a major in the Gloucester Regiment and commanded the school's Cadet Force, which trained in the same way as the Officers' Training Corps (OTC) at public schools. Although by the time they left Colston's boys were mostly 'officer material', I never heard of any going to Sandhurst or Woolwich. Twice a year school made 'official' visits to Bristol. Led by the Cadet Force band on 10th November, the boys marched through the city's streets to attend the Charter Day service of the Society of Merchant Adventurers in Bristol Cathedral and then, three days later, to the Colston Society's celebrations. At this second event they went to the Merchant Venturers Hall, and each was presented with a new shilling and a bun.

There were four boarding houses, each divided for meals into three tables of fifteen. A prefect or monitor sat on a chair at the top end of each table, with seven boys on each side on benches.

The regime at Colston's was austere. A retired sergeant major from the Middlesex Regiment lived with his wife in a lodge at the main entrance gates. He roused the boys in the dormitories at 6.30am with a hand bell. We washed in basins of cold water, dressed and made our beds. Then we went to chapel, where the Headmaster conducted a short service and a prefect read a lesson. After chapel we paraded by houses, divided into tables, out-of-doors in all weathers. The sergeant inspected the parade, at which haircuts were ordered, hands, necks, knees (of those under ten years old, in shorts) and ears were checked for cleanliness, likewise shoes and clothes. Then, to the accompaniment of the bugle band, we marched for breakfast to the dining hall. Meals started after a Latin grace sung to an accompaniment on a harmonium --'Benedic nobis Domine et omnibus donis' and ended with another --'Nomen sanctum tuum Laudamus'.

We ate off enamelled metal places. After grace, when we scraped the benches back, sat down and started eating, the noise of 180 boys was deafening. Food was meagre and most boys eked it out with jam, marmite, eggs, tins of sardines and so on. The school tuck shop was my source for these. Kept by the sergeant, it was in a basement next to the boilers and a good place on cold days. Most boys got regular tuck parcels, but my parents being abroad, I got few. I lost weight each term in my early years at Colston's and was put on to a mug of extra milk, taken each evening at the matron's sick parade, which I hated. It made me the subject of ridicule. I could not have been too feeble, because I did quite well at games and athletics but, being two years younger than the average of my class, I was bullied. I recall being thrown into a holly bush from an upper floor window of a rival house.

After passing School Certificate with exemption from Matriculation I took mathematics, physics and chemistry for Higher School Certificate and was being coached for a State Scholarship to university when, unfortunately, my father's firm went into liquidation and he lost all his money. Modest as Colston's fees were, my parents could not afford them. The school kept me on, exempt from fees, and would have kept me until I took the open State Scholarship Examination, but it was calculated it would cost £250 a year on top of a scholarship to keep me at university and that could not be afforded. So I had to leave and find a job. It was March, 1934.

The Hon. Mrs. Clay and her sister, Heather, attended different boarding schools.

My sister Heather and I both went to boarding school, but to different ones. My parents chose these particular schools because the Headmistresses were both very fine, good leading members of the Girl Guide movement. Heather went to St. James' School,

West Malvern, where the Headmistress was Miss Alice Baird, a leading person in the Guide movement in Worcestershire and on the National Council of the Guides. I went to Westonbirt, in Gloucestershire, where the Headmistress was Mrs. Houison Craufurd, who was from Scotland, and she had been a leading Commissioner in Scotland until she became Headmistress of Westonbirt.

I remember Westonbirt mostly for the beauty of its surroundings. It was a wonderful big mansion, built I think in the late eighteenth century, with a most attractive parkland and laid-out gardens, and an ornamental lake. We had the privilege of living in this lovely house and also of being allowed to wander wherever we liked in these beautiful gardens: the Italian garden with its statues and little grottos -- everything was lovely and I am sure it was very good for our souls.

The education was exceedingly good. We had most kindly and helpful schoolmistresses and matrons to look after us, and the atmosphere of the school was an excellent one. I was very happy there, although, as with most schoolgirls, there were the bad moments.

When I was about fourteen or fifteen there was a change in the leadership of Westonbirt, as Mrs. Craufurd was going to leave and start her own school nearer to London in Hertfordshire. Her assistant, who was the head of our house, was going with her. So my parents decided that it would be better for me to go to a well established school if I were to take my School Certificate, so I joined my sister Heather at St. James'.

I found the rather stronger discipline at St. James' a bit irksome; silly little details irritated me, such as at Westonbirt we used to go up the stairs two at a time, or leap up them three at a time for speed. At St. James' 'You may not go more than one step at a time.' Thundering up the stairs one step at a time took much longer and made much more noise. Of course the other girls didn't mind it so much as they hadn't had the freedom of Westonbirt. Another big difference was that St. James' was in a town with streets running nearby, whereas Westonbirt was in its own glorious parkland and the school boundaries were main roads that were no nearer than five miles. The difference in freedom was quite marked.

As regards school work, I think St. James' did as much good to me as Westonbirt: I was never clever: very average. Towards the time of exams my parents decided I need not take the School Certificate, which was the main leaving certificate at that time, and so I did not have to carry out the set tasks that most of my friends were doing.

I was allowed to take extra French, drawing, music -- all sorts of lovely things, which made my days very happy there, and of course there were games and swimming and the Guides. I joined the Guide Company: guiding was the thing to do in those days at boarding schools of this type all over the country. There they were -- the Guides and the Rangers and the Cadets, learning to be the Guiders of the future. Learning how to lead other girls was important and there is no doubt the Guiders and leaders of the movement in the following years were greatly enhanced by the fact that they had been Guides and Cadets at school. They had thoroughly learnt what those values were, and how to achieve them with other girls. I believe that our boarding schools at that time deserve a great deal of praise for the leadership they gave to the future women of our country.

At those boarding schools I couldn't say that life was spartan. Of course the beds were fairly hard; they were iron bedsteads on wooden floors, but each bed had a little mat beside it for your feet when you first got out of bed. There were cupboards in the passage where we hung our dresses and clothes; we each had a small locker in the dormitory. They were dormitories of perhaps four, five or occasionally six, but there were no big ones. There was one older girl, the leader, who was the head of the dormitory. But we were not coddled and I remember often feeling terribly cold.

As far as I remember the food was reasonably good. It was adequate in amount and adequate in quality.

We did not have at that time Guide camps from school, because rather naturally the Guide Captain, if she was one of the school mistresses, wanted to get home. She did not want to give another week to take the Guides to camp, and most companies were run by school mistresses at that time. So I don't remember ever having a school Guide camp, and of course we were very lucky as we always went family camping. But I believe that from the ethos of guiding and guide camping in later years after the Second War the camping habit spread to ordinary schools. Many of the people in later years who led school camps were those who had done camping as boys and girls in their youth. It was only then that the new regime of school parties going definitely to camp as a school set in.

3. HIGHER EDUCATION

The expansion in provision for higher education which had begun in the Twenties continued throughout the Thirties. Total Government expenditure rose from £3.9 million in 1920-1923 to £9.8 million in 1937-1938 and during this period provision for university places in England and Wales increased by almost 100%. (There was a relative decline in Scotland during this period in higher education). In addition £10.3 million was contributed by local services, mainly rates. Even so, still only a small minority were receiving higher education in 1938 — 2% of nineteen year olds. However, there were many more opportunities for part time education provided through the Workers' Educational Association, which engaged many university tutors and school teachers to run a variety of courses. Also, in 1934 over two million students enrolled at Technical Colleges or Evening Institutes. Most of them chose technical or commercial subjects, but even so music and art accounted for 107,000 students. The trend continued throughout the decade.

In 1937 G. D. H. and M. I. Cole wrote:

One of the most important and least noticed facts of the modern world is the great increase in the number of persons who possess minor technical qualifications which are enough to raise them, both in their estimation and in their earning power, above the ruck of the unqualified or of those whose sole qualification is based on manual apprenticeship. The 'black-coated' proletariat consists to an ever increasing extent of these qualified workers who have laboured away in the evenings to advance themselves, and by that means have in most cases raised themselves a step up the social ladder.

Professor W. E. Burcham is a retired member of the Faculty of Science at Birmingham University. He gives his personal record of some impressions of Cambridge from 1931 to 1939: it is not a general account of college and university life in that decade.

Higher education in the Thirties was not so well structured or financed in the United Kingdom as it is now, sixty years later.

University entrance was certainly not the main object for most of those pupils in secondary schools who were taking their School Certificate examination. But those same schools, even in the face of the deep economic depression of the early Thirties, did everything possible to encourage some of their more academically inclined pupils to enter the sixth form.

In my case the main problem about going to university was not so much the academic qualifications as the question of finance and of the sacrifice that my family would be called upon to make. I had, however, been lucky because the City of Norwich School had given me an excellent start in the natural sciences, and when I took the Higher School Certificate (H.S.C.) examination in 1930 I was awarded a State Scholarship. This provided maintenance support plus approved fees at a university. I had included subsidiary Latin among my H.S.C. subjects because Cambridge, which was our local university, required this for matriculation, and the next step was to obtain admission to one of the colleges of the university. At the end of 1930 I was awarded an Open Exhibition £40 per annum at Trinity Hall, and early in 1931 my father applied for and obtained a grant of £65 per annum from the Norwich Education Committee to cover part of my expenses. The state Scholarship was then determined to include £80 per annum for maintenance, and I was therefore enabled to arrive at Trinity Hall in October 1931 with £185 promised to cover living expenses for the 1931-32 academic year. It turned out to be adequate, though what would have happened had I not had a supportive family to return to during vacations was not clear.

In trying to describe how the Cambridge of the 1930's struck a freshman from the provinces, I ought first to try to clarify the relation between the university and its colleges. The colleges are self-governing foundations, mostly established in the distant past by benefactors with the object of housing and teaching a community of scholars. Within their walls a pattern of life has developed not unlike that of the great manor houses of the Middle Ages and many colleges, indeed, derive substantial income from their estates. Together the colleges form the university, but the university is recognised by Parliament and has an independent existence as a scholarly institution, like the many non-collegiate universities which now flourish. By the Thirties nearly all major teaching duties, apart from personal tuition, had been taken over from the colleges by the university, which had organised its staff into departments and faculties of the sort that are now familiar throughout the whole university system. From a student point of view the university taught, but the college cared.

The undergraduates of the Thirties came from many walks of life. There had always been 'poor scholars' who had subsisted on small stipends, and their number was then increasing relatively to that of the more wealthy but perhaps less academically inclined entrants. It was predominantly a male society, because women could not be members of the university and thus could not be awarded degrees, although they could share lectures and examinations with the men. The two women's colleges contributed probably less than 10% of the total student population. I found that the university, although it existed in the town of Cambridge, was not really part of it, and Cambridge town to me was simply the location of the railway station, of the Mecca cafe, and of Heffer's excellent bookshop, both in Petty Cury, and of a frequently patronized cinema.

My undergraduate work was organized by my college, Trinity Hall. On arriving there I was at once sent to see my tutor, a genial don who was to act 'in loco parentis' to me and to whom I learned that I should report any troubles. My contact with him usually amounted to two brief visits each term, one to report arrival at the beginning and the other to request permission to 'go down' at the end. My tutor immediately sent me to a supervisor, who was in my case not a member of the college but who offered personal guidance in a set of rooms in a house in the town. I went to him as soon as possible and was recommended to attend a number of lectures provided by the mathematics faculty, which I did. He also asked me to attend in his rooms once a week, together with a fellow freshman from Trinity Hall, to discuss the lectures and get practice in problem solving, using old university examination papers. I soon discovered that all university lectures were advertised publicly each term in a special issue of the Cambridge University Reporter. It became my practice to look through this issue as soon as I could get it and to present myself not only at the lectures to which I had been recommended, but also at others to which some special interest attached.

The reason for this behaviour was a realisation of the exceptional opportunities that were offered, even to the lowliest student, in the Cambridge of the Thirties. Chairs or other senior posts were held by men of outstanding ability over a wide range of subjects; in physics for instance, in which I was personally interested, there were J. J. Thomson, Rutherford, Aston and C. T. R. Wilson, all giants of international fame. These people took part in the routine teaching work of their faculty but also gave short specialized courses on their own interests. I saw to it that I missed as few as possible of these classes, and I often take pleasure in looking back on what must have been a unique learning situation. Altogether the three years of study that I spent before taking my degree were busy, happy and exciting because nothing was too closely organised and we were allowed to develop considerable independence in our efforts, using all kinds of books which we could buy in the second-hand shops or consult the (old) university library. Of course, yearly examinations had to be passed in order that our work could continue, but this was simply another task that could be approached in a way of our own choice. In saying this, I must not belittle the help given me by tutors, supervisors, lecturers and laboratory demonstrators, all of whom proved approachable, sympathetic and useful in times of difficulty. I did well enough in my first degree examination to be invited to stay on for what is now called graduate work.

As holder of a college award, I was entitled to rooms in college and I was assigned a set at the top of C-staircase in the main court. I had a sitting room and a bedroom, with a sort of scullery annexe for minor cookery and washing up, and a somewhat distant toilet with even more distant bathroom. Domestic services were provided by a 'gyp' and 'bedder' (male and female respectively) who wakened me each morning with a jug of hot water, and who would bring up coal for the small fire that was my only means of keeping warm in the winter. Meals were provided in the college hall but only dinner was compulsory, and breakfast and lunch were usually frugal because they had to be bought outside and prepared in my rooms. That however was an adventure in itself, at least at the beginning, because I was in no way skilled in the art of efficient shopping and was very susceptible to the numerous circulars from local shopkeepers that arrived continuously throughout my residence. For much of my first few days, too, I was answering the door to visitors representing societies and clubs anxious for my membership. Fortunately for me, perhaps, I was no good at team games and was not recruited to any of the college clubs, but I enjoyed squash, tennis and swimming, and found plenty of opportunity for these pursuits as time went on, particularly during the very pleasant but optional period of summer residence known as Long Vacation Term. I remember, too, that I joined the college play-reading society and the university branch of the Student Christian Movement.

The important thing about life in college and membership of societies was that one made friends with people of like interests. Several of us were fairly regular in attendance at college chapel and from meeting there we began to share other interests. In the end I sensed that a great deal of time could be very pleasantly spent in visiting my friends in their rooms or lodgings, and entertaining them in my own, so for the critical third year, on which my degree would depend, I moved out of college to lodgings in distant Chesterton, with the hope that the journey would deter casual visitors. My own journeys to and fro were made by bicycle, a form of transport that was almost ideal in the flat, narrow streets of the town. Almost everybody cycled, usually dangerously, and I found that the bike, assisted when necessary by the London and North Eastern Railway, enabled me to explore a considerable area of Cambridgeshire and Suffolk at weekends. My expeditions usually had the object of visiting a village church, for I had become interested in church architecture, and in the Thirties churches were usually left unlocked, and even the main roads by which one approached them were pleasantly free of heavy traffic. I have mentioned this activity to make the point that the Cambridge of the early Thirties broadened one's horizons in the most agreeable way. I am not sure that there was anything exceptional about this, but it was important to me and I was glad that I could continue to work there after graduation.

The Thirties marked big changes in Mrs. Mary Horseman's life, as she left school and went on to University, then to teaching.

I left school in 1932, having been in the sixth form for two years, taking the Higher Certificate and Oxford entrance examinations. Thinking back, I am amazed at the sophistication of girls of this age nowadays: I reckon we were probably at the development stage of the present sixteen year old.

Arthur, Rita, Mary, Barney on the river at Oxford.

I didn't get into Oxford, so spent the first two terms of that academic year at Bristol University attending Physics lectures and laboratories, courtesy of my father's friend Professor Tyndall. The following term I was at home helping my brother Charles, eleven years my junior, who had a heart murmur and was 'to be kept quiet' (impossible! Nowadays, of course, this condition is ignored). By this time St. Hugh's had offered me a reserve place in the autumn.

Working in the Electrical Lab., Oxford.

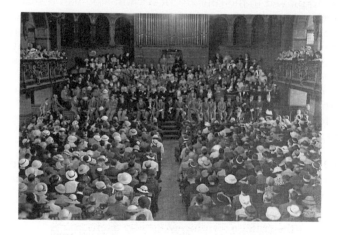

Meeting in the Town Hall, Oxford.

The work was hard -- lectures all morning when you weren't experimenting in the lab, and work for tutorials, and reading to be done afterwards. (I was reading 'Natural Sciences, i.e. Physics). It was in the lab that I met Arthur, later to become my husband. Our apparatus was plugged into the same socket and I asked him if it was O.K. to switch on!

I taught for a year at Queenswood after my finals and they advised me to take a Dip Ed in 1938. So I went back to Oxford and that gave me a chance to get to know Arthur better. He was very persistent and most days called to see me in the lunch hour. Eventually we decided to become engaged and, greatly daring, hired a car for a day and drove to Epsom to tell my parents.

Having trained as a student teacher, Joan MacLachlan was able to go on to a teachers' training college.

I was accepted for Avery Hill Training College, Eltham. The Police Benevolent Fund gave me £40 a year; the Education Committee gave college loans; and the school fund sent me money, so that after paying all the college dues I had 5/- left for pocket money. Avery Hill was in wonderful parkland: a lovely place to live. Discipline was very strict -- no men around, passes only at weekends. Our warden was fierce, but we all survived.

I did a lot of social work in play centres, nursery schools, etc. -- always in the Dockland area. We went to clinics, too, and helped there. I joined the Cadet section of the Girl Guild movement and played in the college cricket and stoolball teams.

We walked miles at weekends and loved the area around Sidcup and Orpington. We were in London for Princess Marina's wedding and the death of King George V: we were always allowed up to London to see the processions and invariably stood by Green Park.

Once, we cut the college photograph day and went up to London to see Edward VIII. He was in full Guard's uniform, mounted, and we were just by his horse when he sent his equerry on ahead to slow down the procession.

After leaving school, Peggy Vanderkar continued her education at the Chelsea College of Physical Education, but war was to change her occupation.

I wanted to do welfare work, but was too young, so Jessie suggested that the college training would be useful in that field later on. Ten years earlier she had been awarded a scholarship to Chelsea College of Physical Education, so I followed in her footsteps there from 1936-1939. During this time I acted as swimming life-saver at a camp for young people from depressed areas. That way I experienced the problems other people suffered.

Then I taught for two years at North Foreland Lodge school for girls before resigning to join the Women's Royal Naval Service. It was quite an honour to have belonged to that service, as it is no longer in existence. My parents were not pleased as in those days it involved them in much expense and sacrifice to send me to college.

I was at 111, the Solkhon family home, when war was declared on 3rd September 1939. Immediately after the solemn declaration by Chamberlain that Germany had ignored the warning about invading Poland, ". . . and so I declare that this country is at war with Germany" there was an air raid warning. We were all reduced to laughter at the sight of lady air raid wardens dressed in tin hats and ankle socks. It was a sunny day and we decided to go for a walk on the Wandsworth Common, but were immediately sent back to collect our gas masks! Air Raid wardens did wonderful things during the war.

College days for Joan Dobson were an enjoyable time.

I had wanted to go to Whitelands College with my friend Truda, but my headmistress persuaded me that Goldsmiths was University of London, and Whitelands was not. Also she said that I would be a pioneer, as I was the first from the school to go to Goldsmiths. So I duly arrived in September 1935.

I was finding college non too irksome. The course was extensively vocational but interesting, with plenty of contact with local schools and demonstration lessons. Unfortunately there was a strong inclination to cut 'dems' and go instead to the cinema. When the lights when up and the mighty Wurlitzer organ rose from the depths for the interval, the place seemed to be full of students. We favoured light musicals, especially the Ginger Rogers and Fred Astaire films.

College life was really very pleasant, though we worked hard. We had to be back in hostel by 8pm or the door would be barred and we had to account to the hostel head for our tardiness. Early evening entertainment consisted of a cup of tea and possibly toast or crumpets in Lyons or the ABC cafe. The cost might amount to 6d, but tea alone was 2d. Highlight of the week was 'Soc-tea' -- tea dancing in college on Friday after lectures.

Jessie Lintern recalls with pleasure the time she spent at a Teacher Training College at Jordan Hill, Glasgow.

October 1937 saw the start of three of the happiest years of my life. The college was built on a hill overlooking the Clyde valley, and I was fortunate enough to be boarding in one of the hostels attached to it. To be treated as a free, independent adult was wonderful! Many of the students were Gaelic-speaking girls from the islands of the Hebrides and would spend evenings in each other's rooms, from which the sound of singing and the soft lilt of Gaelic conversation drifted along the corridors. Provided the general rules were obeyed, relationships with college and hostel staffs were harmonious and cheerful: the only time I was summoned to the college Warden's office was fully justified -- her comments lingered long in my mind. It was at the start of a holiday break, when my friend from the Highlands decided to catch the mid-day train north, rather than wait for the final lecture of the afternoon and take the evening one, which would not get her home until midnight. She asked me to slip off with her in order to look less conspicuous, so with grave misgiving I accompanied her to the station, saw her off, and caught the bus for the hour's run home. The class register was checked at that missed lecture, our absence reported to the college Warden, and a favourite saying of my Grannie's came home to roost: "Be sure your sins will find you out." The Warden's sole reprimand was, "If you cannot discipline yourself, how do you expect to discipline your pupils?" It was a very sound lesson to me, at least.

Lectures were all geared to teaching methods, whether history of education, hygiene, psychology, or mathematics. In the latter, we worked from symbol recognition right through to fractions and compound interest, averages and percentages. If our exam results were consistently high during the first two years, showing real understanding, we were allowed to drop the subject for another of our choice, either English or French. Music covered sight-reading in staff and tonic sol-fa notation, choral singing and the history of composers and their works. Over a three year period we had courses in art, needlework and handicraft, each of two years. By taking two for a year, then dropping one for the third subject, returning to the first for the final year, it was possible to gain recognition in all three. This special qualification was known as 'Chapter III' and its possession was helpful when applying to County Education Departments for an interview. I must say that I even succeeded in art, although the lecturer pointed out that my grade had been achieved 'for quantity, not quality'.

Students were grouped under a methods mistress or master and right from the start spent one complete day each week at a given Primary School, where we were visited by our methods mistress. We had to take at least one lesson on our own and make notes in our methods book of views on class procedure and discipline, attitudes to pupils, subject of and interest in lessons, together with personal plans for the lessons we took and notes of criticism by our supervisory mistress. Later each year a three to four week period was allotted for concentrated teaching practice. In our final year, where a high standard had been consistently reached, the student would be presented with written instructions to attend a hitherto unfamiliar school on a certain date in order to take an unknown class for three lessons, the subjects of which would be notified on her arrival. After a short time in the classroom to make ourselves known to the children, finding out their names from an exercise book on their desks, and looking out any necessary equipment and material, we awaited the appearance of the head of the Methods department. The lessons allocated to me for a class of eight year olds were mental arithmetic -- the score rule, geography -- a first lesson islands and English -- my choice of a poem.

I was delighted that I achieved the coveted standard of proficiency. A few days after my twenty-first birthday, I said goodbye to college and friends and accepted a post offered in an Ayrshire village, with many of whose pupils I still maintain contact. For the next six years I was back in my beloved Carrick.

After she left school, Mrs. Hazel Rolf went to Battersea Polytechnic.

In September 1938, I was admitted to Battersea Polytechnic for the Domestic Science teaching course. It had been a struggle to raise the money but eventually Reading Council gave me ten pounds a year, Green Girls Trust twenty-five pounds, West's Gift sixty pounds, and I had an exhibition from Christ's Hospital of sixty pounds. All the girls living in hostel received thirty-four pounds a year towards fees, but had to sign a contract to teach for at least a year after qualifying.

The first year students were divided into three groups. The building was very old and a warren of rooms, over three hundred, and had departments for Science and Engineering, the latter with just one female student, whose sister was in my group: we were the two youngest. The department of Science included courses for Hotel Catering, School Matrons and Housekeepers. We lived in hostels on the Northside, Clapham Common. Kay Forbes from C. H. and I were in No. 51, newly converted, so the furnishings were modern. I shared a sitting room with two Lancashire girls and one local, but in the second term I was able to change to a cheaper cubicle. On the landing was a cupboard with a gas-ring, and we could put pennies in the meter to boil water for tea or hot water bottles. There was a lady Warden for each hostel and one of them was in charge of the sick room. We paid 5/- a term for a doctor.

At dinner each evening the Wardens sat at High Table and we took turns to sit with them. It was a strain to talk to them as we didn't see them often unless we were late in at night or failed to pay a laundry bill. That first year we had maids to serve meals:

the food was very good as the Head Cook was trained at the Polytechnic.

I was very busy as we had lots of notes to write up and loads of practical work. Our classes lasted all day, from 9.15am to 1pm, then 2pm to 5pm, with fifteen minutes break morning and afternoon. We paid two guineas a term for lunches (supplied by the cookery classes) and 2d for a cup of coffee and 1d for a bun, but I couldn't afford both together so made sure I was in time for breakfast.

College life was very strange to me at first, but not as hectic as at C. H. Our terms were longer than University ones and we had essays, reading and needlework to do in the holidays. I found that difficult as Mum wanted me to help her when the students were away, doing such things as laundering all their bedroom curtains every holiday and also keeping Alan, the baby, amused. So much practical work in term time was very tiring: three hours cookery, laundry, housewifery or chemistry, followed by one hour English, Hygiene or Principles of Education. If the theory came at the end of the day I could hardly keep awake. We were not permitted to skip any classes but the P.E. lecturer told us in our third year that if we felt we had too much work, we could ask to be excused her lecture.

Then in the third term we went into the local schools for teaching practice, in classroom subjects, one afternoon a week. I liked teaching needlework, even to Juniors, but it was exhausting having to account for every needle, etc. at the end of every lesson. At Poly we had to supply all our own materials down to pins and needles.

The London children at that time were well-disciplined and we had a teacher in the room. At one school I taught Gym on the roof, surrounded by wire netting, as it was the only playground. The exercises we had had at C. H. came in useful. The lessons had to be prepared in advance to a special plan, and when a lecturer came to inspect the teaching she corrected the notes. Finding the schools was a problem as they were tucked away among other buildings. The old buildings greeted us with the eternal smell of chalk, disinfectant and bodies as we entered. For teaching we wore ordinary clothes and hats and gloves for the journey, but for all classes we wore a uniform similar to nurses -- blue cotton dress with white stiff collar and cuffs, white aprons; and navy cardigans allowed only for theory classes. For Science we had blue overalls with long sleeves. The aprons were laundered at a Deaf and Dumb institute nearby and also the collars and cuffs, but even their small charges obliged me to try to make two aprons last a week. Stockings were a problem to me as the cheaper lisle ones went into holes quickly at the heels, especially when to save the fare I often walked up from Battersea to Clapham. Then my sister lent me her bicycle, which I kept in stables behind the hostels for 1 shilling a week.

Our lecturers were mostly very competent, especially the two cookery ones, and I am sure our training was far more thorough and up-to-date than any other college in the U.K. We also had the new third year course. If any piece of work, theoretical or practical, was marked below Grade C, the student was warned that failure to improve would mean dismissal. A few had to leave at the end of the first term and several at the end of the first year.

I enjoyed living in London, but the smoky air made all our clothes very dirty. Even after constant washing my petticoat soon had a grey, dingy look up to the waist. We were allowed to do our personal laundry in a basement room, where drying racks hung from the ceiling.

At the end of the summer term 1939 we returned to our homes, leaving our bed-linen and hockey sticks at the hostels. However, at the end of August the news was bad and the BBC announced that London school children were to be evacuated on the Friday. I had agreed to help so went to London to Mabel's flat at Victoria. Early next morning I went to my teaching practice school near Clapham Junction and the teachers and I and the children walked in a crocodile to the station, carrying gas-masks and a small bag of possessions, followed by some parents. What a schemozzle it was as we arranged the children in the train. Luckily they all began with name tags pinned on their clothes. Some older girls had younger ones with them and most had started on their packed lunches and sweets before the train was more than a few minutes on the way. We did not know our destination and ended up at Warfield, near Bracknell: I was thankful to be so near Reading.

One teacher, fifteen children and I were taken to a large house. The cook served a dinner of stew and there weren't enough chairs for all to sit at table. Then the teacher took the children in the garden to play whilst I helped the lady of the house to make up all the extra beds, including four for business friends expected any minute. I ended up sleeping on a couch in the drawing room, but I had a standard lamp to read by and of course, a book with me. That was Saturday, 2nd September, my nineteenth birthday and Pete cycled over from Reading with my cards, but I didn't see him as I was down the garden with the children. On Sunday the Headmistress sent a message that all were to go to church -- a large old one with an ancient vicar who had no intention of pandering to the young, so we were dragging through a boring service when a message came and halted it, whilst he announced that war was declared. The children, most of whom had never been to church before, then realised that they would be staying for some time in this strange place and not just for a holiday, as most had been told by parents. Some began to cry, others were sick.

After dinner, as I was only a temporary helper, the lady of the house said I could return to Reading with her chauffeur as he was going there to buy cakes at Lyon's, which opened on Sundays. I was very relieved. The Polytechnic notified me that the Teacher Training Department was evacuating to Shrewsbury and our belongings from the hostels would be transferred there for us. The college rented four large houses and some of us were billeted out for bed and breakfast. Kay and I were in a small semi-detached house out on the by-pass with a young married couple, no children. They were paid 10/6d a week for each of us and we had to share a double bed. The husband worked in munitions and left early in the mornings, so we suggested his wife might cook our breakfast at the same time as his and leave it on the hotplate and go back to bed.

We had about three miles to cycle every day to the Technical College for classes, down by the river Severn. For laundry classes we had to cycle out above Shrewsbury to Radbrooke Domestic Science College, where the equipment was very primitive, especially the wooden sinks and, in the laundry room, a drain in the floor.

Miss Marjorie Celia Ellis was the middle one of three sisters. Her father was a doctor, who had trained in Aberdeen and then done his post-graduate course at St. Thomas' Hospital, London. Nurses worked very long hours in the Thirties, and did much of the work now done by cleaners.

In those days entrance to St. Thomas' depended much more on the standing of your parents than on your academic qualifications, otherwise I should not have been accepted. I was hopeless at Mathematics so did not pass the General School Certificate Examination.

Florence Nightingale had left money to start a nursing school at St. Thomas' and still exerted a strong influence on the hospital. She said "It is better for beginners to knock the corners off the furniture than off the patients", so during our first year as probationer nurses we did a lot of housework.

We were not allowed to have short hair, and until it had grown to a suitable length we were not allowed to wear the Florence Nightingale hat. The uniform was a pale purple dress, 6 inches

from the ground with a white apron and white pocket handkerchief. We wore black shoes and stockings, with capes, but there
was no special outdoor uniform.

Our rooms were round a bird cage. We were called at 6am,
with breakfast at 6.30, and we had to stand in the centre of the
bird cage whilst the House Sister stood at the door and examined
us one by one to check that we were correctly dressed. Some of
the Ward Sisters were too old to be State Registered.

As well as the Sister, there was the 1st Staff Nurse, the 2nd Staff
Nurse, and three probationers; one of these was responsible for
the dusting and cleaning of the day side of the ward, another for
the night side (fifteen beds each) and the third probationer took
the meals round and also looked after the three fires in the ward.
A man brought the coal and dumped it outside the ward. There
was a ward maid who did the washing up and a 'Pink' (charlady)
who cleaned the bathroom and lavatories. The laundry was sent
to Whiteley's.

At 8 am Sister walked to the middle of the ward and all the
nurses stood behind for morning prayers. This began with the
Collect, followed by the Lord's Prayer and Grace. Then Sister
said 'Good morning'. Some of the wards still had cocoa for breakfast, and some tea. George Ward also had porridge.

If we were on duty we ate any left overs at 10am and put on a
clean apron, then we worked until lunch at 1pm. We were off
duty until 2.40pm, then worked until 5 pm tea and again until
8.30pm, when we went to Chapel. At 9.0 we gobbled supper and
rushed to the bathroom to turn on the water for a bath. Sometimes we were so tired that we fell asleep and the bath overflowed
into the bird cage.

We had one half-day off a week -- once I was so tired I fell asleep
fully dressed and did not waken until the morning bell next day.
Once a month we had a whole day off, with breakfast in bed (provided we had not been late for breakfast that month). We were
paid just £10 a year, so our main recreation was to go for a ride
on a bus for 3d. At the end of our first year we had a month's
holiday, and three weeks the following year. I was due to sit my
final exams. on Easter Monday in 1931, but on Good Friday I developed a very painful throat, but said nothing. Then Sister sent
for me and I fainted in the lift. The doctor said I had diphtheria:
my temperature was 104. I was very ill and my throat was para-
lysed, so I missed the Finals and had to wait another year. I
passed all the examinations without difficulty.

If you broke a thermometer you had to wait outside the Matron's office to be reprimanded. One day I fell and broke seven
thermometers and thought she would be furious. However she

said, "One might be carelessness, but (with a smile) not seven. Did you fall?" She was a wonderful Matron.

When I had qualified I was on night duty as Junior Sister for one year, then in 1936 I took the Midwifery course. When my father went to Australia by sea with the British Medical Association, Matron gave me three months' special leave to accompany him, with my mother and one of my sisters. When I returned, I was Sister on the Eye Ward, then in 1937 I was appointed Sister on Christian Ward, the women's medical ward and the post I had always wanted.

As I was on the reserve, I was called up when war began and in September 1939 I went to France. When the Germans invaded that country we were missing for three weeks, and eventually were evacuated from St. Nazaire by a P. & O. liner.

Margaret Beavis was eventually able to fulfil her ambition to be a nurse.

When I left school, eager to get out into the wide world, I was too young for nursing training, so I had to do a residential Nursery training course for over a year. Then at last I was able to go to Great Ormond Street Hospital for children, training for the General Nursing Council (Registered Sick Children's Nurse) -- a dream I had had since I was about four years old.

It was hard work. The first year we cleaned almost all the time -- sweeping, making up fires, etc. Very long hours for £18 a year, but oh!, so happy. They were wonderful years in such a lovely atmosphere, with never a dull moment. Much energy was expended every moment of the day. The very few hours off duty were crammed with tennis (a mile's run away), dancing, the League of Health and Beauty and much else.

The Coronation of King George VI in 1937 was an outstanding day. From 4.30am we stood in Trafalgar Square. We were granted leave by G. O. S. for the day as we were in the Preliminary Training School and not on the wards. We stood for twelve hours, quite unable to move in the swaying mass of humanity. Of course it was will power that kept us going. All our packed lunches disappeared underfoot! In the end we saw just the heads of King George VI and Queen Elizabeth for a few seconds. A long wait, but it was worth it -- something to tell our children about one day!

On Saturday nights, after day duty, members of the Auxiliary Fire Service came to partner us in dances, or the cast of a West End show came to entertain us, or else we entertained the whole hospital ourselves and made them laugh (very easy for me!).

The London blitz had barely begun in 1939, but we were prepared and ready. Children were evacuated and we nurses, to our great disappointment, had to go to the country ourselves. I moved from Great Ormond Street to another hospital, nursing adults (during my children's training) in Nissen huts, billeted out among the gentry in Sussex -- that was an experience!

We came back to Great Ormond Street in time to see -- and hear! -- an anti-aircraft gun outside the Nurses' Home, doing its stuff, and to swot for finals in a corridor with radios blaring all round us. We were not allowed in our rooms because of danger from the glass windows shattering. We were in the centre of the London blitz, and many exciting things happened, but that belongs to 1940.

After leaving Clapham County School, Biddy Clark decided to make physiotherapy her career.

I passed the Matriculation examination in 1938 and at the age of seventeen wanted to follow a career at no cost to my parents. There were two hospitals in England that offered a physiotherapy training, to be paid for by hard work! I chose Birmingham. Two years were spent in an Orthopaedic Hospital, working long hours and with very little time off. In return we received a physio-therapy training at no cost, provided we worked for a year at the hospital once we had qualified.

During the five and a half years, we had good accommodation and meals. I think we were given 17/6d pocket money a week. I remember saving up for months to buy myself a pair of moun-tain climbing boots. I still have them to this day and they were with me in Africa for eight years. The clinker nails now rattle in the dried up leather, but they are a symbol of the hard work and long hours that went into my training. It was all really worth while, and I have enjoyed my life's work. However, shortly after I began my training war was declared. Our hospital patients were evacuated to make room for war injured troops or civilians. Our first arrivals were refugees from Belgium, sent over by the Red Cross. None of them could speak English and the strict dis-cipline of Matron completely broke down. As trainee nurses we thought it was great fun. Much of our time was spent rolling plaster bandages, ready for casualties.

The blackout was miserable, and when the siren went we had to carry our bedding down to the damp cellars. A huge land mine fell on the hospital, destroying one wing, but miraculously it didn't explode. Even so there were two fatalities from its impact.

Food was very boring -- we had to surrender our ration books to the hospital and had an excessive amount of mashed swede. Our hospital was within smelling distance of Cadbury's factory and it was tantalising to have the scent of chocolate wafting over us when we were only allowed a sweet ration of about 2 ounces a month.

There were only limited vocations open to women in the Thirties, as Mrs. Eileen Davison found! The depression added to the difficulties of finding work of any kind.

There weren't many openings for girls to train when I was young, and I didn't know what I wanted to do anyway. My father suggested a secretarial training, as he said it would always be useful, and I could go on from there if I wished. So I was enroled in Miss S's high class secretarial office in Oxford to learn shorthand, typing, book-keeping and general office routine. Miss S. I found quite formidable, a tall, thin figure with shingled grey hair, pince-nez, severely cut dark skirt topped by a high collared blouse and bow tie! She took in work such as students' theses from the colleges; some authors sent the drafts of their books to be typed before publication; and sometimes there were ancient manuscripts and books to copy out. This work was done by a group of expert shorthand typists in a very small, dark office at the rear of Miss S's. There were four shorthand typists and four or five pupils jammed into this place, which was so dark we nearly always had to have the light on.

Shorthand and typing were taught by rote, and it was a real grind, but we *were* taught! The pupils also had the job of correcting any mistakes the typists might make. No such thing as Tippex -- it was quite a work of art to rub out and then gauge exactly were to re-type. These corrected sheets were minutely examined by Miss S, and if she could see where you had done the correction the sheet was returned with caustic comments and we had to re-type the whole sheet again.

We were also called in to her private office regularly to 'read over', which meant we had to read the original thesis or manuscript, while Miss S. perused the typescript looking for mistakes! I happened to be very good at this job and used to enjoy reading about the different subjects covered, trying to decipher peoples' handwriting, some of it practically illegible! Once a week an elderly retired clergyman came in to teach us book-keeping, but after two months of trying to get it into my head, we mutually agreed it was a waste of time, and I gave it up thankfully. Another failure was French; I had private lessons with an old dear who used to keep on saying 'On peut dire .....' and I was supposed to fill in the gap in French, which I never could do. So that was a disaster too! Apart from reading over, I loathed the whole thing, but we had to persevere in those days, and I left as a mediocre typist and a very capable shorthand writer!

4. EMPLOYMENT

'The Threadbare Thirties' they have been called, and this was the grim reality that those leaving school or college experienced in the early Thirties. The Wall Street Crash of 1929 meant that the British economy was in a dangerous state and with foreign markets hedged around with protective barriers exports had shrunk. Many businesses collapsed, leading to more and more unemployment – the worst this century. Some never found work at all; others had to accept jobs far below their capabilities.

By 1931 unemployment benefit was costing the government £120 million, only £44 million of which was covered by contributions. So that autumn there were cuts in unemployment benefits, including the introduction of means tests on the transitional payments made after insurance benefit was exhausted. The Unemployment Assistant Board Acts of 1934-5 followed: the locally paid transitional payments were to be funded by the Treasury and payments taken over by the Unemployment Assistance Board. However this provoked an outcry when it was found that the rates were sometimes lower than the locally administered transitional payments. So in 1933 a Standstill Act allowed the old rates to be kept whenever they were more favourable.

Many unemployed were still receiving no benefits and there was real deprivation. In 1938 there were hunger marches by the National Unemployed Workers Movement. The Government was afraid and responded by passing the Winter Adjustment Regulations, which gave the Unemployment Assistance Boards powers to award extra winter relief, but even so many did not qualify. Five days before Christmas two hundred unemployed men laid down in front of traffic lights in Oxford Street when they were red, but stayed where they were when the lights turned green. Soon there was a great traffic jam. Police carried the men to the pavement, but they just went back again. Reinforcements from Scotland Yard were caught in the traffic jam and it was an hour or more before they reached the men and removed them.

Then on New Year's Eve a group of unemployed carried a black coffin down the Strand to Fleet Street and on to Stepney. They were not allowed to leave it at 10 Downing Street for the

Unemployed workers march with the black coffin.

Prime Minister, but the message inside 'Unemployed – No appeasement' was delivered. There were no concessions from the Government, but the public and press were sympathetic.

Others took more positive action. Some of the unemployed in Lincoln ran their own nursery school; at Brynmawr a slag heap was turned into a public park and swimming pool; others ran dances, plays and whist drives. An allotment scheme run by the Society of Friends was very popular and fruitful.

Those in work enjoyed better pay and a higher standard of living than in the Twenties and those who had shares on the Stock Exchange found they had nearly doubled in value: they were the fortunate ones.

Once war was declared there was to be plenty of work for all, with women being conscripted as well as men.

When my sister, Jane Madders (nèe Jessie Solkhon) completed her course at Chelsea College of Physical Education, it was the beginning of the Thirties and at the depth of the depression. She had been a very popular and successful Senior Student and the Principal strongly advised her to accept a post for a P.E. mistress at Trevelyan School: this was a select girls' boarding school at Haywards Heath. However, for Jane who had been used to the liberty and joy of life at home, it was a catastrophe. Some of her feelings are revealed in the following poem she entitled:

TREVELYAN 1931.

> And is there honey still for tea?
> I mean at home, for you and me,
> Where folk are kind and words are few,
> And cakes are hot and bread is new;
> Where I may speak aloud my mind
> And not be scorned, or thought unkind;
> Where tea is set around the fire
> And there are songs as flames grow higher;
> Where friends are close, to shut out fears,
> This blank despair, these burning tears;
> Where bathed in love I may forget
> This rankling hate, and deep regret.
> O, is there honey still for tea?
> And will you, sometimes, think of me?

She endured it for two years, and then gave in her notice. She secured a post at Addey & Stanhope, a co-educational (unusual for those days) secondary school, which gave full scope for her many talents. She entered fully into the life of the school and even had the boys enjoying expressive dance.

Then came the formation of *The Central Council Of Recreative Physical Training* and she was offered a place on the staff. Their aim was to improve the physical and mental health of the community through physical recreation. Keep fit classes were introduced, with an excellent demonstration team. When I returned to London Jane persuaded me to apply for training as a Leader, and in 1938 I had a first year at Chelsea College of Physical Education. Having qualified, I was able to have the second year at the L.C.C. College of Physical Education, but air raids disrupted some of the classes in 1940. Taking Keep Fit classes became a very liberating experience.

Staff at the C.C.R.P.T. were sent out in couples, male and female, and they organised events in many parts of the country. It was on one of these expeditions that Jane and Max Madders were working together: they were married in 1940.

Central Council of Recreative Physical Training.
Summer Vacation Course.

Max Madders and Jessie Solkhon.

Max Madders, who died in October 1993, had never felt at home working with his father on the Liverpool Cotton Exchange, where business was to collapse after the 1929 Wall Street crash. His interest was much more in swimming and P.E. and he developed into a talented swimmer. He was able to get a place in a gymnastics school in Denmark, run by a famous teacher, Niels Bukh. He used £200 from a legacy to cover the board, training and travel for one year. At the end of this period he was awarded a certificate to show that he was a qualified P.E. teacher in Denmark.

He returned to England and in 1932 was selected to represent Britain in the Olympics at Los Angeles, but unfortunately the British Olympic Association could not afford to send a full team, and the breast-stroke event was one that was deleted.

In 1936 Max decided to pay his own way to go to the Berlin swimming and athletic events. He was present when Hitler refused Jessie Owens his medal, because he thought he was superior to the black race. Later Max was to become an official British Olympic swimming coach. Then, like Jane, he was appointed a representative of the Central Council of Physical Recreation, travelling around the country trying to persuade the local councils to establish physical training activities in their areas. This was a work they both enjoyed and they were able to organise many athletic events attended by hundreds of men, women and children. Max was to continue this work at Birmingham University.

Gervas Clay read Law and obtained an Honours Degree in Jurisprudence at Oxford. He was still enjoying writing poetry and the following was written in his last year at Oxford.

THE STICK-GATHERER

Beneath the trees they huddle brokenly,
Storm-raddled twigs so short and old,
Lying where the wind's lean hands have shaken them
Upon the autumn mould.

Slowly with syncopated shuffle
The woman is gathering them;
Loosing each one from crabbed old fingers
Within her apron's hem.

Huddled beside her fire in the evening,
Who knows but what she sees
The smoke from the twigs entrancingly taking
Their shapes as heavenly trees?

When I left college I went into the Colonial Service. They gave me another year at Oxford, so I had four years at Oxford before I went in 1930 to what was then Northern Rhodesia, and is now Zambia. I was there thirty-four years. I was in the bush for much of the time but was in the copper belt for four or five years.

I enjoyed my time in Northern Rhodesia. My first district was about sixteen thousand square miles and I was the only European official in the district with about forty thousand Africans. In that area I had to travel around either by bicycle or on horseback. Most of Northern Rhodesia was tsetse fly country and when you were in a tsetse fly area the only meat to eat was chickens -- and very small chickens at that! So when we went on tour we shot an antelope if we had a chance, so that we had meat to eat. The carriers would come with us if they knew we were going to shoot meat, otherwise they were very reluctant.

We had cows, horses and sheep in the Darotse province which was free from tsetse fly, but the rest of the country had fly almost everywhere. The animals died if bitten by the flies, but we went out on our bicycles and they came round us in swarms. They are like large horse flies and they used to bite us furiously: certain areas were known to be badly infested. We were not inoculated against sleeping sickness, but although I was in a tsetse fly area I was not in a sleeping sickness area.

George Tod found that life whilst at university in London was even more miserable than it had been in Edinburgh, so he was glad when his parents decided he should not return but, instead, begin work.

From the Edinburgh Academy I went to London University in 1932 and lived in a small private hotel in Bloomsbury. I had been lonely (mentally) in Scotland but that was nothing to the chilling solitude of London. Living in a tiny bedroom with only a small dressing table, chair, basin, wardrobe and bed was difficult, and although I excelled in maths and chemistry I did not pass all the required exams at the end of my first year (prelims.).

In the summer of 1933 I joined my parents in Haifa, Palestine, and the decision was made that I should not return to London but should get a job and earn my living. My father got me into the M.P.L. (Mediterranean Pipe Line -- this was the name of the company constructing the pipe line which was to carry the oil from the oil fields to the East Mediterranean at Haifa and Tripoli, Lebanese) in Homs, Syria, where my French was useful. Syria and Lebanon were then under French mandate, and it had the added advantage of being far from my father, thus avoiding the label of nepotism.

In the autumn I was called back to H.Q. where the General Superintendent, M. M. Stuckey, asked me if I could calibrate a tank: in my innocent ignorance and without hesitation I replied, "Yes, Sir. Take the area of the base and multiply it by the height." He seemed amused and said, "That'll do for a start." So I was sent to the oil fields in Kirkuk, some 600 miles east across the Syrian/Iraq deserts, to join a team of tank calibrators.

At first I was not even allowed to hold the tape, but there were 60ft ladders and their guy ropes to care for, and simple measurements to take, commissariat and transport arrangements to make, so I was kept busy. Gradually as I learned I was allowed to climb the ladders and take diameters at different heights, calculate the sag of the tape on a 10lb pressure dynamometer, and work out my own tables, allowing for the displacement of the floating roofs. There were six tanks at the oil fields in Kirkuk and two at each pipeline station. These were booster stations along the pipeline between 60 and 100 miles apart, according to the hydraulic gradient of the terrain. Twelve stations in all and, of course, the two terminals on the Mediterranean with twenty-four tanks each, some with floating, others with fixed roofs.

Kirkuk is where the foothills of the Kurdish mountains reach the plains of the Iraq desert, east of the Tigris and south of the Lesser Zab rivers. It is about 1,000ft above sea level. Here the crude oil can be seen actually oozing out of the rock and flowing in tiny rivulets into a wadi, naturally enough called the Wadi Napht (to which our word naphtha is related). Just next to the wadi are gas and oil seepage which, through spontaneous combustion, are always alight. We called them the 'Eternal Fires'. The fiery furnace of Abednigo is part of them. From the air they can be seen from miles away and during the Second World War attempts were made to quench them, but these failed; the gas and oil kept on coming through just as they have done from time immemorial.

A leading Kirkuk family, naturally called the Naphtchis, have the traditional right to collect the crude oil from the seepage, refine it in their rudimentary skills and market it for fuel for lamps, stoves, etc. Lines of donkeys, soaked in crude oil, carrying four gallon tin cans full of the rather dense crude and driven by boys equally dirty, can be seen travelling constantly between the seepage and the town where the Naphtchis have their stills. We used to call it the 'donkey pipeline'.

On Christmas Eve in 1933 the weather in Kirkuk was atrocious, the continuous pelting rain had made a quagmire of all work sites and camps. The Nissen hut which served as our recreation room leaked and the fire smoked. A few of us were huddled round the fire feeling rather miserable when the end door was flung open and the wind blew in a thin young man with a shock of black hair, a pale face, soaked to the skin and with a large sack on his shoulder. He was a new arrival, none of us knew him and for a moment we checked our curses that he should shut the door. He stood there on the bare cement sill and the rain, still running off his clothes, formed a widening puddle round his muddy shoes. He broke the silence by announcing in a firm deep Welsh accent, "My name is Walter Vile; here is your mail from Haifa." He had travelled for three days across 600 miles of desert on dirt tracks. His truck had stuck in the mud in an ancient Assyrian canal in the desert some ten miles south of our camp. In the violent storm he had followed the telephone line which we had installed along the pipeline and had walked the rest of the way to bring us the mail. He had left his own kit in the truck. We all appreciated his evaluation of priorities, and I am sure no-one ever had a warmer welcome or such an introduction. He was immediately one of us. Twenty-five years later he became General Manager of our operations in Syria.

Having gained a knowledge of all tanks, it was a natural step for me to be given the job of tank gauger while the tanks in Kirkuk, on which the tax which we paid to the Iraq Government was calculated, were being filled and before we started pumping down the pipelines. Then the great and dramatic day came. In March 1934 I gauged and opened the valve of the first tank in the I.P.C. (Iraq Petroleum Company Ltd.), and so started the flow of oil from the Iraq oil fields to the Mediterranean. As the oil went down the pipeline at about 4 mph we tested the line for leaks, in all about 1,200 miles of painstaking work, testing not only the pipe but starting new engines and pumps and systems in all the pipeline stations and ensuring that any wrinkles were ironed out.

The pipe and the machinery for each station came before the building of any accommodation. We were still living in tents or Nissen Huts, and conditions were not for the soft hearted -- cold in the winter and infernally hot in the summer, but Stuckey had instilled into us just one aim in life; to get the oil to the coast and to keep it flowing without the slightest hitch.

While we were testing at the Fields end, the final stages of construction were taking place at the terminals by the sea. The submarine sea-lines in Haifa had been completed, had been set on trolleys on rail lines and drawn out to sea to connect with the loading buoys about a quarter of a mile off shore. I was at the Haifa terminal preparing the tanks for the arrival of the oil. The powers that be decided that we should have a ceremony to mark the linking of the sea-line to the 620 mile long land line by the last weld and, consequently, the completion of the Southern pipeline. (The North line went to Tripoli, Lebanon).

Stands were erected with boxes and seats for Government representatives, local dignitaries, religious leaders and senior officials. Flag poles were fixed and suitable and correct flags acquired. Car parks were not easy to fit between the tanks, but as oil and therefore gas had not arrived there was no danger. The site was on the sandy shore, but acres of red carpet covered the sand adequately. We intended it to be a solemn occasion staged to mark, even symbolically, the completion of the biggest construction enterprise in the world.

On the fateful day the sun shone, it was not too hot, the official cars arrived each with its pennant announcing the importance of the passenger, whether he was to be respected or revered. Was he an 'Excellency' or a 'Beatitude', was he 'Your Grace' or 'Hajji'. All were received as befitted their titles, ushered to their seats and a short speech made to welcome the guests and make them feel part of the undertaking which was to have such importance in the development of the Levant as well as the economy of Europe.

The final weld was to be made just in front of the stand where the sea line, still on its trolley, overlapped the land line by about a foot and could be drawn back by tractor to fit the latter and the join welded. The speech ended, the tractor started up and took the strain of the sea line.

Perhaps the noise of the tractor awakened it, but as the sea line started to move a sleepy tortoise crept out of the land line, halted at the lip of the pipe, blinked in the sunshine, looked around inquisitively and slowly turned back into the darkness of the pipe. At first there was a deathly silence but suddenly pomposity became human and turned to laughter. The Superintendent turned to me and in a hoarse whisper said, "Quick, get a broom and get the damned thing out". Now I must admit I had not foreseen this incident; the broom cupboard was in the shore signal station about 200 yards away. I ran, by heavens I ran, got a broom and fished out the poor tortoise amid the advice and cheers of the guests. The lines were joined, the weld completed, and the champagne flowed: a good time was had by all. Later the Superintendent congratulated me on the arrangements, particularly on the novelty of the tortoise!

George Todd in a camel race at Abu Dhabi.

Having his education abruptly terminated due to unforeseen circumstances, Ted Chaplin was denied the opportunity of continuing his studies at university, and the deep depression of the Thirties was no time to be seeking appropriate employment.

When my father's publishing house in India went into liquidation, I was just seventeen and in the Upper Sixth form at Colston's, working for an Open Scholarship. My ambition was to get to Cambridge, where the Cavendish Laboratory had won international fame. My reading in the school library of the work of Ernest Rutherford and Arthur Eddington's book, *'the Expanding Universe'* had fired this ambition. In studying physics and chemistry, I was privileged to use the school's laboratories unsupervised in the early mornings, being exempt from inspection parade and, in the evenings, from prep. So when I had to find a job, I looked for one in a company in which I could foster my interests in science subjects, and take an external degree by studying in the evenings. My family was not of much help, having no useful contacts or influence. I was prepared to be a laboratory assistant, provided I would have the opportunity of studying. To no avail: it was 1934.

My father left India and travelled to Australia and New Zealand, to judge whether the family could settle in either. He was deterred from such a move and returned to England, where he had a nervous breakdown. He never worked again. He was sixty-one. Fortunately, my mother, who was running a successful dressmaking business in Calcutta, had enough money and energy to wind up their affairs in India -- paying all my father's debts -- return to England, and settle the family at Kings Langley in Hertfordshire, from where I searched for work. There was a lot of unemployment, as the country was in a deep economic depression following the Wall Street crash in 1929.

The only job offered was in a large paper making and stationery manufacturing firm, where I became an export clerk. This involved meeting the dates of ships sailing to foreign destinations with manufacturing orders. I had to chase progress through the factory and warehouse. It brought me into close contact with working class people, and I swiftly learned to get their co-operation and help by jollying them along, discussing football, for example. Adopting a superior attitude would have been a bad mistake. My wage was £1 a week. The office opened at 8.30am, and closed at 6.00pm, half day on Saturday, but more often than not I had to work unpaid overtime.

I cycled to work, having bought a bicycle for £2.19.6d, paying for it by weekly instalments of 2/6d -- half a crown (12 p). I cycled home for lunch, a distance of three miles each way, so I had few outgoings. My mother had never cooked before, because she relied on servants in Calcutta and engaged them when on leave. However, she got straight into cooking and housekeeping. I helped by growing vegetables and cycling to a cheap market for fish at Watford on Friday evenings -- fives miles each way.

I stuck this life for four years, having earned wage rises to 35 shillings a week. I was twenty-one and asked to be given a job in India, where there was an office, only to be told there was no chance before I was twenty-five: so I began looking for a job abroad.

I applied for two jobs advertised in *The Daily Telegraph*, one in Bangkok and one in Singapore. I was interviewed for both on the same day and both offered me the job. I asked my father for advice. He did not know Bangkok, but had visited Singapore and recommended it: I took that one. I had to work in the London office, together with other trainees. My salary was enough to pay for a season ticket on the railway, pub lunches, and subscriptions to cricket, rugby and tennis clubs. Life had become altogether more pleasant. In fact, the economy was being boosted by Government money being poured into re-armament. The threatening attitude of Hitler's Germany was causing unease, and recruitment for the forces was accelerated. I applied for a short-service R.A.F. commission, but failed the eyesight test. I then applied to join the Honourable Artillery Company (H.A.C.) and would have

Ted Chaplin and friends.

started my training with them in the autumn of 1938, but my posting to Singapore was fixed for August.

I went out with another trainee on the S.S. 'RANCHI', a P & O ship. We went first class, and it was marvellous for young men of twenty-one, with enough energy and money to enjoy three weeks of unaccustomed luxury, and good companionship amongst the passengers. It was whilst we were on this voyage that the Munich crisis blew up and, after Chamberlain's visit to Hitler, he announced on his return, 'Peace in our time'. But when we arrived in Singapore, we were amongst people who had no such feelings. In fact, within two days we were enrolled into the local Volunteer forces, in preparation for the Japanese attack which most people foretold.

We worked hard and played hard, and I saw out the Thirties in Singapore. The Forties brought that Japanese attack, and it was an altogether different story. I suffered three and a half years as a Japanese POW and often felt that Colston School's austere regime was good training to endure the hardships then!

In Germany the spread of Nazism forced Mrs. Juliana Ray to leave school early and look for a suitable training.

When it came to the time, at the age of twelve, for me to go on to secondary education, the obvious choice was the Veres Paine Grammar School where my mother and her sisters were students. The Deputy Headmistress remembered my mother, so it made it easy for me and I also found a master and a mistress who had taught her. The atmosphere at the school was delightful, but then after two years conditions began to change.

Shari mama warned me that we Jews were more and more disliked because of the propaganda disseminated in Germany that was affecting Hungary. That meant I had to work and behave exceptionally well. Gradually almost a military rule was introduced and our uniform changed to blouses that looked almost like hussar tops, with cravats and Hungarian style hats.

When I was in the sixth form and still two years from matriculation, matters came to a head. I disliked school life more and more as politics dominated all subjects. Suddenly a very dear form mistress of mine was forced to retire because of her anti-Nazi views. I decided to finish school at the end of the year.

My father considered the possibility of emigrating, and decided that sewing, dressmaking and fashion designing was a trade that would be useful anywhere in the world. Accordingly he arranged for me to join the Salon Rosenthal, a big fashion house in the best part of the shopping centre of Budapest. Because of my higher educational qualifications I would be able to take the professional exam in eighteen months instead of three years. Then in the evenings I attended language courses, as well as going to concerts and reading to make up for the missing years at school.

[Much of this information will be found in Mrs. Juliana Ray's book and I am grateful that she has given me permission to quote from it: *By Grace Alone* - an epic journey of faith through three generations of a Jewish family].

John Magee knew from first hand experience the devastating results of unemployment on education in Hull during the Thirties.

The effects of unemployment in the Thirties were far worse than those of the Nineties. Far fewer married women worked at that time, so the number of families without a breadwinner was much greater. The unemployed got little help from the state or any other source. With the decline in trade, many ships were laid up and the crews were paid off and got no further wages until the ship sailed again. My father was a marine engineer and during long periods from 1927 onwards he had to take the job of watchman on his own ship laid up away from home. Those circumstances led to his early death in 1932. My wife at about the same time was the first to discover the suicide of another seafaring man who had lost his job. Many fully qualified graduates could not find teaching posts. My own headmaster told us that in 1932 he had two hundred applications for one post and that the applications of all but those with first class honours went into the wastepaper basket. Mathematics posts advertised said that an interest in music and drama would be helpful, and that experience in scouting etc. would be useful. One heard the comment, 'Only the Almighty need apply'.

My wife and I both started teaching at this time and each of us made sixty applications for posts without success, in spite of the fact that we both had good honours degrees. With my father's death, I had to take a post under the elementary code, with less pay than in the grammar school I had hoped to enter. We started at the time when there was a 10 per cent cut in all teachers' salaries.

Secondary education was not free. Fees to all but scholarship boys and girls were about £8 a year, which in present values would be over £200, and a special school was available for those who could not afford this amount. Later I was fortunate in getting a post in a technical school which used a building condemned as an orphanage and was badly maintained. It had no place for a school assembly but did a very good job in spite of circumstances which would not be tolerated today. In addition to major trials, the minor difficulty of classroom ink will long be remembered by both scholars and staff. The pot inkwells were often treated with wads of blotting paper, or carbide, and broken pen nibs could be made into darts which adorned many classroom ceilings. When the school was evacuated during the Second World War we taught under far better conditions that we had known at home.

When the children in the elementary schools left at the age of fourteen, most of them took jobs which would be regarded as unskilled now. The cane then was not just a last resort!

During this decade the three municipal grammar schools in Hull made remarkable progress, using modern methods and giving an education comparable to that of the public schools. They were able to send increasing numbers to Oxford and Cambridge and other universities. They also supplied most of the teachers needed in Hull schools.

Before the recession of the Thirties deepened, plans were already advanced for new buildings for the two co-educational grammar schools. These were on the outskirts of the town and had ample playing fields. They also had up to date science laboratories and light airy classrooms. In those days, however, the sexes were segregated for teaching and indeed it was a rule that boy and girl were forbidden to walk home together! These schools had the great advantage of being socially comprehensive, a virtue which is lacking today since most comprehensives are neighbourhood schools, drawing mainly from the same class of people.

Children generally were encouraged to be more socially conscious, and League of Nations Association groups met in some schools. This was the era of the 'Peace Pledge Union' and many young idealists spent much time in promoting it. This waned, however, as the war clouds gathered. One commendable aspect of school life is much weaker today: the members of a school class made a social unit and the friendships formed within it often lasted a lifetime, to say nothing of the romances which were more stable than those of today. I believe that children were more honest then, for it did not appear to be necessary to lock up cupboards and other things.

The tremendous expansion of secondary education after the war showed much native talent had been wasted, because so many people wanted their children to be earning as soon as possible instead of going to grammar or technical school. The night technical schools catered for those at work during the day, but in a three hour session I have known students fall asleep with fatigue.

In spite of the high unemployment rate during the Thirties, Joan MacLachlan gained a school teaching post.

After leaving college, I was appointed to a senior girl's school in a mining area. I earned £21.17.6d a month (I repaid £2 a week on the college loan so the total was £19.17.6d). My bus fare was 12/6d a week and I had a two mile walk each way to catch the bus, which left at 7.30 am.

The girls were splendid, but we had a terrible Head. She was a big, overpowering woman, and the younger staff were terrified of her. I was too popular and she seemed to resent that. I often met the girls on Saturdays and we went to exciting places like Hardwick Hall and to my uncle's farm.

I escaped after two years, with my spirits almost broken, but I got a wonderful post in a local senior girls' school and stayed there for twelve years.

After successfully completing her college training, Joan Dobson had to face the problem of finding work during the depression of the Thirties.

College course over and teaching certificate obtained, it remained to search for a post. It was even more difficult to find employment in the Thirties than in the Nineties. There were thirty or more applicants at each interview, plus many more who had not been put on the short list. Most education committees favoured their own county students, but I was a London student and London jobs were open to all comers. My young man of the time quickly obtained a job in his own county of Kent, but then he had been given a student loan and they were anxious to get their money back. I had been given a London Senior Scholarship for my training and had nothing to repay. While waiting for a successful conclusion to interviews, I went on supply. This entailed sitting in a large hall, signing on and waiting to be called for a day or two's teaching in local schools. At the time it felt like a cattle market.

Jack Solkhon was also unemployed then and we often accompanied each other to the cinema, sitting in the 6d seats. I finally obtained a job in a junior school in Surrey, on the borders of Hampshire. This involved a journey in the morning of trolley-bus (which had recently replaced trams in Wandsworth) to Clapham Junction, commuter crammed train to Waterloo, another to Woking and finally a bus to Knaphill. All this had to be repeated in reverse in the evening.

The journey to my teaching job finally proved too much for me, and I moved to digs in a nearby village for a while, but in 1938 I left to get married to a fellow student who had taken a similar course to mine at college. Within just over a year we (the Allies) were at war. My husband volunteered for the R.A.F. and for quite a long time awaited call-up. We were living in Canterbury when Neville Chamberlain made his fateful announcement, followed very shortly after by the air-raid siren. We lived by the cathedral and our air-raid shelter was in the cathedral crypt. The 'Red Dean' had had the King's School green dug up to provide a deep pad of soil above us in the cathedral nave. I believe he was never forgiven for that. I have a mental picture of him during a night time alarm clad in pyjamas with his priestly stole round his neck!

My husband's call-up papers came, and I was expecting my first baby, so we decided to pack up our furniture and put it in store and that I should go back to London and the family home. Everyone had said the war would be over by Christmas! A faint hope! When the time came to store our furniture, no Pickford's van arrived. I waited and waited -- to no avail. All available transport had gone to the coast to bring back our returning defeated army. It was the hour of Dunkirk. The next decade had begun. The time of Winston Churchill had arrived. This was really 'growing up'.

Mrs. Kittie Webster says she had no formal training but she had that wider education that comes from travelling abroad and mixing with people from many nations.

I came to England on my own in 1937 for the coronation. At that point my mother and I had come back from the States to Ireland: my mother had property and family there. I joined the Youth Hostels Association and did a lot with them. First of all I stayed at Oxford with some friends and helped there, and then I came up to London and started to train in dress design and dress making. In those days the Youth Hostels were run chiefly by people on a voluntary basis with accommodation provided but no pay. Any money they made usually came from serving meals. So I stayed in the London Youth Hostel at Great Ormond Street, where the staff were paid: there were six of us - two students at the Royal Academy of Music, two other girls who were in the Civil Service, and another worked at the British Museum. We were allowed to stay there for the modest sum of 10 shillings a week, provided we lent a hand from time to time. We paid for any meals -- about 1 shilling, or got our own meals in a kitchen provided for self-cookers. In my spare time I did a lot of relief work at other hostels including Holmbury St. Mary in Surrey and Colchester. I often went at weekends so that those in charge could have some time off.

Then the war came. At that time I had a friend who was articled to become a solicitor. We probably would have married but unfortunately on one of our outings he was knocked down by a car and killed, which was a great shock. That was in the Spring of 1939 and I was very upset. His sister was Headmistress of a school in Richmond and she applied and was appointed to a school in Birmingham, to start in September that year. So when war was threatened and evacuation was arranged she did not know her teachers or any of the children. She had moved to Birmingham in the holidays and she sent an SOS to me to go up and help her. I knew I would be called up in due course so I went and we duly assembled and evacuated the children on 1st September -- but they only went to Bromsgrove. The children were billeted in various houses round about and my friend, her mother and I stayed with the local Headmistress. But it wasn't very long before the people in Bromsgrove found that the children from the slum area of Birmingham didn't quite fit in. They had all kinds of problems and the Billeting Officer was tearing his hair: by the time little Billie or little Jane had been round to several houses, people wouldn't have them.

So the Medical Officer of Health for Worcestershire said "What about setting up a home?" My friend -- (two Headmistresses in the same house was not easy), thought it was a good idea. So the council took over two council houses which happened to be empty. My friend and her mother were installed in one and I in the other. She of course was teaching, but I took charge and did all the catering and cooking and looking after the kids, though she was there to help with the discipline. We had about ten children the other people rejected. People were very kind when they hadn't got the children living with them. They would give them presents and toys and they were very happy. We had a severe winter that year and we built snowmen etc. As we were only a bus ride from Birmingham some parents visited at weekends to keep in touch.

Then because Bromsgrove was only twelve miles from Birmingham the evacuees started drifting back, and the school in fact was reopened, so my friend travelled to Birmingham every day, leaving my mother and me in charge. The Medical Officer of Health appeared one day and said "Come with me. I want you to have a look at a house." So I went with him and he took me to one of the houses, Stoney Hill, that belonged to Bromsgrove school, a boys' public school that had been evacuated to Wales. The India Office had taken over most of the houses. He said, "That's fine. There are about fifty children from Clacton and Felixstowe arriving this afternoon", and I was there in an empty house. So I said "What about my children? They won't know where to come." He replied "We will sent the W.V.S. or someone to pick them up from school". In the meantime the W.V.S. and other people had been alerted -- it was Dunkirk and all the people who had been evacuated to Felixstowe and Clacton on the east coast had to be hastily removed. Local government officers and the W.V.S. rallied around and in a matter of hours the empty house was furnished with the necessary equipment, but for the first week or so -- in glorious June weather -- we had most of our meals on the lawn because we had no tables or chairs.

The Hon. Mrs. Clay was able to spend time at home as well as travelling abroad when she left school.

Heather left St. James' in 1932: she lived at home and had a very very busy social life. She also did sculpting and drawing with my father, and in 1933 she had the honour of being presented to His Majesty King George V and to Queen Mary at Buckingham Palace. She had to wear an amazing long dress with a train, and a headdress made with ostrich feather, and an ostrich feather fan. My mother who was dressed in similar clothes, presented her. That was a very great occasion. They gave a party afterwards in London for their friends and relations to see Heather and my mother in their presentation robes. I was allowed off from school for the day and went up to London by train to see them. I didn't actually go to the presentation but I was able to go to the party afterwards. So that was an excitement at that time.

Lady Baden-Powell presented at Buckingham Palace.

Then I left St. James' in 1934, I was not yet old enough to be presented, but my mother had received an invitation to take her daughter to a Buckingham Palace garden party. So instead of taking Heather she filled in my name. The day I arrived home from school I went by train and got out at Reading. Mother met me there; took me straight to a dress shop, and we bought my dress and hat -- a beautiful full length swirl of mauve and blue and pink chiffon over a satin underskirt, and a dark blue straw hat, with a wide brim and a great big mauve velvet swathe round the top of it. I remember it perfectly well: I looked wonderful! My first real long dress, and I was just seventeen! A few days later we went to the Buckingham Palace garden party and I wore this dress. Awful to say so, but I don't remember anything about the Party -- though I have been lucky enough to go several times in later years, and have treasured memories of these gracious occasions.

After we left school, our education continued with a course of shorthand and typing in a school at Farnham, only five miles away from home. So Heather and I went in the little car she had been given when she left school and went to Farnham every day. I never completed the Pitman's course, but I did do enough of it to be competent as a secretary to my mother, and Heather was secretary to my father. She was always much better than me at everything! She had had a bit longer at shorthand and typing than I had.

Betty Baden-Powell = Hon. Mrs. Clay.

Two months later in September they took us as their secretaries on a world tour, from 1934 to May 1935. That was the most marvellous experience of my life, going with these two wonderful people as they set about helping Scout and Guide leaders in all the countries we visited; advising them, helping them and inspiring them to go on and develop their movement and bring more and more people within its fold of goodwill and opportunity.

The main goal was to be in Australia for the Jamboree, and having visited other countries on the way there, we went on to New Zealand and across the Pacific and Canada for three months, also visiting places in the United States of America. Then back home in May 1935.

That summer we stayed at home. Heather had started a little job in London working as secretary for Lady Hilton Young. She was the widow of the famous explorer Captain Scott, who had died in the Antarctic. She was a sculptress by profession and talented, and Heather was enchanted watching her modelling people. Lady Hilton Young made a statue of her husband, which is erected in London. Her son was the famous Peter Scott, who does wonderful paintings of birds. He founded the Severn Wild Fowl Trust and other places of sanctuary for birds. I remember Heather, who was living with them as she was secretary, saying Lady Hilton Young said, "Oh Heather, go up and tell Peter it is time for dinner. Tell him to come down please." So she went up to Peter's studio and knocked on the door and said "Excuse me, but would you please come down. Your mother says it is dinner time." "Oh yes. Well I think I will just finish this whilst I am doing it. I've only got a couple of birds to put in." And there and then with the utmost skill and expertise he painted two more exquisite birds into this picture. My sister was so entranced with his skill and his ability.

Much later, when I was married, Heather bought a print of one of Peter Scott's paintings and gave it to us as a wedding present. So we have it to this day, with Brent geese flying.

In the summer of 1935 I was jaunting about at home, living at Pax Hill; I think I helped briefly with a Brownie Pack but then the summer holidays came and that stopped. Meanwhile I was having a lovely social life -- tennis parties (I was a rotten tennis player: exceedingly bad and one week I would say "I hate this game", and the next time, "What fun this is" when I played better).

Departing for Kenya, October 1935.
Station Master on far right in top hat.

Then there were lots of parties and dances and jollifications, and it was all such fun. Meanwhile I was secretary to my mum and doing quite a lot of work there, really trying to earn my keep. She was so wonderful to me and gave me so much freedom and fun. Of course we had our visit to the Gilwell reunion and other camping excitements; then in October that year we set off once more for another tour, this time to Africa for a Jamboree at East London in South Africa. There was also a lovely tour all through the winter of 1935-36. We went to various places where my parents saw Scouts and Guides.

In January 1936 the country and the empire had the sadness of the death of King George V, so of course we had to go into mourning straight away. We were staying in rather posh places at Government House, Pretoria, and Government House, Salisbury, so we had to rush out immediately and buy black dresses. We put black armbands on our uniform because we were in mourning, and everywhere we went when the union jack was put up, it was pulled down again to half mast, to show that we truly were mourning our sovereign.

The bursting of the financial bubble in America during 1929 spread ripples of depression and unemployment throughout the whole world in the early Thirties, and England did not escape.

I was completing the course at the Triangle Secretarial College in 1930, and was advised by the Principal to accept a temporary post with the British American Tobacco Company at Millbank, London, although I should have had two months further training. Jobs were so scarce that it was unwise to turn down any reasonable offer. The salary was 50 shillings weekly, plus a lunch in the excellent canteen; good in those difficult days!

The office was large and airy, overlooking the Thames, and my two colleagues were both very helpful to a timid newcomer. I was working for the Traffic Manager, who had to arrange transport for all the employees who were travelling abroad. There were three bells on the wall in our office, and we each had our own signal, but the noise always made me jump and palpitations followed. Most days I could not face having lunch in the canteen, and went without and sat on the green opposite the office watching the ships pass up and down the Thames. Fortunately it was summertime.

At the end of the three months of temporary work I was offered a permanency, but refused as I felt too ill – it was the beginning of a nervous breakdown. The rest of that year I was at home, looked after by our most understanding mother, and by the beginning of 1931 I was ready for work again. Unemployment was rife, but the Triangle had a good reputation and I was invited for an interview with the architects Wimperis,

Simpson and Guthrie, South Molton Street, off Oxford Street, and duly appointed.

It was much more interesting being in a small office, and the junior architects were very friendly. All went well until my colleague was off sick for a week. As well as being secretary to the three partners she manned a small telephone exchange and had given me only very brief instructions about using it. The partners insisted on knowing the name of the caller before accepting a call, and one day I was sure the man wanting to speak to Mr. Guthrie was saying he was Havannah. I knew that couldn't be right, so asked him again – and again. Then one of the junior architects came into the office and I asked him to find out, but he was as much in the dark as I was. So again I asked and received the answer "Oh, tell him it's the owner of the Cambridge Theatre." I learned later that he was Sir Harold Werner! I expected Mr. Guthrie to be upset about it, but he never mentioned it. Perhaps he was amused! We were all invited to the official opening of the theatre, but I declined.

I usually went to the ABC restaurant nearby for lunch, and had a poached egg or baked beans on toast. That left plenty of time to explore the many different shops in Oxford Street, some large stores like Selfridges (the nearest) but also many smaller ones.

I had only been there for three or four months and was quite enjoying the work, when out of the blue I had a letter from Mr. Arthur Millbourn, Headmaster of Colston's School, Bristol, (and later ordained). He was an Old Blue (from Christ's Hospital, Horsham) and as his previous secretary was an Old Blue from Hertford he had written to ask Miss Craig, the

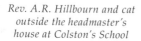

Rev. A.R. Hillbourn and cat outside the headmaster's house at Colston's School

Headmistress, to recommend someone else and she had suggested me.

Knowing the health problems I had had at school and since, Miss Craig felt that it would be better for me to live in semi-rural surroundings, with no travelling, and urged me to accept the post. It was a plunge in the dark. As I received full board and lodging the initial salary was only £60 a year, but I decided to accept. The architects seemed sorry that I was leaving and gave me a very generous cheque although I had been there such a short time.

After years at a girls' boarding school it was a shock to be living among boys and staff – all men apart from the matron, but the Headmaster and his wife, who had no children, treated me more as a daughter than an employee. I had my own sitting room and bedroom, with a maid to look after everything. Breakfast and lunch I had on high table with the staff, but dinner and meals in the holidays with the Matron in her room. When Mr. and Mrs. Millbourn were on holiday I was able to invite one of my sisters or a friend to keep me company, and they usually overlapped a few days so were also 'adopted'. The Millbourns were very musical and invited us to listen to classical music from records or their pianola, and I enjoyed being allowed to play the latter. We also had some enjoyable picnics.

The resident staff, all housemasters, soon got to know me and invited me to join them when they went to dances at the Bath Pump Room and elsewhere, or plays at the Little Theatre, and concerts at Colston's Hall. A visit to Oxford for Eights Week was another special event. They also taught me to play badminton, which I enjoyed. During my time there sufficient funds were raised to build a school chapel, an outdoor swimming pool and a pavilion. Rugby matches were always supported enthusiastically, and Colston's often won.

As well as the staff, I got to know many of the boys: it was a friendly place, but by 1938 rumblings of war were growing louder and louder, and I felt I should be in London with my parents, so very reluctantly I gave in my notice. It was the Principal of the Triangle Secretarial College again who recommended me for a post as secretary to the Managing Director and Secretary of May and Baker Ltd. at St. Paul's Churchyard. I thoroughly enjoyed both the work and the opportunity to explore the city of London. It was the time when their discovery, M & B 693 (2-p amino benzine sulphonamido pyridine) had revolutionised the treatment of some illnesses, including pneumonia and gonorrhoea, and I was much involved.

Grace in the study at Colston's.

Sixth-formers at Colston's School.

Colston's School swimming being built.

Colston's School swimming pool in use.

Then came a complication. The Managing Director at May & Baker's chemical factory at Dagenham, Essex, decided to form his own company in the north of England, and his secretary and accountant joined him. That meant the Managing Director and Secretary from London had to take over and asked me to go with them, promising to pay my fares. This was at the end of 1938, when the threat of war had receded, and I foolishly agreed. It meant travelling right across London from Wandsworth to Dagenham. It took an hour and a half most days, but once air raids began and railway lines were bombed that journey turned out to be a nightmare.

However, it was a very interesting experience, and among other things I discovered that my predecessor had been responsible for engaging office staff when necessary. In peace time that was a fairly rare occurrence, but in 1939 when war was imminent many of the young men who were on the R.A.F. and Territorial reserve lists were called up at once, and I found that much of my time was engaged in finding replacements. Some of the women left for various reasons, too, so much so that I had to appoint a secretary to do much of my work for the Managing Director.

I found that the personnel and welfare aspects of the work were what I was really interested in, and having survived much bombing I was selected to take a London School of Economics course at Cambridge University in 1941 for Personnel and Welfare Offices: I realised what I had missed in not going to university when I left school.

Eileen Davison had trained as a secretary and describes her first job.

Just before the Second World War I started my first job as secretary/general amanuensis in a small Cement Works' office, working for my father, who was manager and a director, and the managing director. I was very happy there, although I should have preferred some kind of work on the land to office work, and longed to exchange my typewriter for a tractor! The office block was set amidst fields and from my office window I could watch the farmer at his work and, if the window were open, I heard the skylarks singing. In the summer my father and I would cycle the five miles from home, taking a sandwich lunch with us, and cycle back in the late afternoon. I remember the joy of those cycle rides, the beautiful unspoilt countryside, the quiet roads, the wild flowers spilling over the banks, fields of corn liberally besprinkled with poppies and cornflowers, the lush hedgerows, and the birds!

It was a very friendly office, everyone helping each other out in times of need. Pay day and the 'end of the month balancing the ledger day' were usually pretty hectic and, if I were not busy myself, I would lend a hand: the rest of the staff, all married men older than myself, were very good to me too and bent over backwards to help me. Of course, we had no sophisticated office equipment as they have today. There were manual typewriters, an adding up machine and a franking machine, and that was it! There was also a very leisurely approach to life generally, becoming to those who are countrymen by birth and nature. I well remember one little man who was a hunchback (due to the fact that during his work on the railway he had been crushed between two wagons), he was so kind and cheery, and a wizard at figures. Then there was another, who couldn't file correctly, and whose typing and spelling left much to be desired; he had such a leisurely approach to life it was unbelievable! This outfit was presided over by the managing director, who also had difficulty with spelling, was highly eccentric, and had a wonderful sense of humour, which kept everything ticking over.

Mrs. Betty Forsyth was living in Dundee during the Thirties and lives there still.

After leaving school in 1936 I went to business college, which I found boring. In the mornings we learned shorthand and typing; in the afternoons book-keeping. The register was taken in the morning, but never in the afternoon, so it was common practice to miss classes after lunch. I saw many films (I saw 'Firefly' four times!), but I'm afraid my book-keeping never really got off the ground.

When I started work I earned 12/6d per week, but could make a little extra by working in the evenings, typing envelopes for 1 shilling per hour. More profitable was the payment for Saturday afternoon or evening work. Taking down football reports in shorthand over the telephone in the afternoon was paid at the rate of 2/6d per hour, but working for two hours in the evening for a Sunday newspaper meant 10 shillings for the two hours' work – almost another week's pay! Every Saturday evening on the way to the office I treated myself to a quarter of a pound of chocolates, which cost me six old pence – real extravagance!

Mrs. Jean Gillis first met her husband, Val, when she was only ten and he, at the age of seventeen, was playing the saxophone with a dance band.

After winning a scholarship to Ensham School, I left at sixteen and went to work for a firm of solicitors in the City Temple. I remember I was paid £1 a week, of that 17/6d was for Mum and Dad towards my keep, leaving me 2/6d for myself. This enabled me to pay my fares to the office and to have some over for myself. I had to leave home early in the morning to catch what was called the 'Workman's' tram to the Embankment: the fare was 2d for a day return ticket!

It was during this time, from 1936 to 1940, that Uncle Val (as I called him) kept appearing outside my office in Sergeant's Inn, to accompany me home. In 1940 during the war we became engaged to be married. Val was a carpenter by trade and was found fit and well for the Services, having passed A1. However, by the Lord's mercy as he was in a reserved occupation he did not have to go to war but was employed on the more urgent work of building aircraft and Admiralty launches.

Brai Harper did not have long to appreciate being employed before the outbreak of the Second World War disrupted his life and that of many others.

At the age of seventeen and a half, I was apprenticed as a cub reporter on the local paper. This meant learning to ride a motor-bike, and then doing a weekly tour of the nearby villages to collect news from whoever was willing to give it. Sometimes it was rather eccentric rectors, or hall secretaries, or the cobbler or baker. In the summer, I attended village fêtes or concerts in the hall. Back in town for the rest of the week, I attended annual general meetings of the many societies, anniversary celebrations at the Methodist Church (which seemed to happen every month!), and I also inherited the children's corner and the entertainment page. The latter I particularly liked, because it took me round each week to the four cinemas to get details and adverts for their forthcoming attractions. I also had a free pass to see the films. When the fire maroon went off, so did I on my motorbike, listening for the fire engine's bell and trying to get onto its tail. There were never any big fires; just frying pans or gorse bushes or bonfires out of control. In odd moments, I dropped in on the undertakers, who would tip me off on any death which might give a story. It was not too productive to ring the police station or the hospital: they were terribly cagey.

After the 1938 crisis, when Chamberlain assured us of peace in our time, my older brother and I joined the R.N.V.R. to ensure that when the peace ended we would be in the Navy. We attended every week at the depot in Newhaven, where we did gun drill round an obsolete 1916 gun, and had lectures round a similarly obsolete mine, not realising that Hitler had a whole new range of mining tricks for our delight. In 1939, when they felt sure we were really interested, we were issued with our uniforms. On the 6 September we were mobilised to Portsmouth and went on the longest train journey I had had, all the way to Thurso in Caithness, where we embarked for Scapa Flow.

We were berthed in the old battleship *Iron Duke,* a whole big mess-deck of R.N.V.R. rookies, used for the next two months for various working parties, replenishing the stores of the cruisers and destroyers when they returned from operations. I managed to dodge much of the heavy stuff by being appointed to the crew of a small speedboat, which took sailing orders out to tankers and supply ships, at any hour of the day or night in all weathers. After that, I was put into the Captain's office, because I could type and spell. Then *Royal Oak* was sunk not two miles from us, and a few days later the bombers hit the *Iron Duke* and we abandoned ship. A happy boyhood ended with a bang!

Shortage of finances prevented George Topping from going on to university when he left school.

I was in a science group and hoped to be a doctor, but when we added up the two free bursaries (because of Dad's low wages) and the three I qualified for in examinations, the total income from all five was £70 a year and I needed a minimum of £85, so I could not at that time go to university in Glasgow. Only the richer people went to Edinburgh!

Later I sat an examination for Lanark County Council in Glasgow and came out top. I was offered a position in what was to become their Social Welfare Department, and accepted it at 17/6d per week, but with 'good prospects'. But after two to three years war was declared and we were called up -- me on 8 August 1940 into the Scots Guards for six years.

I attended Glasgow University as a student 1937-1940 for a Diploma in Poor Law, but by the time the war was over everything had changed and by 1946/1948 it was renamed a Diploma in Public Administration, which, in the Civil Service proper, (which I had joined in July 1948) was of no use to me!

Andrew J. Blair was one of the many youngsters trying to find their first job during the great depression of the early Thirties.

With a great deal of luck and after written applications to every branch of all eight banks in Greenock I eventually got a job with the Bank of Scotland five weeks before my sixteenth birthday. I was taken on as an apprentice for four years (the first 'year' lasting eighteen months!) on a salary scale of £30, £50, £70 and £90 per annum (NOT per week!), which of course was not a living wage. The expectation was that at the end of the apprenticeship I would be retained on a salary of £110 or £120 on which a single man could live – just. By the age of about thirty one would expect to be earning in the region of £200 per annum, the salary which would support – just – a married couple. Before marrying one had to have the bank's permission! Few females were employed and they had to leave when they married.

Probably I was naive, but I do not remember any bowing, scraping or genuflection by anyone to anyone. Certainly one had to defer to one's elders, seniors, bosses and important persons generally. But that seemed more a matter of manners. In a way all were equal but some were more important.

George Campbell was another who was fortunate to find employment during the early Thirties, although the salary would be considered derisory nowadays.

In 1933 I joined the Insurance Brokers Willis Faber and Dumas in Leadenhall Street in the City of London, as a junior clerk in the Accounts Department. The offices were Victorian, with long, high, double-sided desks where the clerks, six each side, sat on high long-legged chairs facing each other, working on heavy ledgers. My job was to lift the ledgers on to the desks and to make the tea. Discipline was strict but I was glad at least to have a job, even though the salary was only £1 per week.

Travel from my home in Finchley was by bus, route 144A. The cost for the week, which included Saturday mornings, was 6 shillings. I gave my mother 7/6d, which left 6/6d to spend on riotous living! Lunch usually cost about 6d or, on rare occasions when I indulged in steak and kidney pudding and chips, 9d. This was usually taken in the basement of the Express Dairy shop.

Kathleen Stirzaker had to leave school when she was fourteen.

I was fourteen years old in 1935 and had to leave school. Getting a job in the Thirties was as difficult as it is now in the Nineties, but I got a job as a domestic help. In the afternoons I had to take the baby of the house to the park. I worked from 8.30am to 5.30pm and had my dinner and a cup of tea in the afternoon. I was paid 5 shillings a week for this: I worked every day except Sunday and Thursday afternoon. I was very grateful for this job, but I was always on the look-out for something better. Although I did many domestic jobs I was eighteen years old before I got work in an office, which is what I had wanted to do all the time. This was at the local swimming baths. I had to write down the ticket numbers so that we knew how many were sold, then the money had to be counted so that we knew that the correct amount had been collected. On Friday mornings I took the week's money to the bank. I think my wages at this time would be about 30/-. It was 1939 by then and the Second World War began.

Because she was half Jewish, Mrs. Margaret Willis was not allowed to proceed to university, although she was well qualified, and instead had to look for work.

I got a job in a firm that produced chemical additives for the building trade. I started work on 1 April 1933, the very day Hitler ordered a boycott of Jewish shops, showing by action what he meant by 'doing God's work in fighting the Jew'. My reaction was to purchase a fair-sized Magen David, which I wore with pride and as an act of defiance.

The boss was a Christian and a friend of the Jews, but some of the employees were fanatical Nazis. One day the leader of our department did not turn up. He did not come the next day either. What happened to Karl Heinke? Little by little we got to know the truth; his communist leanings had been uncovered and he had been taken to a labour camp for political retraining. When he returned after months he was a changed man: no longer a sparkle in his eye and a joke on his lips. He never said what had happened; he never spoke about it.

The firm I worked for expanded rapidly with developing industry. The products were needed for buildings, bridges, autobahn and fortifications. Both the Siegfried line and the Maginot line used them, as I was to discover when I -- against all the machinations of the Nazis in the firm -- became the private secretary of the boss. He was a Christian, and took other Jews into his firm, including my friend Mirjam.

Also in October 1938, my brother Hans was able to take up work in our firm. I was no longer the only bread-winner in the family, nor the only one feeling responsible for our parents.

In the meantime, we had moved to a smaller flat in the house, making use of the attic rooms. On 9 November 1938 we had a visit from a Jewish Christian Pastor, Dr. H. E., who was going to stay the whole day, but shortly after 11am we heard a tremendous noise of shattering glass, which went on and on coming nearer and nearer. The Nazi hordes had entered the road from either side, making for the centre where our house was. We felt helpless and frightened, but before they could reach us the attack was called off. Our visitor phoned his wife in B and heard that the same systematic destruction had been carried out there, even in their home. On returning home he himself was arrested and put in a concentration camp. The Nazi explanation for this destruction of Jewish shops and homes all over Germany was that it was the 'outburst of spontaneous anger of the people' for the death in Paris of the German ambassador. In history it is called the 'Crystal-night'. Many Jews were arrested that night and put into concentration camps.

At the beginning of April 1939 the young people in England with whom I had corresponded were married, and they invited me to visit them in their new home. The invitation was for Bank holiday (at that time at the beginning of August). I had a contract with the firm that I would give three months' notice. If I were to leave for good, I would have to act quickly to be free to travel in August. "Please God, help me and confirm your calling: give me a sign!" Two signs were given, one at the embassy where I got my tourist visa, and one at the firm. Having access to confidential correspondence, a file came to my notice which showed that negotiations were afoot to transfer the business to a younger relative. Even though the boss, who had been so kind to us Jews over the years and was now in a nursing home, should recover from his serious illness, the firm would never be the same again. I could safely give in my notice. When I visited him in the nursing home he wished me God's speed, and I could thank him for his protection over the years. I did not know then that six weeks later he would have closed his eyes for good.

The last few weeks at the firm were occupied with writing or typing the secret recipes of the firm's products. Just to show that Nazi propaganda had lulled the German people into a false sense of peace and security, I may mention the fact that the contract made with an English business consortium contained the phrase 'in case of war the recipes will be theirs' -- not realising that war was only four to six weeks away.

I myself left on 3rd August 1939, exactly a month before war started. I was met at Victoria Station by one of the business friends of the firm who helped me with money, as we were allowed to take RM10 only out of the country.

Before he died in 1986, Bob Rutty wrote his family saga. His earlier life is described in *Growing Up In The Twenties*. In 1926 he began work at Fleurets in Bloomsbury Square but changed jobs in 1930.

In 1930 I took a job at Douglas Young & Co. This firm was a well established and respected one, with offices in Coleman Street in the City. I was a successful negotiator. Wages 50 shillings a week, plus commission and bonus (the latter never very much).

There were three of us -- Gordon Youngman, the manager, myself and eventually Youngman's brother-in-law, Jack Early. I was ambivalent to Youngman, but he was very good and I eventually learned a lot from him. The office had primarily been used for rent collecting - originally opened by Douglas Youngman. He raised the earnings of that branch from £100 per month to over an average of £1,000 per month (multiply it for present day inflation).

Sometimes accounts weren't always paid in relation to the due monthly commission cheque, so when at the end of the month I was short of income I used to pocket the shortfall from rents of the properties I managed and then pay it back when my commission came through. The governors eventually cottoned on but were very decent about it and I got a rise. Very naughty, I know, but as Fagin sings *'You got to pick a pocket or two'*.

I have never forgotten that when I was taken on by Wallace Young he said to me 'We really wanted a Public School chap you know'. Well, who could have been more public than me?

At one time a dear old chap who owned a large chunk of property and land on the Embankment (South), by the Fire Brigade Headquarters, said he was going to leave part of it to me, but alas.... Another client, Jacob Zuckrow, and his wife allowed us the use of his corrugated iron bungalow at Canvey Island for holidays: free! I remember the first time we went on holiday and took Brian on to the sea wall he said "What a lot of water".

At the outbreak of war in September 1939 my employment ceased. While I was waiting for call up (when they decided my entry would bring about Hitler's downfall) as a member of the Red Cross I joined the A.R.P. (Air Raid Precautions). I was second in charge at the Edonton Eldon Road depot for the princely sum of £3 per week.

At the Eldon Road Ambulance Station we had six lorries converted into ambulances, a number of cars used as ambulance cars and about ten squads of stretcher bearers. We had the whole of the ground floor school rooms, hall and playground. I used to drill the men in the playground: great fun ordering them about. During the year I was there we were called out to three air raids: Halstead Drive, Harrow Drive and another I can't remember. Luckily there were only injuries and not deaths. Then there were the loose telephone wires. Anybody who adopts sangfroid over this is wrong. It was blooming frightening with all the bang bang overhead, the searchlights and everything.

My friend Jimmy James, who was with me at Eldon Road, waiting to be called to the Merchant Navy, helped me. I had a tough four stretcher bearers who one night got drunk and I ordered them off the station. One of them took out a knife and came at me, but Jimmy gave him a left to the stomach and a right to the jaw, and saved me and the day. They never came back to my station.

After a time I was moved from Eldon Road to Ridge House, which was on the site now occupied by the Library at the end of Ridge Avenue. The air raids were fewer. Then on 11th December 1940 I was called up to the Sherwood Foresters, an infantry regiment, and stationed at Derby.

When Mr. John Wallis of Wiveliscombe left school it was the beginning of the Thirties and extremely difficult to find work, as the slump had hit the U.K. very hard and millions were unemployed. His father was a dentist so he was able to help, as John explains.

My father, knowing other people through his practice, got me into a warehouse in the City. I started off in the basement. We boys had to go up into the various departments and collect the goods people had ordered, then get them back to the basement, where they were all checked and put into willow skips on wheels. We fllled up a skip with all a customer's goods and pushed it through to the packing department. There they used to take the mickey out of us, sending us for such things as glass tacks and rubber hammers: when we got back they asked if we had got any. I was up to their game and used to spent half an hour or so in the loo or somewhere, and would answer, "No. Nobody had any."

The worst part was the packing department because skips were in short supply, so we had to stand by a skip while they packed the contents. They let us stand there and wait, then when it was empty and we wanted it take it they said, "No, you can't have it. It's wanted." So we had to start all over again. It was so stupid, but it wasn't my fault if I wasted a whole morning.

Then we went up to the gents clothing department; there I tied up parcels and at the end of the day I swept the floor. Sometimes

I took parcels down to the packing department. We had a lift but it was a string affair and often got stuck. The lift man used to give us snuff -- some of it was all right. We could also have a cup of tea in the lift. It was allowed but it was also meant to be secret.

This job was going on and on for ever until someone died, and I didn't fancy waiting for that, so I went round to another warehouse in the Cheapside. When I went in the Manager asked, "What are you doing now?" When I told him he said "I'm sorry, I can't take you from another firm, but if you were out of work I would take you straight away." So I went back and gave in my notice and returned to the firm and was accepted. I worked in Ladies' Underwear. Mostly it was spencers and vests and panties, made of wool or cotton. I was in charge of the stock and I was very happy there. We were very busy until Christmas and then it was stocktaking. As soon as that was completed they gave me my cards. I assume they took on somebody else the following September.

A friend of my father's had a furniture shop and factory in Streatham, where we were living, and he offered me a job in the factory, in the manager's office, costing up all the materials used for each piece of furniture. I was not interested in money and did not remember how much I was paid, but I know I was given an extra 7/6d once because I was able to replace the mother-of-pearl and veneer that had been damaged on an inlaid clock face. When I had finished it looked as good as new!

Alison Hudson's first job at Galashiels.

I was almost sixteen years old when I got a job in a tailoring business employing about one hundred men and women. We sang at work, enjoyed going to the pictures, small dances, and occasional trips to Edinburgh to see plays and operettas. Life in general was rather good.

The company I worked for had a very friendly atmosphere. It was very high class work: suits, coats, ladies' costumes being sent all over the world. Names I remember are 'Cabbages and Kings' of America and 'Wessel and Vett' in Scandinavia. Most staff worked at ordinary sewing machines, but I was employed on machines which did special work. One, with a curved needle, 'padded' and shaped the curves on lapels. Another did an oversew stitch fastening Melton collar lining to the neck of jackets and coats. Yet another machine did zigzag stitch, again padding inside some parts of garments. Buttonholes were mainly done by hand sewers, but trousers were done by a rather large, noisy machine.

143

Most pressing was done by hand, but a large steam-pressing machine, trade name Hoffman, was used for some parts of garments.

We worked in rows of machines, with girls on hand sewing at benches and stools. There was at least one tailor who sat on his table doing very special hand-made garments. The firm actually made a winter coat each for the Princess of Wales and the Duke of York, using Kashmir and pure silk.

Pride meant that girls dressed very well and vied with each other to see who could be smartest! In those days to have a bathroom and even an inside toilet was undreamed of! But this did not deter most people from being smart and even glamorous, and many a working girl married into the so-called upper class. Some people were wealthy through business and had big houses, but those we worked for were friendly and always acknowledged us when we met.

Lilian Smith much regretted the fact that she was deprived of a grammar school education because of the financial stringencies of her family.

I had to go to work from the age of fourteen as Dad could not afford to keep me at school, although I was offered a place at High School. I was very upset and resentful for a long time.

I began work at Reeves and Sons, Artists Materials, spending my day between 8am and 5pm hand-polishing brush handles and set squares -- this for the princely sum of 10/6d, 9 shillings for mother and 1/6d for me.

Kit Hull started work as soon as she was old enough to leave school.

My father bought me a second-hand bicycle in 1937. I was fourteen then and started my first job at a printing factory. My father took me the first day. There were long benches with a trolley run on rails along the side of them. We were what was called 'tearers'; we had to put the paints on the blocks and then tear it over with a brush, more like a scrubbing brush. Then the men put their print blocks into it, on silk -- Paisley patterns like you get on scarves. When the whole sheet of silk was finished they pulled it up above to dry. I earned 15 shillings a week, and gave my mother 10 shillings; my 5 shillings went on stockings and I saved the rest towards new shoes. Later we went on to half time and were paid only 7/6d. That's when I went into the laundry for ten years.

We didn't actually wash the clothes: they were put into big machines, then spun dry in hydro machines, called spinners today. Big articles were put through a calender (that's what they were called -- like a mangle, but ten times bigger).

I went through the whole procedure from sorting, packing, ironing and folding. It was very cold where the sorting was done. We used to put brown paper round our legs and wore mittens and our coats sometimes. Then on Friday we used to scrub all the bare boards on the floor. We wore a sack for an apron.

When war broke out in 1939 we laundered the soldiers' washing. I think a lot of them were lonely as they used to put notes in their parcels. When the sirens sounded we all went down the air raid shelters; we took our knitting and lunch.

Work was tough when Ian MacLachlan was young.

I was born and brought up in Ballachulish, Argyll, on the shores of Loch Leven, twelve miles from Ben Nevis. I was eighteen when the Thirties began and worked in the slate quarry with my father, brother and uncles. The work was hard and exacting: finding a profitable seam and coping with the hazardous weather made men of us -- no weaklings could survive.

Wages were low: we were paid by result. There were no unions so we were at the mercy of the owners. However they did build new houses for the workers, and we were lucky enough to occupy a top flat, with the luxury of hot water, a bathroom and extra rooms.

In 1933 my elder brother was killed. He went to investigate a faulty charge for a mate but he didn't get away in time and was killed by the blast. I had the task of going home to tell my mother. The whole village was in mourning; the schools and shops all closed on the day of his funeral. My mother was diabetic and never recovered from the shock. She died just four years later. By 1936 the quarry was declining so I moved to Kinlochleven Aluminium Works along with other young men. The quarry was worked by the older men, who just eked out a living for a few more years.

Don Clark began earning his own living as soon as he reached the minimum school leaving age.

I was sent to work on a Welsh hill farm at the age of fourteen. I had recovered from TB but my father did not want any of his children to work in the pit. I would be in the fresh air and earn 5 shillings a week, plus my keep.

I had one day off a month, but I was given food, a training in farming, and a good pair of boots. I was always hungry and would pinch an egg each day and eat it raw to give me strength!

It was hard work but I enjoyed it and went to a neighbouring farm in my free time to learn how to be an expert on hedging.

When war broke out the farmers were told to kill the bracken and grow more food. Five hundred tons of stone lime were delivered to the farm, but as there was no extra labour it was impossible to spread it. When it rained the lime expanded to ten times its original size.

During the war even on a farm food was short, but I was able to kill a rabbit occasionally and send it to my mother in a parcel with its head sticking out. It went by special rabbit post for 6d, and was much appreciated back in the valley.

Mr. Alfred Ridpath was fortunate to be employed during the great recession of the Thirties.

I was already in the Merchant Service with the Cunard White Star Line in 1930 and was a seaman for two years. I have always been grateful for the six years of world travel in the Merchant Navy, as I was able to learn so much of the world and of the lifestyles of many other nations.

Three and five masted ships were often seen sailing up and down the Mersey in the Thirties, even though the days of the steamships were coming in rapidly, but at sea they were a magnificent sight, passing at a distance of around a mile from us. Crews were enrolled from the age of fourteen upwards, and at this age they were frequently sent up the mast in the sailing ships. In rough weather the chance of survival was slight. On my first trip to sea, I had to carry my own mattress; seamen in those days carried their own beds with them, just as a hiker would carry his pack. A board, or a portion of deck, or sometimes a hammock were provided on which to put the mattress.

Refrigerators were installed on the Cunard White Star Line ships, but of course no such refinements were available on the sailing ships, and salted food was predominately used.

There was no sex education in those days: information was picked up in the playground. Homosexuality was rife on board ship and young people were subject to abuse. It was not tried on me as I was a big lad, but the thought of participating I found revolting. America had burlesque shows which seamen regularly attended.

The Revd. Alan M. Sax had to leave school early, but he was able to overcome that handicap in later life.

I left school when I was fourteen and worked at various dead end jobs. I was sixteen when the Second World War was declared and, prior to my army service, spent a number of years in the Rest

Centre Service caring for people who had been bombed out of their homes. When I was seventeen and three quarters I began to volunteer for military service. Both the Air Force and the Army passed me C4 when I went for the medical check. Then on 4th December, a few days after my eighteenth birthday, I was conscripted by the Army, saw the medical board as on the previous two occasions and was passed A1. It seemed there was a different standard of medical fitness when it came to conscription!

I was at Gordon Barracks, Aberdeen, for six weeks training, and thereafter was transferred to Catterick in Yorkshire and then to the Middle East. After spending six years in Her Majesty's Forces I was discharged as C2. I sought to apply for an army pension: the papers were torn up by my father -- no son of his was going to apply to his country for a pension. Whatever happened was because of loyalty to his country.

Barclay Hankin describes the day he joined the Army.

I had been in the Signals Platoon in the Christ's Hospital O.T.C. and I had obtained a Communications degree from Imperial College. London University Joint Selection Board, who had earlier placed a call-up reservation upon me to finish my degree, thought I should join I.C.I. I had managed to get back into the Post Office Engineering Department (forerunner of British Telecom) and after many months of badgering the Personnel Department my wish was eventually granted. I was instructed to report at Catterick Camp on 7th November 1940.

The train from Kings Cross was full of soldiers and others in civvies like myself, being called up. We were keenly apprehensive of what was to come, but certainly excited. We changed at Darlington, a busy war time interchange with W.V.S. canteens on every platform, in great demand for tea and buns. Then to Catterick Camp (or was it Richmond?), where army lorries transported us first to the reception hut H.Q. and then to the quartermaster stores for immediate kitting out. The battledress, boots, gaiters, pants, vests, shirts, socks, greatcoat, towels, etc. all seemed of good quality, although the boots were exceptionally hard and stiff, and were clearly going to take much breaking in. The kit included a 'housewife' for sewing repairs and a brass button stick for cleaning buttons! A cocky Corporal, determined to establish his authority at the start, marched us to our barrack room. He told us we had arrived in the Royal Signals depot and all would be well if we were always on time, did as we were told, were invariably clean and smart, and that we should address him as Sir! Tea would be at about 18 hours, but before that we would have to parade for inoculations. We were due for a 'full house', which meant at least three separate jabs, one of which was the dreaded TAB, which made you feel ill with a temperature for a while. We would get the evening off to relax!

The M.O. was very busy jabbing dozens of new arrivals, so it was a matter of luck whether you got a new needle or one blunted by much use on those before you. We were then marched to our first meal and found ourselves sitting at tables for twelve soldiers. We collected a huge aluminium tin with the food and helped ourselves in a mad grab to get a fair share of cottage pie and, later, jam roll. There were no plates. We had our own mess tins and knife, fork and spoon. In these circumstances reasonable politeness did not really pay off! It was a little like those modern T.V. advertisements for cat food, where several cats all advance to feed from the same dish.

We returned to our barrack rooms to make our beds with three biscuit mattresses and two dark rough blankets. There may have been sheets and pillowcases, but I cannot remember them. The Corporal had told us we could go to the N.A.A.F.I. to supplement our meal if we wished, but that the tea was better at the Church Army Canteen. I retired to bed without further ado, as the TAB was beginning to work and we were to be on square bashing next morning, before breakfast. I was elated to be a signalman at last!

5. CLASS DISTINCTIONS

Introduction

The fusing of differentials between the classes, which had begun during the First World War, continued into the Thirties, but the distinctions had by no means vanished.

The following extract is from *'Out of the Dolls House'* by Angela Holdsworth:

Diana McClure, setting up her own establishment in the Thirties, had servants to cater for nearly every whim. But her generation did not take their staff for granted and she was less of a grande dame than her mother. She lay awake at night rehearsing speeches before ticking off a servant. Unlike her mother, "I didn't have cook into the bedroom. I used to go and see her in the mornings and we'd discuss things and then I would go and do my own shopping. I was very bad at it at first and didn't know what sort of joints to order. It was becoming more the norm for people to do more than, certainly, my mother did".

At the other end of the scale was the abject poverty like that suffered by Helen Forrester's family after her father was made bankrupt. (*Twopence to cross the Mersey*, by Helen Forrester).

Along the pavement men in shabby cloth caps shuffled from litter bin to litter bin to sift through the garbage for food and cigarette ends. In the gutter stood four unemployed Welsh miners, caps held hopefully out while they sang over and over again in sad tenor voices 'Land of our Fathers' and 'All through the Night'.

As Helen Forrester's father had been self-employed he was not entitled to Unemployment Benefit, so had to rely on Parish relief, which had replaced the much hated Workhouse. For two adults and seven children he received the princely sum of 43 shillings, out of which he had to pay the exorbitant sum of 27/6d for two filthy, poorly furnished rooms and an attic, all bug-ridden. Coal had to be carried up 64 stairs, and their meagre food cooked on the fire. The pennies needed to feed the gas meter lasted only a very short time, so there was very little money left to pay for milk (especially for the baby) and other food. Unfortunately both her parents had been heavy smokers and craved cigarettes, so some of the precious money was spent on them. They could not even afford to buy soap.

In 1931, because of the effects of the slump on the economy, the National Government decided to make cuts in unemployment benefit, so they introduced the much hated Means Test. This was imposed after six months' unemployment benefit had been paid, and reduced the transitional benefit which normally followed, if the claimant had savings or relatives who could support them. The money they received was sufficient to keep them from starvation, but that was all. Those living in the country and others with allotments were slightly better off, as they could grow their own vegetables and perhaps do some poaching.

Women were still discriminated against. Teachers and those in other professions were forced to resign when they married, so losing their own income. Also, they had to live where their husbands chose, which often meant leaving their families and friends and living a very lonely life. If they had children, they were even more tied. In earlier days, it was often the husband who died first and it was the norm for the widow to live with one of her daughters. This meant there was always a baby sitter handy, as well as companionship. Now with smaller houses quite often she was not welcomed by her son-in-law.

King Edward VIII talking to the unemployed at Abertillery.
1936

By 1939 many people owned a car and most homes had a radio, but television sets were rare. Two-thirds of houses were wired for electricity, and 68% had electric or gas cookers, but only 10% had vacuum cleaners. For those in employment the standard of living had improved considerably, and once war was declared and many men were called up to the services, there were many more jobs available.

John Magee describes the crippling effects of poverty on the lives of the people in Hull during the Thirties.

Of course, unemployment was a major cause of poverty, but not the only one. Housing conditions often made the pub more attractive than home. The cinema was in its heyday and many adults and children went to the 'flicks' two or three times a week, partly for the warmth and partly for interest! It was the same with the libraries, though borrowing was limited to one book at a time, with one added for students.

There was a good deal of 'respectable poverty', meaning those valiant women who fought a courageous battle against dirt, especially during the November smoke-laden fogs, which the clean air laws have now eliminated. By modern standards Hull was a dirty place, though not as enervating as places like Manchester. The nearness of these made Hull certainly healthier than many industrial areas. Housing in Hull was distinguished by the great number of its terrace houses. Terrace to some may mean the magnificent crescents of the wealthy city of Bath, but in Hull a terrace was an opening off a side street containing eight to twelve small houses round a flagged rectangle, sometimes containing minute gardens. Usually the front door opened on to the living room. Each terrace housed a small community, almost like an extended family, in which people cared for each other. This alleviated some of the worst effects of poverty, especially during illness and old age. At this time vast housing estates were being built around the city and people were removed from slums, due for demolition, to good houses with baths, proper sanitary facilities and gardens. Although these provided conditions for a better life, people felt the loss of that neighbourliness they had known in the terraces. The poor found the expense of travelling to work a burden. Schools were provided, but it took some time before churches, pubs and social amenities arrived. I was concerned with a boys' club which Toc H. had started in a slum area. This met in part of a disused paint factory with a tortoise stove for heating. Some of the boys were very poor, and those who wore sandshoes all the year round had sores on their feet in the winter. The summer camp was the only chance some had of enjoying a

151

holiday away from the town. When these slums were cleared, the club migrated with the boys to a housing estate and prospered with the aid of the local education authority.

There were many homeless in Hull, some amongst the casual dockers, and a community of nuns of the Church of England ran a dockers' mission to accommodate them. They also maintained a free haven for those who needed shelter for the night. Amongst these the meths drinkers and the inadequates were the most difficult to help, as those from Toc H. found when they were helping there.

Making wireless sets was a popular hobby and home entertainment by radio and the gramophone was universal. The use of loudspeakers had made thousands of pairs of headphones redundant and Toc H. collected enough of these to begin the first hospital radio service in Hull. They also started the Hull blood transfusion service.

During the Thirties working people generally had a hard life demanding physical stamina and long hours. They were remarkably tolerant of conditions. They waited patiently at the frequently closed level crossings, which had a strangle hold on Hull's traffic. The fish meal factories in a west wind distributed their odours and, worse still, there was a tannery near the middle of the town.

The cheapness of fish and chips in Hull saved many children from malnutrition. Hull's excellent parks provided quite literally a breathing space outside the crowded areas.

Alfred Ridpath was born in Liverpool in 1910, and experienced some of the worst effects of the recession there after the First World War.

My home and family were quite poor, very characteristic of much of Liverpool in those days. It was the proprietors of the Liverpool Echo who provided me with my first footwear (a pair of clogs) when I was ten. Barefooted children were very numerous in those times: Sunday best clothing was regularly pawned on Mondays!

I left school at sixteen, after completing two years of a scholarship at Bootle Technical College, where I studied engineering. During the General Strike poverty, degradation and violence were endemic. Most of my recreation was running and athletics: I was a very fit young man, which probably accounted very largely for my survival. I was one of the few fortunates that had a job during the Twenties and Thirties. Pubs and pawnshops and soup kitchens were part of life in Liverpool in those days. Christian mission sought to alleviate some of the worst poverty, but hardly made much impact. Even for those in work the wages were very poor -- employers everywhere exploited men and women desperate for work.

Lilian Smith now living in Devon had been happy at school but suffered from the snobbish attitudes of her contemporaries.

I liked school, unlike my brother who played truant at the drop of a hat. The school board man was a regular visitor to our home.

The school consisted of infants, juniors and seniors, all in one building, a playground with outside toilets and no playing field. The cane could be used by teachers, and was! Talking in class usually meant standing in the corridor with hands on head, but I still remember my teachers with affection.

If you worked in a factory, as I did, you were considered lower than an office girl. School also had class distinctions. At the age of eleven I was asked to my one and only birthday party by a classmate who lived in a smart house: I was a council kid. We were actually called that. She and the rest of her smart friends wore party dresses and soft shoes: I wore a home-made dress and my one and only decent pair of Sunday shoes. I was made to feel as small as the present I took -- it was one of the most miserable experiences of my life. At home we did not have parties -- just friends to tea.

An anonymous contributor from Croydon describes some of the deprivations and difficulties of the Thirties.

The houses were full of bugs and often with rats running around. We put goose grease on bedposts and legs to stop the bugs crawling up. We had overcoats for blankets on the beds and had to pawn things to get food. There was no water in the house and we had to go into the street to a water tap and carry it in buckets.

Men did not live to old age in the Thirties: many died around forty-five years from heart attacks.

If you were on the dole, for which you got 5/3d, and they found that you had received 1 shilling for acting as a caddy for a golfer they had a means test. They came round to your house and if you had four chairs and there were only three in the family, they made you get rid of one and you got 2 shillings for it. When you couldn't pay the rent you moved out in the middle of the night, taking your belongings on a hand cart.

It cost 2/6d, if you could afford it, to go to the doctor. When children had whooping cough their parents took them into the street when the men were tarring the road and made them breathe in the tar, or they put goose grease and brown paper on their chests. Babies' bottles were made with Nestles milk. In 1936 they introduced free dinners for the poorer children. We cooked pigs heads to make brawn. A cheap meal.

Another anonymous contributor describes her young days in Lancashire.

This county, where I was born, was noted for the high quality of its woven cloth. The weavers all wore clogs, and the first sound I heard every morning was the clatter of their clogs on the stone-flagged footpaths as they made their way to work at about 6am. 'Knockers-up' were employed to go round from house to house, tapping on the bedroom windows with a long pole to ensure that the workers were awakened in time to get to the mill for the early shift. Lamplighters also came round each night and morning with their long poles and tapered ladders to light or dowse the gas lamps, by which the streets were lit.

My father worked in the office of a cotton mill, where Mother had also worked until her marriage. Married women did not go out to work in those days--at least, not in my experience. There was strict discipline at home and at school, with a great awareness of moral values. Obedience was demanded and received without argument.

I found school most enjoyable. I was able to read before I went there, so was put in the second class instead of the 'play' class. Mother taught me to read, though I can't remember how. She was not a teacher but I had no difficulty in learning and have always been an avid reader. We used slates for our school lessons. They were etched with parallel lines on one side and squares (for sums) on the other, and were framed in timber.

Jim Finlayson was fortunate in the grim days of the depression to find a job, even though the pay was very low. He highlights the difference class made.

I began work on 10th January 1930 in a Glasgow wholesale leather and grindery warehouse. The going rate for a fourteen-year old school leaver was ten shillings (50p) a week. At the same time the proprietor's son was sent off to a fee-paying school in Edinburgh. That was my introduction to class distinctions. This was not resented then: working class parents could not afford to patronise fee-paying schools, and that was the end of it. By the inverted snobbery of the times, I was actually sorry for this lad, sent away from home. My parents were envied because their child had gained employment when so many were unemployed.

The proprietor was not to blame for the actions of his syco-phantic employees. At the age of fifteen I was sent with a parcel of leather and grindery to the Glasgow docks. It registered 109lbs on the dock scales. The clerk remarked, "The bloke who sent you with that should be blankety well shot." Man's inhumanity to man was fostered to some extent by the class distinctions of the era, plus the constant fear of unemployment. 'Twas ever thus in the Thirties'.

Mrs Anne Docherty now lives in Australia but was brought up in Scotland.

In the Thirties Glasgow suffered as much as most working class areas. Housing was terrible: 90% had no baths, and there was only one toilet for three families on each landing of a tenement.

Children from the working class were three to four inches shorter than those who attended good schools, and only between a half and one per cent attended university. Worst of all was the apathy towards science and engineering. The church opposed this and possibly the upper classes were afraid that the lower orders would know too much. If the U. K. had observed how the Germans treated these subjects perhaps fewer people would have died in the Second World War due to obsolete equipment. Working class children could have absorbed training if it had been available, but with overcrowded classes, poor diet and dreadful housing, most of them had no chance. The attitude of some of the better-off folk to those on the dole was terrible: there were no secondhand clothes shops to help them, no St. Vincent de Paul, and no soup kitchens.

I lived in Glasgow at that time, and the memories of the men at street corners with their dejected faces will live with me for ever.

Anna McCubbin Cunningham MA Hons. (Glasgow) is now living in Johannesburg, South Africa, but was born in 1927 in Port Glasgow: the only child of Marion and Archibald Dunsmore.

My father's family were middle class, my grandfather owning his own joiner's business. The family lived in a villa in one of the elite areas of Port Glasgow. My mother came from a lower rung in society, mainly because her parents separated and her mother had to bring up a large family on a small income. They lived in an apartment in a tenement. My parents both came from large families, perhaps that is why I was an only child.

We lived in a council housing estate built after the First World War, on the hills behind the town. When I was two we moved to 7 Farquhar Road, which was not so far to climb and was regarded as quite a superior address, as there were privately owned houses on one side of the road. Last but not least, it was nearer to the bowling green for my father.

There was a magnificent view of the River Clyde from the house but, in the days before people had cars, it was a considerable climb from the town to reach it, and even worse if you were carrying heavy bags of groceries. Our block consisted of four units; each unit had a fair sized garden. Rent was paid to the Town Council, which was responsible for repairs. A Tenants Association, something quite innovative in the Thirties, was formed to protect the interest of the tenants. Our unit had a living room, which also served as dining room and bedroom for my parents (with a divan bed); a sitting room, bedroom, kitchen, pantry, bathroom, hall and coal cellar. It was comfortably furnished with good quality furniture saved for during my parents' long courtship. I had a bedroom to myself.

Anna Cunningham (middle of front row) with family.

There were coal fires in each room, but generally only the living room one was lit. In winter my room had a paraffin heater, and I can still visualise the pattern cast on the ceiling by the heater, which I watched from a bed warmed by a plump eiderdown and an aluminium hot water bottle. The fire heated the water and had a hob on which kettles or pots could be placed to keep warm. Bread was toasted at the fire with the aid of a long fork. This worked very well except when the bread fell into the fire! My parents could not afford any domestic help, and I remember the somewhat dismal Monday dinners when washing day made a lot of cooking impossible.

For the Thirties the kitchen was quite well fitted out, with a gas cooker, boiler for the washing, double sinks and a pantry. If the clothes were very dirty they were boiled, then rinsed at the sink and put through the wringer, before being hung outside. We had no pulley, but there was a small clothes-horse on which the ironed items could be aired. The grate and metal surrounds of the fire had to be black-leaded, and it was a great day when the old fireplace was removed and a tiled one and mantelpiece installed. I remember my mother's horror at cleaning the chimney flues. It was an equally great day when electricity was supplied to replace the gas lighting. Baths were weekly events, although we had to wash well every day, including scrubbing our knees.

My family was not poor, but my mother had to be very careful. My father lost his job as mercantile clerk with the Gourock Ropework Company during the depression. He was lucky to find work fairly quickly as a clerk in the Poor Law Assistance, which meant he had a small but steady income. There was no money for frills and nothing was bought unless we could afford it.

Jill Clarke was very much aware of class distinctions whilst she was at school.

School life was very class orientated. Children from well-off homes went to private schools and had better opportunities to get on in life. All other children went to state schools. If they were very clever they could get scholarships to go to grammar schools, but even if they won one lack of money was still a disadvantage. The same applied to university scholarships.

Class distinctions were really quite ridiculous. Children from private schools were not allowed to play with children from the state schools in my area, which of course made it a rule that it was exciting to disobey. How people spoke, their table manners, the clothes they wore were all deemed to be very important. It was considered vulgar to talk about money. Although some of the people we knew were really quite hard up, this was hidden. I can remember my mother cleaning the step to our house early in the morning so that she would not be seen by her neighbour, who had a maid.

Different social classes in his area are described by William Findlay.

We were basically a village, surrounded by fields belonging to farmers, all of whom were well-known in the village. Although the farmers must have been relatively well off, they were accepted as being 'one of us'. This was probably due to the fact that they performed manual work themselves, alongside their employees.

The only other bosses who were accepted as being of the people were the owners of the few small shops which served the village. Other shopping needs, so far as food was concerned, were met by the Co-operative: a much larger store. Clothing and larger household goods had to be bought either at a neighbouring village, or in Glasgow.

Very few married women worked, but almost all able-bodied men were employed. Very few actually worked in the village. A number were employed on the neighbouring farms; but most of the farm workers lived in tied cottages.

Another group of workmen were the miners; they resided in miners' rows, streets of mainly inferior houses, often detached from the village. Such houses were generally the property of the mine owners. Miners' children attended the village schools and the miners' wives shopped in the village shops. Nothing derogatory was ever said by either side, but the miner families tended to keep themselves to themselves.

The vast majority of men from our village, Auchinairn, were employed by the Railway companies at their Springburn Works. Some, however, were employed in Glasgow, mainly by engineering companies. A few men worked locally, in quarrying and in the brick works.

The village had a primary school: secondary school pupils had to walk to the neighbouring village of Bishopbriggs, about two miles away. The village school was always well run. The authority of the teachers was unquestioned -- most of them could emphasise this with the words, "I taught your father". The headmaster was one of the Big Three, to whom all deferred; the other two were the doctor and the clergyman. Our neighbouring village had a J.P.: he ranked a close second to the three. There was a district councillor and a county councillor but as neither lived locally they were seldom available for consultation.

Next in line of prominence were the village policemen and the district nurse: both always appeared calm and casual, but never seemed to be off duty. Further down the line, but still respected, were the water man, the lamp lighter, and the road sweeper. I also have vivid memories of the man who drove the steam roadroller.

I did not realise it at the time but the best years of village life were already over by the late Thirties, and probably before that. My father and many of his neighbours who had been brought up in the village could tell of earlier days when the village had its own football team and its own silver band. Both were financed by the villages, who also made the football pitch. There had been a quoits pitch and other local amenities. Regular dances were held in a local hall, but by the late Thirties the young people were travelling to Springburn and Glasgow for their entertainment.

The football team, Auchinairn United, no longer existed and the field was used by one of the Bishopbriggs' Boys' Brigade companies. A number of the Auchinairn boys joined the Boys' Brigade and learned to play the pipes. Three brothers of Highland Stock, the Hardies, had come to live in Bishopbriggs and they formed the nucleus of a very fine Boys' Brigade pipe band.

Auchinairn was on the decline. Towards the end of the Thirties a large number of houses in the village, ours included, were condemned, and we were assigned newly built council houses in Bishopbriggs: the only concession was that we could attend Auchinairn School. This we all did, with great pride.

Although there were differences of status, there was no feeling of class distinctions in that part of Scotland where Ian MacLachlan lived.

Highland folk were genteel and although there was a lot of activity in the summer when the gentry went to stay in the country houses, we never felt inferior.

My aunt was housekeeper for Lord Strathcona and Mount Royal at Glencoe House. She lived in an estate house (a big, beautiful house) in the village with her brother. When she retired Lord Strathcona had a bungalow built for her. She was well spoken, a splendid scholar, and was very highly thought of. Her sister lived nearby as she was housekeeper to the Dean of Glencoe: she was treated as an equal.

Labour was the popular party amongst men who worked hard for low wages.

We were aware of the fact that things were not going well in Europe and followed developments on the radio. When war was declared the Territorials assembled in the Drill Hall and men were dispatched to their units. Most belonged to the Argyll and Sutherland Highlanders.

Pauline Thompson was not aware of any class distinctions when she was young, although they were there.

I cannot recall any class distinctions. All the villages at South Heindley helped one another when a crisis arose. Families and communities were close knit, especially in a colliery village or a mill town. There were the workers and then only the other class --colliery owners, mill owners, the landed gentry (country squires, estate owners, farmers and the titled people) -- the rich!

Our village had a bus service, about three buses a day to the nearest town (Wakefield); other transport was by horse and trap, or motorcycle with sidecar. The nearest railway station was in the next village (Ryhill) approximately a mile away. Walking was a way of life in those days, an enjoyable experience and good exercise as we went from our village to another to shop and/or visit friends and relatives.

The annual holiday in the Thirties was only one week. For us it was always spent at Blackpool because, if the weather was wet, we could always go into the Tower and spend a full day there: sixpence each for entrance fee and that covered going up the tower, ballroom, fun fair, aquarium, and listening to the famous organist of those years -- Reginald Dixon. Our accommodation was what was termed a one room lodging, and the food Mother brought in was cooked for us each day at no extra cost. We travelled to and from holiday destinations by train, as special trains were put on to such places as Blackpool and Scarborough from local stations in villages and town when the collieries and mills had their annual holiday week. Other outings during the year would be a horse and trap ride into the countryside for a picnic.

Shortage of money meant that Alan Sax's family were not able to enjoy the little luxuries most people took for granted.

Holidays were non-existent for us. Living in the East End of London meant we were working class: poverty was at our door. Mother's skirt was torn up to make my shorts for school. Visits by the National Assistance Board Relief Officer meant that anything valuable was hidden under the large plush table cloth (wireless, etc.) -- otherwise valuables were to be sold before relief could or would be granted.

The only time I went on holiday was with the Country Holiday Fund, and I was very homesick. Theatres and cinemas were also barely part of our lives. On one occasion my father, who always gave his unopened pay packet to my mother, took my sister and me to the cinema and found that he didn't have enough money to pay for the performance. We had to walk all the way home! From his pay packet all my father received was money for his cigarettes, his newspapers and his fares to his employment.

In spite of their poverty, Kit Hull and her family managed to enjoy life in the Thirties.

In 1930 I was seven years old. I had three sisters and we lived with my mother and father in one room in south-west London: we slept there as well. Bedtime was a scramble as we had camp beds. They folded up like concertinas and if you moved about too much they gradually folded up.

There was only fifteen months difference between us girls, so we all went to the same school, although my eldest sister didn't attend much because she suffered from asthma.

My mother made our clothes -- hand sewn -- she dressed us all alike. We all went to the Public Baths on a Friday night. The taps were on the outside and you had to call out to the Attendant for more hot or cold water. We all got in the same water because it cost sixpence and that was a lot for my mother to pay.

We had a penny a week pocket money most weeks if my father was working, but he took it back if we didn't eat our dinners. On Sundays we pushed the doll's pram down to our grandma's with the meat and potatoes for her to cook, as we had no cooker in our room.

When our hair needed cutting my dad put a small bowl on our heads and cut round it, the back and sides the same length as the fringe. We were all glad when it grew: other kids used to laugh at us.

We went to Sunday School. It was only a small hall. I was so proud when I won a New Testament for reciting by heart three verses from the Bible, and I was also given a story book.

When I was eleven years old the Council gave us a flat. As my parents had to pay more rent I used to get up at six o'clock and queue at the bakers for stale bread and cakes, which were much cheaper than fresh ones.

Mrs. Vera Markham is now living in Mitcham, Surrey. Although she has M. S., is confined to a wheelchair and her husband died some years ago, she is a joy to visit because of her positive outlook on life. She recalls with pleasure the Keep Fit classes she took part in. Earlier life was not so good.

We were a very poor family and when we asked for help from the Council we were subject to a means test. A man came to the house to see what could be sold. There were some pictures which my father had painted, and for one of them he offered a few pence, but as we couldn't accept the offer he cancelled it. We had a mahogany piano which he suggested we could sell, but as two octaves in the middle were missing we wouldn't get much for that. So I'm afraid we lived very poorly. Electricity was one shilling in the meter, which we couldn't afford, so we used candles. Gas was a penny in the slot and it lasted for quite a time.

I had to wear plimsolls because we couldn't afford to buy shoes, and we had 'let downs' from our brothers and sisters to wear, and went to Jumble Sales to get a few things cheap. Milk was about a penny a pint and bread 3d a loaf. We had no cakes unless we bought stale ones -- and they *were* stale. No sweets, but we went carol singing one Christmas and we managed to get four farthings; we bought four hard sticks of liquorice for a farthing a stick.

The milk came round called Courts milk, and we used to run out in the street with a jug and the milkman baled it out with a tin can. Imagine how hygienic that could be! On Sundays we had an oven buster for dinner, which was mostly beef fat, and we had to cook it over the fire range, but we couldn't afford enough fuel to cook it properly, so the Yorkshire puddings were flat.

If we went to Egee's Market in Tooting Broadway, London, we could buy 40 eggs for a shilling, and if they were cracked they would be even cheaper, so we would come home with cracked eggs and in order to cut out the smell and taste we used lots of vinegar and pepper. Cheese was too expensive but Egee's Market sold chunks of cheese which was very ripe and we made Welsh rabbit (rarebit), again on the fire.

We kept eight chickens, and as we couldn't feed them too well my mother found some old bottled beans and we gave them to the chickens. But they were too salty and the birds died in the night because they couldn't get any water. There they were with their beaks open and their legs upside down. They all died and we ate them.

We mainly had blackberry and apple jam for dinner, made with blackberries we had picked in the summer on Mitcham Common.

My father used to repair our boots on a three legged iron mould. He would cut a piece from any old lino so he could cover our soles with holes in them with lino and tintacks.

If you could afford to go to music lessons they were 9d for half an hour. I did have a few music lessons when I was about fourteen, but my teacher could not understand why I played with my hands so far apart -- it was because of the missing two octaves in our piano!

My father was a painter and decorator, and when there was a slump he couldn't get any work. We had a wireless set (radio) that was accumulator operated. I used to get into trouble if I put it on as the accumulator would run down and it was 2d to recharge it, and we couldn't afford even that. When my father couldn't get a job painting and decorating he worked as a postman at Christmas time and he earned 26 shillings a week. There were six of us in the family -- my parents and four children. I had a younger sister and two younger brothers. When there was no money coming in we had to go to a Poor Man's lawyer (?) at the Cricket Green, Mitcham. At one time the family might have been split up as we were so poor, but we didn't want that. We were given food. Our rent was 15/11d a week. My mother didn't do any work -- it was unheard of. The only work you could do was taking in washing. Also some women were paid 1 shilling for laying out the dead. It was called the 'underground movement'. You were also paid ld for cleaning the front door step with hard-stone. Unfortunately my father drank. Beer was 2d a pint and he often came home drunk. There was a soup kitchen at Mitcham Grammar School, that provided free soup, and that was a help.

I went to St. Mark's School at Mitcham, and had no breakfast before I went, so I fainted. The teacher gave me an apple and a banana.

We paid 1 shilling a week for the family to the Hospital Savings Association, also 1 shilling a week to the doctor. If you wanted a home visit he charged 5 shillings. We treated measles, etc., our-selves. There was a diphtheria scare in the street so we kept sucking peppermints to ward off any germs.

We had two bedrooms. My younger brother Raymond slept in my mother's room with a curtain, and my older brother had part of the other bedroom where my sister and I slept curtained off. We had no blankets and used coats. Everyone in our area of Mitcham was poor, but we helped each other when we could.

Once a year we went on a Sunday School outing, and also there was a Busman's outing. If you knew someone who worked on the buses you could join the outing for a picnic at Ashstead.

I learnt swimming at school. You had to lie across the chair and do the breast stoke with arms and legs. If you could co-ordi-nate them in six weeks you were given a free pass to Mitcham Baths, and I became a good swimmer. I won the Junior County 100 yards flat race. We had to wear spiked shoes and my mother could not afford to buy a new pair, so she got some that had a long split in them that she bought at a Jumble Sale.

You used to be able to buy a pair of spectacles in Woolworths and in those days, nothing sold cost over 6d. Shops were very different in those days. Most of them were small and nothing was prepacked. The grocer would pat up the butter or margarine and wrap it up. Other food was weighed out according to the quan-tity you wanted and put into bags or, if it was only an ounce or two, it was put into paper folded into a cone. We could buy 1lb of pot herbs. We used wrapping paper as writing paper. I had a bicycle that someone gave me and my father told me I was not to carry June, my sister, on the back. But I was naughty and did so one day and we crashed into a lamp-post, and both had grazed knees.

We made up our own games, and used Co-op tin money for playing at shops. We never had a doll -- we made our own toys. Mother gave us security but she was often ill and had lots of miscarriages. When I grew up I was big and tough and took up nursing: my Dad respected me.

Mr. R. Cunningham (Dick) from South Africa has his roots in Scotland, where he was born in 1920.

My family might be classified as middle middle-class. During the Thirties my father was the Glasgow University Librarian and Keeper of the Hunterian Books and Manuscripts. He could afford a house in Holyrood Crescent, one of the Crescents and Gardens which adorned both sides of Great Western Road. Our house was in the middle of a terrace; it had a ground and first floor and, above that, an attic floor with two large bed-sitting rooms and bathroom, all with excellent dormer windows, also a storeroom.

The ground floor consisted of a long hall, the stairway on the left and under it a roomy cloak room, which served as our air-raid shelter from 1939 on. On the right was an umbrella stand, a large wooden settle with a big oval mirror hanging above it; then a semi-circular gate legged table with a silver salver and a bowl of flowers. Next there was the door to the lounge/study and, at the end, a very large ornamented wooden trunk, with enough room behind it for us to park our three bicycles. On the right was a doorway into a small passage, from which opened off the dining room. This had a window overlooking the spacious back garden on the left; the pantry and the kitchen and, from the latter, a couple of steps at the back down to the scullery. On one side were the dish washing sink and the copper and, on the other, the twin clothes washing sinks with a mangle attached to their top. There was also a double door opening on the back garden, with a gate to the lane at the bot-

Dick Cunningham's home, 16 Holyrood Crescent, Glasgow.
Twin sisters on tricycle.

tom. Large horse-drawn carts came either to remove the refuse or hand deliver the coal, 20 bags at a time, each weighing a hundred weight. This went into the cellar underneath the dining room.

The first floor contained the drawing room at the front over the study, both having tall bay windows overlooking, as did my small bedroom next to it, the Crescent garden, enclosed in a high metal paling with barbed wire on the top and a locked gate. I am glad I have been able to look out at trees from my bedroom virtually all my life. There were also two much larger bedrooms at the back, one for my parents and the other for my twin sisters, and the bathroom, all overlooking the lane on to the impressive but appalling wall of Coopers' factory and our coalman's yard. Opposite the bathroom was the linen cupboard.

As my parents entertained their friends to Sunday afternoon tea parties and an occasional dinner, and the whole family to Christmas dinner, the furniture in the drawing and dining rooms had to be of a certain standard. The former had an exquisite Indian carpet, a three-seater sofa and four matching armchairs, with a number of decorative portable chairs with rounded backs scattered about the room. There were also a pleasant writing bureau and a square revolving bookcase containing the mainly leather-bound sets of Scott, Thackeray and other 19th century writers, my mother had inherited from her father. Early in the Thirties my paternal grandmother contributed a grand piano, a gift to my sisters, while my mother's youngest brother brought her home from Burma a beautiful teak coffee table, inlaid with ivory, which stood on top the Indian rug, in the bay window. This room, my bedroom and the study were south facing, so they enjoyed whatever sunshine there was. However, winter afternoon tea parties required a roaring coal fire in a tiled fireplace, with attendant gold coloured fender, coal scuttle and fire irons, the whole surmounted by a white mantelpiece with appropriate ornaments on it. A few pictures hung at strategic points around the room, but I'm glad to say the heavily bearded portraits of my grandfathers were consigned to the attic bedsitting room.

Below the drawing room was the study, used as the family sitting room. Its huge windows looked out on the small front garden, consisting of a hedge to hide the railings and four rhododendron bushes. There was a small lawn in between and in front of the window a narrow flower bed, with a climbing rose and a few annuals planted by my mother. The study contained my father's large roll-top desk, with a table in the bay window on which he did most of his writing. A three-seater sofa with a fold-down arm, which could be used as a spare bed, and two armchairs surrounded the fireplace. There was a large table in the middle of the room, with glass-fronted bookcases housing hundreds of books all round it. In spite of having the resources of a university library to hand, my father had his own excellent reference library (many good quality secondhand copies). When I asked him a question I often got the answer "Look it up in So and So". He reviewed quite a number of books, mainly historical, and he was allowed to keep the review copy, which added to the collection.

When my father bought the house, it had no electricity, just gas for lighting and cooking, a range in the kitchen for cooking and heating the hot water system, and coal fires in every room. Before we moved in, my father had electricity installed for lighting and plugs for lamps and electric fires. My mother retained the gas cooker, and gas fires with gas rings were installed in the dining room and our parents' bedroom. The kitchen range was lit early every morning, as was the fire in the study, but the other coal fires in the house were left untouched except for the drawing room when visitors were due, and the bedroom fire of a child who was ill. In those days influenza was a serious illness and could mean being confined to bed for a fortnight or more.

In the mid-Thirties an electric water heater was installed in a new water tank; also in the kitchen a more sophisticated range, which did not need to heat the house water supply. In the late Thirties my mother had a small refrigerator, made by a reputable company, installed in the pantry. She discovered she was the first in her circle of friends to do so, but it was not a success and kept breaking down. The company supplied her, gratis, with two more but when the third broke down it regretted that, with a war newly on, it could not replace it and returned her money.

We had two live-in servants, a cook-general and a housemaid, who shared the back bed-sitting room on the attic floor. Their bed-linen, towels and food, on the whole on a par with ours, were supplied by my mother. The 'general' addendum to the cook's title was important as it required her not only to cook but also to wash up the pots and pans, keep the kitchen clean, stoke the range and help keep her room tidy. They were usually Highlanders and were paid £4 - £4.10s per month. The house-maids were aged fourteen to sixteen, and usually came for interview accompanied by their mothers. They had to provide their own uniforms, one for cleaning work in the mornings and the other a black dress, frilly apron and cap for afternoons and evenings. As they usually had little or no experience, they began on a monthly wage of 12/6d - 15 shillings, but this was quickly increased as they improved towards the high standards demanded by my mother.

They each had a mid-week afternoon off and alternate week-ends, once monthly. The housemaid was faced with a list pinned up in the pantry of the jobs she had to do each weekday afternoon, e.g. 'clean the silver'. My father worked and my mother shopped on Saturday mornings, but they and the servants all enjoyed a lie-in on Sunday mornings, and it was my responsibility to take up my parents' breakfast on separate trays, and thereafter to provide my own and my sisters' breakfasts in the dining room. I was taught how to boil eggs (my mother's eggs always having a different timing from everybody else's) and cook sausages, to make the tea properly and not to burn the toast. My mother had fresh butter and home-made jam or jelly (quite an industry in our house at the relevant seasons), and my father salt butter and marmalade, so it wasn't all that simple. The servants sometimes accompanied us on holiday when we rented an unserviced house.

In the early Thirties a cousin of my father persuaded him to instal a telephone in our home. Being a senior technician in the telephone department of the Post Office, the cousin had the installation carried it quickly. My parents decided it should go in the dining room - the least used public room -- and it was stood on a two-tier table beside the fireplace, with the directory on the lower shelf and an armchair alongside it. The instrument had a long stem with a large mouthpiece at its head and the receiver set in the cradle just below, with a long cord to let it reach the ear. We children and the housemaid were taught how to answer it and, if we had to call someone else to the phone, *not* to put the receiving back in its cradle but to lay it on the table.

Another revolution at home occurred about the same time. A friend of my mother from Edinburgh arrived one Friday evening with her two sons, about my age, to spend the weekend. On Saturday morning the two boys showed me their weekly pocket money (1d). I said I hadn't received mine yet: this was untrue as none of us received pocket money, being told that anything we needed would be supplied by our parents. So I rushed inside, told my mother, and was also given 1d. Thereafter I asked for and was given it every week, as were my sisters. I also began to earn 2d weekly by cycling from school to rugby practice and back home pocketing, with my father's knowledge, the Corporation bus fare each way, which he gave me. He also believed in National Savings and we were each given a 15 shilling certificate every month, provided we remembered to ask for it by the 3rd of each new month.

Although Bexhill-on-Sea, where Brai Harper spent his childhood, was very much a 'middle class town', he was not aware of any class consciousness.

In the Thirties, the middle class was still running things. Plays and films were mostly about educated, well mannered people in opulent surroundings. On variety stages the entertainers all wore evening dress; so did dance bands, cinema managers and even, I'm told, radio announcers! Bexhill was a very middle class town, with many retired colonials who had spent their working lives in jungles, growing palm oil, tea, coffee, cocoa, coconuts or rubber -- or even indigo - and they wanted a quiet retirement, insulated from the madding crowd with whom they had nothing in common.

Bexhill was ideal! There were no noticeably mean streets, and the council estates were at the back of the town, out of sight. The shopping centre was for well dressed and well mannered people, moving purposefully about. The Elvis and Rambo look alikes, sucking their lager tins and leaning in every shop doorway, had not yet emerged.

Yet I don't think I felt any class distinctions. The working class were the people who painted our house, delivered our bread and milk, coal and groceries, mended a burst pipe or broken gate, emptied our dustbin, and were always polite and good humoured. They were just doing a different job from my father's. When I joined the Scouts in 1933, I found that one of the patrol leaders was the boy who patted the butter in our grocery store; another was an errand boy whom I had often seen swaying round the town with the big basket bulging with merchandise on the front of the bicycle.

Betty Forsyth was quite unconscious of the deprivations many of the poorer members of society suffered during the Thirties.

We lived in the country until I was eleven in 1933. We were fortunate to have proper sanitation, as many of the cottages in the village had only dry or chemical lavatories and cold running water. We had no electricity, however, and depended on oil lamps and candles for all our light. For heating we had only coal fires, which had to be cleaned out every morning, and even when they were burning they were totally inadequate for a moderately sized house. All the cooking was done on a kitchen range, which was also used to heat the black iron. Washing was done in a couple of large sinks, with a hand-operated mangle. Our radio was operated by batteries.

I was very envious of an aunt who had gas in her house, and could turn on a light by pulling a cord which ignited the gas burner -- I thought that was the last word in modem living! Although I lived in Dundee throughout the Thirties, I am ashamed to say that I had no conception of the hardships experienced by workers, especially in the jute trade, in that city. I lived in a comfortable suburban area and went to a fee paying school, and it was only when I experienced the real world of business that I began to have some little idea of how other people lived.

My husband, who was brought up in a small town in the north of Scotland, can remember the depression much more vividly. He recalls the soup kitchens, with queues waiting each day for their fair share, and the children who came in from outlying districts with very little for their packed lunches, often wearing no shoes in the summer and heavy boots in the winter.

Lucy was one of the relatively few youngsters who enjoyed a high standard of living during the Thirties.

Our family life in the Thirties (as we experienced it in our fairly remote part of the West Country) was more or less usual for the locality --the way of life of a small landowner and country squire, as my father was, and his family.

We lived in a medium sized country house, which was part Georgian, part Victorian. It had a small garden of shrubs and lawns, a kitchen garden which was let out, and my father also owned some village property and a few hundred acres of farm land. All of this was let at very low rents, which covered the cost of essential repairs.

We were near enough to the town of Plymouth to do our occasional shopping there, all supplies of food, etc. were delivered to the house from more local sources.

Ours was a comfortable life, if somewhat restricted: we were protected by the isolation of the immediate environment. We had plenty of friends to stay, mostly of my parents' generation. We had maids and a cook, so we did not actually do the housework, although we were taught to understand exactly how everything should be done. Home discipline was quite consistent concerning all behaviour, punctuality, tidiness, manners and respecting other people. It was a secure and practical upbringing in those days; much more relaxed, slower, and everyone knew his or her own part in the scheme of things.

Life in the Thirties was comparatively simple and straightforward, with much less bureaucracy and form filling. Although we had a fridge and a hoover in those days, all the other cleaning was done by hand. There were no dish washers or washing machines and tumble dryers. There was also a great deal of making and mending clothes and stocking darning. There were no Supermarkets or the variety of throw-away clothes and household effects we have today; no fast foods -- just good plain English cooking. I believe we were happier, as there were not the same pressures, conflicts, tensions, rush, and all the complexes and disasters of family life such as take place nowadays at all levels. Marriage, home and the bringing up of children was the accepted outcome, which was usually successful - separation and divorce were very rare. Those who did not marry found a place either within the family or in some career, or they shared their life with another single friend or relation.

There was no equal pay for women, nor were women expected or encouraged to take jobs: that was man's prerogative. Women's job in life, if married, was the priority of their home, where domesticity was a paramount responsibility and highly exacting; full time work seeing to the comforts of the husband (the breadwinner) and the welfare of the children and extended family. There were local public duties; fund-raising and other outside interests were encouraged.

Social life became possible or not, on a financial basis according to the number of servants employed, as hospitality at home was the accepted thing: only hotels, cafes and larger shops provided restaurants. There was no frozen or junk food in the varieties we have now.

Socials, get togethers, villlage occasions of all kinds -- seasonable or religious festivals -- took place then as they do now, and there was every opportunity to join in. People were aware of their neighbours' needs and were more involved and helpful than most people are today. Welfare was an individual concern, neighbourly, not 'organised' as it is now into groups for specific problems.

The Hon. Mrs. Clay was not class conscious, but probably considered her family to be upper middle class.

I lived with my parents, Olave and Robert Baden-Powell, at a house called Pax Hill, Bentley, Hampshire. This house was called Pax Hill because my parents were house hunting at the end of the First World War. They were on their bicycles and cycled along from Farnham, through the little village of Bentley, and came to a FOR SALE notice at the end of a long drive. They rode up this long drive and had their picnic lunch on the grass at the side. At the top was this charming house and they said "This is it". It was! It had a different name, but because the day that they chose it was Armistice Day, 1918, they named it PAX for peace, and it was a place of peace for the rest of the time they lived there.

There are many houses belonging to scouts and guides all over the world called Pax Hill, or Paxlease, or Pax Lodge, or Pax House, or Pax something, named after this home of scouting and guiding. My parents lived there for about twenty years, and only left when the Second World War began. They were in Africa for the winter. When mother came back to England after the war she gave Pax Hill to the Girl Guides and they used it for very many years.

Pax Hill was a large house by today's standards, and I suppose now it would be classed as a small country home. They did alter it after they had been there some time: they built on two wings, one wing was for the servants to live in, and later on when the house became too small they added another wing on the other end of the house, which included a large music room, or barn, and my father's study and studio for his art work. Above it were three bedrooms and bathroom for the guests, so that was the guest wing. It became a house of about eleven or twelve bedrooms and the equivalent number of bathrooms.

Pax Hill from the West , the Baden-Powell home.

To work this large establishment we were very fortunate to have a staff of four or five maids indoors, living in, and we had three fulltime gardeners, two of them living on the premises and one living further away. These people were very contented to work for us. There was a lot of work, as can be imagined, but they lived well. The gardeners had a complete run of the garden to grow any food or to take the reapings of the garden that they wanted for their own families, and of course the indoor servants had much the same food as we had. They lived very comfortably in that nice house. We were very lucky because at some stages many of them were of the same family.

It might be interesting to see what we did have in the way of staff. The flrst one to come was a young woman called Annie. Annie had come to my mother's family as a girl of fourteen, when mum was fourteen too. When my mother married, Annie asked if she could come with her as her maid, aged twenty-two. She did that and was Mum's first maid. Later on she seemed to gather round her other members of her family. When somebody was needed as cook Annie said "Oh my sister could do that". She seemed to have an inexhaustible supply of brothers and sisters. So Annie's sister came as cook for a while. Then her brother, Ernest Court, came as chauffeur. Later Annie married a coal merchant and he came as gardener Scofield. Then Lily came as housemaid for a while: she was another sister. And when one of them had to leave Annie's mother came -- old Mrs. Court, a dear little smiling Devonshire person. So we were surrounded by this wonderful Court family

Beside the cook and the housemaid, there was the parlour maid, who did the dining room and served the meals and looked after all the china and silver. Then of course there was a kitchen maid to help the cook. There were always masses of vegetables in the house, because there was a big family: Dad and Mum and my brother Peter, my sister Heather and me; then my mother took over the care of her three nieces, whose mother died when they were tiny. We nearly always had at least one of them living with us, and usually two. They were the Davidsons. Christian and Yvonne were almost permanent members of the family, Clare didn't come to us very often, as she went to her other grandmother. So besides the housemaid we also usually had an assistant housemaid, because there were always so many beds to be made. In those days we didn't usually make our own beds, but if there were a lot of visitors there was a request: 'Please make your own beds tomorrow.' So it was an unusual thing for us to have to clean our own rooms and make the beds, as we had these marvellous helpers to do it. It was interesting about the gardeners, because one was Ernest, the brother of Annie. We had a nanny when we were very small and she was called Hilda. Ernest Court very cleverly courted Hilda and won her. We always called him Bear. He went off to the war and joined the Flying Corps. and came to visit in a furry flying coat and furry flying helmet.

We were quite frightened of him when he appeared and thought he was a bear; we called him 'Bear' ever afterwards. They married in the late 1920's and a cottage was built in a field for them. Of course it had to be called The Bear's Den and that little cottage was always known as the Den. In 1932 their second baby was christened.

Scofield was head gardener. Then there was another gardener called Raggett: he had been in the First World War and been very badly gassed. He always had breathing problems and a bad chest, but my father employed him as a gardener to do whatever he could. He really worked as hard as he could and seemed to enjoy the work. He lived in a bungalow in our grounds. Then there was another one, Brooker, who had been a soldier in the First World War and my father gave him a job. He had been badly wounded and wasn't awfully strong but he had a wife and four or five children. He lived in a cottage further away and my parents were assiduous in taking care of their people. Mother used to send us with the donkey cart full of gifts for them; there would be something that had been cooked in our kitchens, a chicken or plum pudding perhaps. Particularly at Christmas time there would be presents for everyone of the children -- clothes, and a toy of some sort, as my parents really believed in looking after the families of those who worked for them.

Even after all these years I can remember their faces and their voices, and Scofield's laugh -- he had a very merry laugh -- we were very fond of them and I am sure they were fond of us. They were happy working in this household at Pax Hill.

6. TRANSPORT, TRAVEL AND HOLIDAYS

Although the railways continued to play a large part in the transport of goods and people during the Thirties, the internal combustion engine was beginning to erode their domination. Already during the Twenties the family car and the motorcycle were increasingly popular.

Air travel, too, was attracting more customers, and there were great expectations for the airships that were being built. Barnes Wallis designed the R100, which was built privately and in July 1930 successfully crossed to Canada and back. However, the R101 crashed over France, killing forty-four people. No more airships were built in Britain. Then in May 1937 the German airship *Hindenburg* crashed in New Jersey after crossing the Atlantic. The *Akron* and the *Macon*, the largest airships belonging to the USA had also crashed, and this meant the demise of this form of transport. However, in 1936 a long distance aircraft capable of landing on water made its first flight to Australia from England in nine and a half days. Soon the flying boat, which was considered much safer than airships, would be increasingly used for travel across the Atlantic.

The 'Royal Scot'.

However, in the Thirties most people who could afford it preferred to go by train and sea: in 1934 the luxury liner the *Queen Mary* was finally launched. At 76,240 tonnes it was the largest ship yet built and in 1936 it created a record by crossing the Atlantic in just under four days. That same year a British pilot, Beryl Markham, was the first woman to fly an aircraft single handed across the Atlantic from Europe, although Amy Johnson had made a solo flight to Australia in 1930.

1936, The Queen Mary sails.

The increase in road transport was causing havoc on the roads and in 1934 Oliver Stanley, the Minister of Transport, began drawing up various schemes to reduce the casualties. However, he was replaced by Leslie Hore Belisha and it was he who introduced them. They included new road signs, roundabouts, authorised pedestrian crossings, and it was Belisha's name that was given to the orange beacons that marked them. Driving tests were introduced for the first time – before that anyone could buy a car and drive away with a minimum of instruction. Signs such as *Major Road Ahead* and *One Way Street*, and 30 m.p.h. speed limits in built-up areas, helped to reduce accidents as did the law to make cyclists have more visible rear lights. It was possible to buy an Austin Seven or Ford Eight for a little over £100 in 1931 and in spite of the depression more and more of those in work were investing in a car of some kind. This meant visits at weekends as well as holidays to the country or seaside were increasingly popular, and many others were able to travel by charabanc (coach) or motorcycle. There were also special excursions by train. The demand for overnight accommodation led to the creation of more hotels and seaside landladies doing bed and breakfast or providing other catering arrangements. It was in 1930 that the first Youth Hostel (based on their success in Germany) was opened at Winchester, and others followed. They charged only 1 shilling a night, with the provision of a cooked breakfast and evening meal at a small extra cost, or self-catering facilities for those who preferred to cook their own meals. They only accepted those who arrived under their own steam, walking or cycling, but it opened up the countryside to many who could not afford the luxury of hotels.

Although some employees already enjoyed a week's holiday with pay, it was not until the Act of 1938 that this became a standard industrial practice. Holiday camps had already been introduced by Butlins in 1937, with chalets and modern catering, also leisure facilities that catered for all age groups. So the leisure industry had greatly increased during the Thirties.

Biddy Clark describes a fuel used for transportation during the Second World War probably unknown to many of the present generation.

I met my late husband, Joe Shillito, when I was nursing in 1938. He was a graduate at Birmingham University and was researching into the uses of alternative fuel, to write his thesis for an MSc degree in Fuel Technology.

With the possibility of war, the problem of importing fuel for transport became critical. Petrol was stringently rationed and we saw taxis with large bags on their roofs filled with town gas produced from our own coal.

Later on, attention was given to the use of 'Producer Gas', which could be made from indigenous smokeless fuels such as coke and anthracite. The principle was to feed a reduced amount of air to the hot fuel, which was then combusted to carbon monoxide instead of the usual carbon dioxide. The resultant produced gas still had a heating value and could be combusted with additional air in the engine of the vehicle, instead of the normal petrol or diesel fuel.

Joe was asked to research into all the problems involved in producing efficient fuel, to control the system and to solve the problem of corrosion in the engine, which could result from producer gas.

The university provided a long bus; one side was cut open and various bottles, tubes, tanks etc. inserted so that it looked like a mobile laboratory. Towed behind the bus was a 'hopper', which was filled with anthracite to be fired.

Several hundred miles had to be test run each week, and as these were my courting days much enjoyment was had travelling through the countryside in this immense vehicle. To test its hill-climbing capacity, Joe decided to take it to North Wales. As we wound up the narrow mountain lanes, sparks flew out of the hopper, setting light to a hedge -- much to the consternation of the Welsh villagers! Many recordings were taken on the journey and most of the problems were solved. Later the Western National Bus Company converted many of their buses to producer gas. There were warning signs on the back of the bus regarding the hopper that was being towed and was full of burning anthracite. One gentleman ignored the warning and as he jumped off the bus his trousers were ripped by the hopper.

The alternative fuels filled a large gap during the war years, but they were never as efficient as petrol or diesel.

Joe Shillito - gas producer for bus.
Research at Birmingham University.

Aircraft and flying proved a fascination for Dick Cunningham during the Thirties, but he also enjoyed other forms of transportation.

In 1930 the huge airship R101 flew low over Glasgow during a round Britain trial flight, shortly before her fatal crash in northern France. She was clearly visible from my bedroom window as she flew behind the spire of St. Mary's Cathedral. The following year

I undertook the longest tram drive of my life, to an airfield near Renfrew, to watch a hair-raising display of aerobatics by a small plane, including the pilot removing his control stick as he flew past and also walking on the wings. The following year, when holidaying in Oban, the new small flying boat *Spirit Of Iona* landed in the bay and took passengers (about eight to ten at a time) on short flights. This allowed them to see Lismore Island, up Loch Linnhe, across to Mull, and down instead of up to McCaig's Folly. My father provided the 10 shillings which allowed me to enjoy my only ever trip in a flying boat. A small one-passenger plane landed in a field near Blackwaterfoot in 1935 and took a passenger on a five minute flight, high enough to see most of Arran and across to Campeltown. We were holidaying there at the time, and again my father produced the necessary 10 shillings.

In 1936 our father's Camberley bachelor friend gave me and my sisters each a new bicycle. I chose the biggest Raleigh -- guaranteed for fifty years -- and insisted on having a three-speed gear and a mileometer added, also a large saddle-bag. My Saturday morning shopping messages for my mother became even more involved. In the days of small, specialist shops my mother decided that fresh eggs were best from one shop, fresh butter from another, and so with scones, cakes, my father's potato scones, honey, potatoes, green vegetables, fruit. I did more stopping than riding, but the service was always good and little waiting was necessary.

Besides using the Clyde steamers for destinations such as Dunoon and the islands we also, on pleasant Sundays in September in the mid-Thirties, used the LNER steamers for cruises from Craigendoran pier, to the top of which the train from Glasgow ran, to the Kyles of Bute or Loch Long, or the Cock of Arran.

The excellent tram service around Glasgow was acknowledged as being the best in the world. Stops were not far apart and trams were frequent. In the early Thirties the driver's cab at each end, together with the seating area on the top deck immediately above them, were open to the elements. If it was not wet or windy, as children we opted for the open seats, often to the annoyance of the conductor. He had to climb upstairs and go to the front just to collect 'a ha'penny half' or 'a penny half'. The cabs and the upstairs seats were soon glassed in. The routes were designated not by number boy but a broad band of colour around the tram, between the lower and upper decks. You caught a 'blue, green, red, yellow or white' tram, and it was only in the centre of town that you might find yourself with two of the same colour going to different destinations. You had to know where you were going!

Although there were increasing numbers of cars on the roads in the Thirties, they were still a luxury for most people; Mr. Barclay Hankin managed to invest in a cheap second-hand vehicle.

I had learnt to drive whilst still at school. In 1937 I bought my first car for the princely sum of £10 from a second hand dealer in Shepherds Bush! It was a 1927 Austin 7 with a 'special' body, a hood, side screens and a small dicky. It was green and looked like an insect, so soon became known as 'the bug'.

I knew that second hand dealers had a bad reputation and that one could not expect a great deal for £10! It proved to have only one fault, and that was its huge consumption of oil. It went merrily along and just managed 50 miles per hour and 50 miles per gallon of petrol on long journeys. Unfortunately the oil seemed to get used up at the rate of 50 miles to a pint! Cleveland petrol was only about 1/2d per gallon, and cheap oil about 6d per pint if you bought it in a 5 gallon drum. It would have been expensive to cure the oil problem, so I decided to accept it as fuel and carry supplies with me, checking carefully every 50 miles or so.

This car was a huge joy, taking us everywhere, including two trips to Scotland. Two people could get to Oban (500 miles) for less than £2, but it usually meant camping for two nights on the way. Side screens were difficult to repair, as the talc went brittle and it required a struggle by two people to sew them in with a very strong needle. In winter it was distinctly cold, so we wrapped legs and shoulders in rugs and, if necessary, stopped at a convenient town and walked round Woolworths to get warm! After about two years, the back axle gave up the ghost, and she was sold for £5. Motoring in the Thirties was cheap, enormous fun, and with far less traffic than nowadays. Pound for pound, that £10 was probably the best investment I ever made.

The Bug.

The Hon. Mrs. Clay describes transport at Pax Hill in the Thirties.

We were very lucky as we had cars. There was the Rolls Royce that was given to my father at the 1929 Jamboree, which was therefore called Jamroll. It was a lovely car and we had a caravan with it called Eccles. We also had at that time the last of the Standard cars we had always had. It was called Jimmax, as all of our cars had been called Jim something. This was the biggest of the lot, so it was called Jimmax, but Jimmax was not a success: it was always breaking down and letting us down all over the countryside. So my parents decided we must have another car besides Jamroll that would pull the caravan so it must be a really strong one, as Jimmax had found it rather an effort to pull the caravan up the hills, especially in Devon.

In 1931 my mother and father went to Australia and while they were away Mrs. Wade, Dad's secretary, who knew they were looking for another car, found a Rolls Royce -- quite an old one -- that looked in good condition. The garage strongly recommended it so she cabled to them and they cabled back 'Buy it'. So (it sounds awfully posh!) they bought this second Rolls Royce. It had to begin with a J, so was called Jaus (aus for Australia). Jaus was a marvellous car. We all learnt to drive in it: it pulled the caravan and was very strong and very reliable.

Later on, when my sister Heather left school in 1933, they bought a little secondhand car, a Standard which we called Jummy.

Pax, home of the Baden - Powell family with their two Rolls Royce cars, Jam Roll and Jaus + Eccles caravan.

Lilian Smith was able to travel around with her father and family, and also to enjoy holidays with her grandparents.

Dad did not have a car -- a Ford 8 -- until 1939: before that he had a motorbike and sidecar. Mum rode pillion and we three children in the sidecar. Dad was a devotee of speedway racing and we travelled to different events. My memories are of noise and dirt.

Holidays we spent with my maternal grandparents who lived at Southend-on-Sea. When the tide was out all you could see was mud! I also went to the school camp at Dovercourt. 6d was paid weekly into a fund for this. Outings consisted of days in London with the family next door, visiting museums, art galleries, the Tower of London, etc.; then we had tea at Lyon's Corner House. I was taken to keep their daughter company and I enjoyed the outings greatly.

Mostly Hazel Rolf used a bicycle to travel around, but in 1931 her father bought a car.

Dad bought a secondhand Morris Cowley car for thirty pounds and we sometimes went in it from Reading to Chertsey on Sundays to visit my Grandma and aunts. The first time we had planned to go we were all waiting in the drive and the car would not start. Dad worked on it for a while and then fetched a neighbour: eventually they got it going but we were about two hours late. The number of the car was MO 3311; it was brown with a rain hood and celluloid window frames to slot in. As it was a lengthy job getting the hood up and the windows fixed, it had to be raining very hard before Dad would stop and see to it. Later Dad bought a secondhand Morris Oxford saloon, No. PX 8961, which was entirely enclosed so more comfortable.

When our college was evacuated to Shrewsbury at the outbreak of war in 1939, I needed a bicycle. As it was going to be cheaper living there than in London, I decided to buy a new bike and was lucky to find one in a shop in town for £7.10s. However, my enjoyment of it was short lived, for it was stolen from the front garden of the house, 'Twyford', where we ate our meals and did our prep. Mine was the only new one among the twenty others there and we had nowhere else to keep them. I reported the number to the police, but of course they had many such thefts reported and they were in short supply. So once again I borrowed my sister Vera's bike and enjoyed many rides in the countryside.

In Scotland there were various means of transport available in the Thirties, as Jim Finlayson describes.

Trams were a familiar sight in Scottish towns during the Thirties, as they had been since the turn of the century. Naturally, for me as a Glaswegian, the cars were an important feature of my daily life. It is difficult to give a phonetic rendering of 'caur': perhaps our Cockney friends come nearest with the 'cor' in 'cor blimey'. Anyway, when we had boarded an over-full caur we were given the classic instruction, "Come oan, get aff" (Come on, get off). This seemingly contradictory instruction was well understood by the public.

It is almost beyond belief that it was possible to travel for two hours and close on thirty miles for 3d (old pennies): there is no equivalent in today's currency. One needed to be very patient and have a good bladder to make such a journey, as it was not possible to leave the car for the call of nature without paying again on the next car.

Many of the tram journeys were short and charged by stages. A stage was about a mile, price a halfpenny. During school days if I was late or the weather wet or slushy my mother found a halfpenny to take me to a tram stop near to the school.

Dependent on the nature or mood of the driver, goods were sometimes carried on his platform. I was a piper in a pipe band and my friend was the big drummer. Jimmy lived at a tram terminus and would load the huge bass drum at the driver's heels and take it off at the next terminus, which was near to the band headquarters some six miles distant. The process was reversed to convey himself and the drum home after the parade: total cost less than half today's 5p. One tram route was past a famous market called 'The Barras' (Barrows). It was not unusual to see a roll of linoleum propped up beside the driver, one of a happy breed! 'The Barras' still exist: sadly, not the trams.

Even the giant Cunard shipping line was short of capital in the Thirties and earlier. The keel for the world's largest ship was laid down at the yard of John Brown at Clydebank, but work was halted, then started again. The colossal hull was eventually completed with government help, largely due to the efforts of a Scottish M.P., David Kirkwood. Many people thought the ship might be named after him. In the event, her majesty Queen Mary launched the ship and called it the *S.S. Queen Mary* in 1935. It was a great day for the Clyde, Clydebank and Scotland. The great ship, hitherto known as No. 536, was waterborne. She took the Blue Riband of the Atlantic in the face of competition from the lovely French vessel *Normandie*.

The *Queen Mary* plied the Atlantic faithfully through the years before and during the Second World War. I believe she is now permanently moored at Long Beach, California, USA, where she is a tourist attraction with shopping malls and accommodation.

During the depression of the Thirties quite a few young unemployed men camped near Loch Lomond. They were as fit as

fiddles and cycled in to Glasgow to sign on at the Labour Exchange or 'The Burroo' (Bureau). This was the era of the infamous
Means Test, which could split up families.

My first new bicycle was the best model in the Rudge Whit-
worth catalogue, the 'Celerity lightweight', price £4.19.6d. I paid
for it at 5/- (25p) weekly and was incensed that I was charged an
extra 5/6d. I rode this bike to work every day, thereby saving
tram fares, until the outbreak of the Second World War. In addition it was my transport cheaply and silently into the country.

Cycling club runs in those days were well attended and could
muster upwards of sixty members. Those were often split into
two sections, the fast and the slow, which latter included some of
the ladies. Of course, the stigma of riding in the slow section was
offset by being with the ladies!

**Kenneth Beck is now living in Manchester, but grew up in
Scotland. He has happy memories of travel and holidays
during the Thirties.**

My earliest memories of transport in the Thirties are of open-top
tramcars, on which I travelled to and from school in Dunfermline,
Fife. I recall climbing the stairs to the top deck and the way the
tramcar used to sway.

Steam trains, of course, were no novelty in the Thirties and I
enjoyed many trips to Edinburgh from Dunfermline, the crossing
of the Forth Bridge being the highlight of the journey. As a special
treat, my father took me on the ferry boat which plied between
North and South Queensferry, with spectacular views of the Forth
Bridge from the river. We walked through the Earl of Roseberry's
estate at Dalmeny to Cramond, and then boarded the bus for Edinburgh. The return journey was usually by train.

Another Sunday outing was by tramcar to the Rosyth Dockyard, where there sometimes were interesting Royal Navy ships
to visit.

I recall sailing to Belfast from the Broomielaw in Glasgow. It
was a novelty sleeping in a cabin and wakening next morning as
the boat sailed up Belfast Lough.

When I was about eight years old, my father took me to London. Instead of going by train, we sailed from Leith one Saturday
afternoon and docked at London on the Monday morning. That
was probably in August, but the sea was surprisingly rough, especially near the Wash. There were not many passengers in the
dining saloon that Sunday! I shall always remember hearing the
hymn *'For all the Saints'* on the wireless that Sunday evening as
the boat sailed up the Thames -- so calm after the North Sea! Going to London was, of course, a big adventure, with the sight of

Tower Bridge, the Tower of London, St. Paul's Cathedral, Westminster Abbey -- places I had only read about in books at school. I remember hearing a Guards' Band playing in Hyde Park and a visit to Gamages, where my father bought me a Hornby engine, which I treasured for years to come.

Another holiday we enjoyed was a round trip from Dunfermline to Aberdeen, by train to Inverness and then we sailed to Fort William, through Loch Ness. The scenery from Fort William to Oban and then to Glasgow was very picturesque. This was a round trip, as we returned to Dunfermline by train from Glasgow. It would cost a substantial sum of money nowadays!

1935 was a sad year, as my mother died from T.B. in December, when I was almost twelve years old. The following year my father took me to Llandudno in August. We spent two happy weeks there, and I have treasured memories of the boarding house where we stayed in Trinity Square and of walks along Llandudno's pier to hear the orchestra, led by David MacCallum, whose violin solos were memorable. On Sunday evening, of course, there was hymn singing on the prom. We enjoyed the Pierrot shows in the Happy Valley, a trip by tramcar to the top of the Great Orme, and by a small one deck tramcar (called 'the Toastrack') to Colwyn Bay. We had several enjoyable coach trips to parts of Snowdonia and the surrounding area. Llandudno has remained my favourite holiday resort in the north, and I often wish I could, by some magic, have that holiday, or part of it, again.

It seemed to Andrew J. Blair that not many people travelled as far as England from Scotland, where he lived in the Thirties.

Except for short journeys, there was only one way to travel and that was by rail. Probably the majority had holidays *without* pay. Most Scots holidayed in Scotland near or far, for a day or a month according to means. To go to England or further was unusual. For outings we in Greenock were fortunate in being able to walk into the country or by the shore. Forays might be made by bus or train or, joy of joys, by one of the many steamers which ran timetabled services, like buses, or pleasure cruises round the spacious waters of the Firth.

In Jill Clarke's experience transport always seemed to be reliable in the Thirties.

Few people had cars in the Thirties, and those who did were the very rich. Public transport was cheap, and seemed reliable. I went to London by Underground to school each day, and I do not remember there ever being delays or breakdowns. Children were always taught to stand up and give their seats to grown ups, which I did with some reluctance at times.

Train journeys were exciting, and planned well ahead. We used to have a fortnight in Cornwall with an aunt: it was an important event in the year. Mother booked our seats on the train and our luggage was sent on ahead. A cabin trunk was packed and collected by the railway the day before our journey: on our arrival it would be waiting for us at our destination. It cost 1 shilling.

We had very little money to spend on our holidays. I don't remember having any trips or meals out, but we had a wonderful time, just being by the sea.

Families often went to holiday camps, or boarding houses at coastal resorts. Only the wealthy went to hotels. I did not stay at one until after the Second World War.

For Lucy, in her fairly remote part of the West Country, Plymouth was the main centre of entertainment, shopping and services.

The train and ferry services to Plymouth were good, with small local lines still providing a good service. Local buses were probably better than they are today. There were few cars as they were a luxury for those in the higher income groups, although some of the young invested in old bangers. There were also trade vans and lorries, and a few horse-drawn vehicles. The roads were wonderfully empty and a delight to drive on, and to be able to stop wherever you liked. No motorways or dual carriageways, roundabouts, or confusion of lights and directions.

For day outings there were charabancs (coaches). It was not until after the Second World War that high powered travel agents made their appearance. Charabanc trips were a popular pastime in the summer for all those who could not afford a car: they took people for day outings to the coast, to the moor, to village functions, county agricultural shows, Navy Week at Plymouth, point to point races -- in fact any event that the public enjoyed.

Plymouth was our town for recreation of all kinds as we grew up: cinema, theatre, dances, tennis, and all the entertainment provided by the army, navy or air force. There were dances on ships, boat trips, and launching of ships from the dockyard. Friends from the service, often came to our house; they were a migratory population as their term of service was about two years only. We, as a family, had plenty of these enjoyments and brief friendships, with the social entertainments they provided.

Our holidays as children were limited to two a year, when we went to a rented house on Dartmoor: we looked forward to these for the whole year. My parents took their holidays together, either abroad or to Scotland or Wales to fish in the rivers and lochs, or to play golf. We never went with them. We were left with the maids (who were a nice lot of girls and provided a good deal of comfort in our young life, as also did the current governess). We had dogs, and I had a pony.

We had a good country life, with plenty of scope within its life-style. The way of life of the small county squire went out completely with the onset of the Second World War. The larger estates still survived, or became resuscitated after the war if they could be turned into a viable asset, or turned over to the National Trust. The West Country boasted few large estates but many smaller ancient properties which were already, between the two wars, getting very run down and existing on capital (we were among these). The Second World War was their death knell, and this included our family.

There were still not many cars around in northern England during the Thirties, as an anonymous contributor remembers.
Most people travelled about on trams, although there were plenty of bicycles in use, too. I had one as a present on my fifth birthday. My family had a car, a Wolseley 9, 1935 model. There were few cars on the roads and none of my friends' families owned one. We went for outings into the countryside or to the seaside. Holidays were for one week only, and always in this country.

During the Thirties a special Bob holiday was spent at Lucy Summers' beautiful old country cottage 'Vrede' at Cudham, near Green Street Green, Kent. Marjorie and I were both recovering from illnesses, and as Lucy was going abroad for two weeks she invited us to look after her house and dog, Sally, whilst she was away. Amazing trust again! Marjorie was reading English at King's College, London. I was nearing the end of my secretarial course, and we both delighted in the beauty and peace of our surroundings. Marjorie kept a diary (with a little help from me) for Lucy on her return and extracts from it will give a more vivid picture than my ancient memories of those magical days. Although we were alone at first, others joined us when they were free, especially during the second week. Both Lucy and Marjorie died some years ago, as have other Bobs.

Monday, 31st July: Horrid, flat feeling after you (Lucy) had gone. Bestirred myself and wandered down a windy, sweet-scented lane to Green St. Green, saw a silky, tremulous rat escape the heels of a clip-clopping pony and trap, opposite

Snag Lane. Met Grace and shopped comprehensively between 11.00 and 11.30. Instructive conversation with
butcher. Two large, brown 'Mummy Solkhon' cakes added to
the larder: cherry and seed. Evening walk across Angas Home
drive -- larchwood; home through Lett's Green and Horn's
Green. Plantations of giant willow-herb in misty openings in
wood. Picked honeysuckle, enough to fill the big bowl in the
dining room. Grey, heavy sky made woods and lanes appear
greener than ever. Sudden sideways outpouring of stormy
yellow light from the edge of the greyness as we neared home,
catching treetops at a queer angle. Oil-stove and all lamps,
except dining room one, managed quite intelligently. No ray
of light, intellectual or material, shone on us where the latter
was concerned, so we decided to sup always by daylight.
Grace retired to bed soon. I wandered about, feeling the
complete house-owner and reluctant to bury my new importance in sleep. Sally charming all day; determined to make us
feel at home.

Tuesday, August 1st: Walked down to Green St. Green and
ordered leg of lamb - 4/6d.; shopped generally and caught
11.30 'bus back - rather proud of our ability to fit times of
'buses in so neatly. Pretended to read and tried not to sleep
in the afternoon. Tea in the garden. Evening walk along New
Barn Lane, past farm, up hill, then turned right across the
fields. Several picture-postcard views of 'Vrede' through
openings in wood. We lost ourselves occasionally in hazel
and ash plantations, owing to winding, indistinct paths.
Found a field of tall yellow plants with thick patches of thyme,
which we picked in armfuls, and later cut lots of dogwood with
berries shading from cream to crimson and black. Followed
always, and sometimes forcibly propelled, by faithful hound.
My argument is that it doesn't matter how many times one
appears to be lost on a walk, one is nevertheless a competent
guide if home is reached before midnight, without retracing
more than a quarter of one's footsteps. We did, so I am! THE
event of the day -- we broke away from the maze of young trees
by stepping over barbed wire into the large, one horse field at
the bottom of the green hill in front of 'Vrede'. Half way
across Sally discovered a baby bird, which we carried home in
addition to our burden of flowers. We climbed the almost
perpendicular slope with the bird in one hand and branches
in the other. Examined it: no injury, but claws limp and legs
of no use. We decided to ask advice next door. Mrs. .... felt
the bird, which she said was a baby woodpecker or tree
creeper, and she thought it was in good condition but prob-

ably starving, and its legs were limp from weakness. So we made a nest for it in two pairs of my stockings and fed it on milk and sponge cake, which is consumed greedily after first fluttering its wings. I might have guessed it was a woodpecker for the painful jabs it gave to the palm of my hand! We left it in the spare bedroom, shutting the door in the face of the cat. Some time after going to bed we visited it by candle-light, as we heard it tapping on the wall. We fed it again and it seemed stronger.

(After thought. Fat lady requiring cloak-room, in middle of jelly-making during the evening).

<u>Wednesday, August 2nd:</u> Cook's field-day! Managed oven as if born and bred amongst Valor Perfections. Lamb roasted most successfully (fat red cookery book in top cupboard clear and concise); left too much fat in gravy – otherwise good. Only cause for grief – no room for peas to cook at same time as potatoes, so with masterly decision decided to cut peas out of menu. Pride hurt but dinner to time, Grace having fetched Mummy Solkhon and Nancy (Marjorie's sister) up on 11.30 'bus. Dinner at 1.00pm. Sweets – pears and apricot jelly mould made night before. Guests revelled in sun and deck-chairs. Picnic planned, but garden tea too attractive. Evening walk, straight over brow of hill opposite, past Christmas Cottage, to left through woods. Lost again, but most attractively: beginning to pride myself on casual artistry (artistic casualness?) of my walks! Up and down many brambly, slippery slopes; Sally bursting with joy, did each perilous descent three times to our once, at lightning speed. Brought home more flowers. Sultry night: four search-lights chasing one aeroplane, which looked like a fragile, white moth when it was caught. Wandered in and out of garden in pyjamas watching excitement in the sky. Stood the candle on the bathroom window-sill and left the window and door open while Nancy came in to talk. Result -- the curtain flared up. Between us we released it and flung it out of the window; secured charred fragment to match in Bromley. Afraid that the white paint is marked.

Lay on bed, semi-naked, and watched the moonlight grow stronger and searchlights paler. Sudden spasm of energetic conversation, then sleep.

Baby woodpecker thriving before breakfast – dead afterwards. He probably choked as his neck was twisted and very little sponge-cake left. Disappointing! The floor was plentifully bespattered with white marks: surprisingly extensive mess, which took us some time to clear. We buried the soft, fluffy little thing in the corner of the rose bed.

The laundry man, whom we missed yesterday, called and retrieved clean washing from next door for us, where he had left it.

Borrowed large, horn-handled carving knife from next door. Had to shave Sally close on one side of chin to remove large, ridiculous burr.

N.B. No connection between last two remarks!

Thursday, August 3rd: Lovely larch wood - honeysuckle walk again. Grace turned back soon after starting: still very tired. Mummy Solkhon, Nancy and I continued, with Sally, whom Nancy had rechristened Shadow and fallen in love with. She certainly has been charmingly obedient all day, and irresistible in her affectionate moments. Armfuls of honeysuckle for visitors to take home this evening, gathered from both sides of the hedge. Home at 1.15pm for lunch. Mummy Solkhon explained the working of the sewing machine. Pretended to be more intelligent that I really was, it seems a horribly complicated business. It took four of us to get a spool wound, then Mummy S. machined merrily away, after removing half an inch of leather to tighten things up. Intimidated by her capable manner. Grace and her mother went on 4.10 'bus, Grace returning on circular tour at 5.10. Nancy and I went down on the 7.10 'bus, but had to let one Green Line coach go as it was full up: she caught the next one.

Sally rounded up a field full of sheep, beyond Angas Home, before we or the men knew what she was up to. Streak of sandy yellow hair moving at lightning speed. She returned when satisfied, quite unashamed, and continued on her walk with us.

Friday, August 4th: Valley full to the brim with milky mist. Sat up in bed early and gloated over long day ahead. Lazy morning in the garden and I darned all the stockings I possess. Between 2.10 and 5.10 visited Bromley on a shopping expedition and returned laden with fruit, etc. Grace spent the afternoon sunbathing in blue swimming costume on the lawn. Made a large savoury omelette for supper. Curdled a whole pint of milk by pouring it on to pineapple jelly, which was solid instead of diluted. Rather a shock!

Bought remnant for bathroom curtains at Medhurst, and three pairs of socks and innumerable odds and ends at Boots. Great temptation to buy lots of unnecessary things in sales.

Postcard from Salzburg. Very glad – strange impression that you were still in the air some vague where.

Saturday, August 5th: Woke simultaneously at 4.00 am and descended with candles for water. For a few seconds a rainbow-coloured halo encircled each flame as we stood in the kitchen, then disappeared. We both saw them, so not an hallucination. Was it morning mist, dispelled by warmth of flame? Leg of lamb going well – keeping well. Arrival of 4lb 2oz sirloin ordered on Tuesday rather staggering. Consulted red cookery book again and cooked it for one and a half hours. It looked really handsome when done. Beans and potatoes as well. Polly Mitts (Molly Pitts) arrived after lunch at 2.10pm, having come the long way round. The afternoon simply melted away in the garden. Polly wandered round the house, crowing with delight and talking appreciatively to herself. Put her in Joan's room. Tea in the garden, then we watched the cricket match between Bromley and Cudham. An elderly Bromley batsman was winded badly, doubled up, but he nobly took the field again at the end of the innings. Shocked Polly by showing very inaccurate knowledge of scoring. Sally enjoyed herself immensely, fielded a few balls, fortunately boundaries. After supper she took a long time decided between going to bed with a large mutton bone and coming for a walk with us. Finally dropped the bone and came round the cricket field. A full moon, with a theatrical circle of black trees. We played slow-motion, phantom cricket, which sent Sally nearly crazy with excitement. Made several really good puns and was quite witty: inspired by cooler, night air. Had a fairly appreciative audience. Put family to bed, plus mutton bone, and went out again, this time dropping into the mist in the valley below; came back by steep Christmas Cottage Lane, because of Polly's rheumatism and night-mists in fields. Grace has taken to sleeping head to foot of bed. Interesting discussions beneath our window:
  (a) the wife's illness, neuritis, erysipelas;
  (b) drunken insistence on being 58 years old.
Sunday, August 6th: Brilliant sunshine at 6am. Only a faint streak of mist across trees. Descended for two apples and 'The Fleeting' and consumed them until Grace rose to go to the 8 o'clock service. Then went to sleep. Woke to find breakfast laid and Polly in a very handsome green and yellow flowered silk dressing gown, bought for visit to Paris last year. Had leisure to enjoy the *Observer* for the first time for weeks. Hot. Sat on slope of hill; too hot, so came in. Made a fruitless effort on sewing machine. Read *'The Fleeting'*, then continued abstracting Sweet William seeds. Sally too hot: flopped on the floor and wherever I went the silly thing followed, even

when she had found a cool patch under the bed. Campaign on blue-bottles and flies. Thought it wiser to get rid of last few slices of lamb -- suggestion of animation underneath the bottom slice. Otherwise, catering going well. Series of small boys, with baby sister in bathing costume and fat tummy, calling for water in thermos flasks. Gave them glasses, too. Finished 'The Fleeting'. Too lazy to say anything about it now. Read myself into a stupor. Supper in garden -- junket and plums. Junket sour, so plums and milk. Getting cooler. At last up to date with diary. Evening walk through beech hangar to New Barn Farm, then home, with armfuls of tall, yellow flowers; sap sickly sweet, like coconut.

Monday, August 7th: Visited Miss How... who was open for an hour in morning (Bank Holiday). Bought another fly-band especially for Polly to walk into – it gives her a peculiar, horrid sensation to be caught up among flies and stickiness. Three times in rapid succession!

Hundreds of hikers all day long, many in bathing costumes and shorts; some lovely, tanned skins; one beauty in backless bathing costume on back of motor-bicycle.

Machined one very crooked seam, then decided to do the rest of the nightdress by hand. Polly spent the afternoon in the garden room reading 'Villette'; Grace in the garden sunbathing; I in dining room for the pleasure of overhearing comments of passers-by. One wild looking gang of scantily-clad hikers with concertina chanting primitive songs. Lady: "Lovely house - sweet border of flowers". Ever so many similar comments.

Several little boys for water. One anxious woman with large can and small ginger-beer bottle for water for car a mile and a half down New Barn Lane, which had "made a contact" (??). Two very nice girls for water in bottles: gave glasses of water also. Toasted scones for tea in garden. Finished curtains after tea. Expecting Jane all day. Had supper by 8.00pm, then waited for 8.10 'bus, but Jane not on it, so then we set out for a long walk via larch wood, etc. At the other side of the recreation ground I remembered I had left the kettle on the stove, so went back. Found Jane on the doorstep, having missed the 'bus and walked up the hill. Providential return, otherwise she would have had to resort to the inn for an hour or two. The original purpose of evening walk was to bury the beef, because we had allowed a blue-bottle to lay eggs on it after only one day's meals. Very reluctant to confess this failure to estimate endurance in hot weather, but this journal's only ideal is honesty. After second supper the Burial

Party set out, with torch and spade, body in brown paper bag. Sally and Jenny, of her own accord, escorted us. Full moonlight – cat leaping sideways, with feathery tail aloft. She seemed to suspect our sinister purpose. We found a suitable spot on the edge of the cabbage field by the larch wood, and dug a hole with difficulty. Polly pronounced the epitaph: "After life's fitful fever ....." Continued our walk via Mace Lane, home. Much cooler – gusts of friendly wind through the house. Woke during the night and saw Grace lying in full blast with nothing on: meant to cover her up, but fell asleep in middle of intention.

Tuesday, August 8th: Jane's advent meant a considerable increase in back-chat, repartee and gossip. Four a nice number. Considered cancelling other invitations! Ironed frock, etc. Shopped in village. Returned shilling which Mrs. H. had overestimated in our change yesterday. Had huge dinner. Wrote home and elsewhere. Garden. Sun. Wind. (Following written in field half-way between Leaves Green and Down). Tea with large fruit and nut cake (from Mummy S. again), and much hysteria. Planned walk at 6.30pm, then remembered fat lady who came for cloak-room before going to the Angus Home in the morning and asked if she might call in on her way home in the evening; so waited for her. Heard a commotion and saw Sally tumbling headlong into a saloon car. Occupants and I stared at one another in dim recognition – Mr. and Mrs. Cooper, little boy and young woman. They had seen the notice of car accident in paper and thought you were damaged too extensively to go away, so called back today to see. Reassured them and invited them in, but they continued on their way.

Selfridge's van delivered two large parcels for 'Vrede', Green St. Green – Mr. Fisher. I told the man of plagiarism and sent him down to horrid little house at bottom of lane. Fat lady having paid us another visit, we set off on our evening walk. Glorious, mellow sunlight, crystal clear sky; shortened our walk, cutting out Lett's Green by path through Newyear's Wood. Brought in a quart of cider from the Inn next door; made savoury omelettes. Jane succeeded in lighting dining room lamp. Convivial supper – wit warmed by cider, lamplight casting a soft glow over variety of courses. Anti-fly cream (one of my many Boots purchases) in much demand. Have come to the pitch when we scratch, meals or no meals. Glass of water-jug in your bedroom broken. Accidental - no ragging.

Wednesday, August 9th: Village shop: Mrs. H. a dear. Everyone in the village is worth talking to. Old man discussed

Sally, Sealyhams, and dogs in general. Love this leisurely life
– wish I were a villager. Packed dinner and set off for Down
and Leaves Green, where we ate a complete new loaf bought
in Down between us, and a quarter of butter, etc. Invested in
a lead for Sally for main roads in Down: it looked beautiful,
but snapped off about ten minutes later. Still quite useful.
Glasses of cider at King's Head Inn, after seeing Polly off on
her walk to Keston and Hayes, where her newly married sister
is setting up house after their honeymoon. Expect her back
any time this evening. Wandered across glorious links, up
steep, leafy beech lane with charming white house converted
from two cottages. At top of lane a huge new building with
elaborate outhouses and a figure of St. Francis on front.
Hospital? Sanatorium? Dairy-farm? School? Now grilling in
a field facing woods blue with heat mist.

Tea at Hostye Farm: recommend it heartily. Fresh scones,
butter good, interesting cakes, comfy chairs and pleasant
hand-painted china to match colour scheme. Found two very
welcome p.c.'s on return. Jane is lovely: golden brown and
ruddy, with twinkling blue eyes. Grace has beautiful V-shaped
peach stain on her back from sunbathing. Sally too lovable --
shall hate not seeing her inquiring tail in front of me next
week.

Thursday, August 10th: Jane and I kept house, while Polly
and Grace went to bring Biddy and Joan back on 11.30 'bus.
Sudden influx of extreme youth and high spirits on their
return. Red check blouses and grey shorts: tanned skins.
Dinner for six. Caught the 2.10 'bus to G. S. G. to get family
shopping and to save Sally from starvation. Shops supercili-
ous at mention of Vims. Finally got some at ..... Had tea at
Mecca Cafe, round corner from Medhursts. Spent every
penny, then found two books in Smith's and simply had to ask
the man to keep them for me until Monday: 'Alice in Wonderland', illustrated by Rackham (6/- reduced to 3/6d) and 'Gob-
lin Market' 1/-d. Missed 'bus because of secondhand book
shop by Bromley Station. Five minutes after I arrived at G. S.
G. Jerry got off 4.11 from Sidcup; came straight on from Miss
Ockenden's wedding. Back at Vrede by 7.10pm. Jerry wanted
to know if we always lived in such elegant style. Explained it
was the effect of room, polished table, etc., rather than high
living. Very hilarious meal. Soon dispersed to bed. Biddy and
Joan slept out.

Friday, August 11th: Biddy and Joan still sweetly sleeping
when I arose. Breakfast grew and laid itself by magic and
combined fooling. Everybody marvellously at home. Took

193

Jerry for a walk while others prepared appetizing dinner of roast lamb, roast potatoes, beans, plums, custard, etc. Saw a dead mole; renewed conversation with old man, this time on osier beds. Jerry reacting adequately to loveliness of Vrede, of country and of Bobs. Sally behaved like a catapult or Bif-Bat, hurling herself forward and backward and forward without ceasing. Returned to scrumptious dinner. Took Jerry by 5.10 'bus to G. S. G., where she soon caught 'bus to Orpington. Walked back in rain, under someone's blue umbrella, found in hall. Very refreshing walk; dove-grey sky with pale, lemon curdled clouds. Gentle grey donkey in one field, untidy rooks in another, and innumerable large plovers in another. Met a strange man descending stairs, on returning to Vrede, with accumulators for wireless. Said he called once a fortnight. Told him you were having it seen to, so he said he would call on Tuesday. Jane all but succeeded in Singing Hinnies, but they crumbled almost entirely. Ate the majority of crumbs. Very nice. Retired to Garden Room to work out accounts. Bobs cleared dining room and Jane taught Country dancing, mainly for Betty's benefit, but to everyone's delight. Strains of singing floated up the stairs. If only you could see everyone's glowing, joyous faces! Fire lighted, as thunderstorm cooled people too suddenly. Kitbag has sticking-plaster where a plate struck her on her forehead at camp. Otherwise everyone bursting with health. Biddy and Joan leaving at 8.00pm, walking to G. S. G. to get Green Line. Registered envelope containing car key. Plug in bathroom basin slipped into pipe. Sally consumed four bullseyes, first sweet things she has had. Made a speech at dinner, forbidding any more sweets for her. Am getting really domineering. 12.0 midnight. Woke to see light from policeman's bullseye flash across room. Jessie and Grace heard knock and Sally bark. Went to get Polly's moral support (she sleeping in dining room). One of the windows had been left open purposely, and he called to inform us. Polly woke up after all was finished.

<u>Saturday, August 12th</u>: Cooler. All went for leafy walk – much appreciated. Ate much chocolate and apples. Two cow's in Mr. Harris' field cut Betty and me off from rest of party. Manoeuvred them successfully. Basked in sun all afternoon. Ate Star Bars and talked. Sally consumed large portion of Betty's costume coat: complete square out of back. So awful that we laughed hysterically for some time. Tea in garden. Betty and Molly went on 7.10 'bus; I stayed in and read three detective stories, while others called on farm in

333333333333

Cacket's Lane and talked with very pleasant mother of Mr. Harris. Jane identified as school-mistress at once! Long but not silent session in mauve bedroom. Sang everything possible – laughed ourselves ill listening to discussion on dogs – Gypsy Race, Egg Whip and Mrs. Freeman between Scotsman and another man beneath window. Mrs. F. apparently a marvellous runner. Quite an amicable conclusion.

<u>Sunday, August 13th</u>: Small party of six. Grace up and out to Church by 8am; rest still lost in slumber. Bread and milk very low, but nobly encouraged appetites – which grow more and more outrageous – until, when breakfast was finished, there remained but one corner of bread for dinner, tea, supper and tomorrow's breakfast. But trusted in the Lord and packed as much food as we could find for picnic. Glorious sun-and-wind day. Picture of Mrs. Stanley chasing determined, ridiculously small calf round Recreation Field. Continued by footpath to Lett's Green, Knockholt, and Knockholt Pound. Here we stopped to think. Went to bakehouse and captured two loaves; knocked up General Stores and secured half a pound of butter. Faith rewarded! Then took a marvellous, beech-shaded lane (quite a mile) down the side of Chevening Estate. Not so marvellous when we found no opening in fence on either side and were growing more and more famished. Finally, just as Chevening village came into sight we found an open gate and an oat field. In spite of very prickly stubble we fell on our food: two loaves, etc., rapidly reduced to two crusts. It really was shocking to see unashamed appetites. Some wanted to lie and sleep it off, but Grace wanted to catch 4.10 'bus, so we went on, through lovely village, through Chevening Estate, higher and higher with lovely view behind and to our left. Saw lots of baby pheasants. Sally remained quite ignorant. Came out on secondary road, leading us into main road just by Knockholt Church, through the churchyard as we had come in the morning. Went back by morning footpaths after that and arrived home at 4.00pm. Grace caught 4.10pm bus. We ate a huge tea: made a second pot of tea. Revelled in raisin jam (about which many surmises before finally identifying). Went on eating and drinking, then withdrew to garden. On the way home Sally had emerged from a ditch with a black nose and four black tightly-fitting legs. More hysteria. She looked as if she had done it as a joke, and laughed with us. Washed her in the sink after tea, then played ball on the lawn to dry her. Molly walked out of Garden Room and joined us until 10.00pm. Ripping to see her again. Laughed, and laughed, and laughed! Made omelettes with

dripping for supper: much nicer than with butter. Sad discovery of mouldy cheese. Burial party in orchard after Cissie and Kathleen (Ward) had caught 7.10. Laid it to rest in rotten tree-trunk. Continued with trowel, and Sally on my belt, to Hostye Farm to buy bread. Secured, from very nice girl, half a quartern loaf. Faith rewarded further! Returned along Mace Lane. Our first really late night – to bed after 11.00pm.

<u>Monday, August 14th</u>: Three left – Jane, Kitbag (so-called because her real name was Kathleen Bagg) and Marjorie. Tried to remove all signs of invasion. Marvellous team-spirit shown in housework. Interval for lemonade at 11am. Noisy thunderstorm and heavy rain at 7.30am (which failed to wake Kitbag) left the valley full of mist, and intense and oppressive heat. Visited Mr. Howard about seven times, each occasion supposed to be the last – long conversation each time. Mowed lawn. Jane and Kitbag tried to catch 2.10, 3.10 and 4.10 (then tea with 'lashings' of raisin jam), 5.10, finally made themselves go on the 6.10 on which Clara returned.

9.05pm Sally and I saw headlights of car come round bend in the lane. You had returned safely.

Another very special holiday was the 'FAMILY CAMP' at Thakeham, near Warminghurst, Sussex. Mr. Harris, the farmer, was well known to some of the Bobs through Guide camps on one of his fields, and we were good friends. So he

Family camp, Thakeham, Sussex. Arrival.

Family camp at Thakeham.
Filling paliasses with straw.

Family camp at Thakeham.
Grace   Marjorie   Jack   Mummy & Daddy
              Kitbag   Biddy

kindly gave permission for the family Solkhon and friends to camp there during the Thirties. We arrived with all our luggage, tents, cooking utensils, food, bedding etc. in a lorry we had hired. Soon tents were pitched and we filled our palliasses with straw and made our beds. For my mother it was her first experience of camping, but she took to it like a duck to water, and managed some excellent meals on the open wood fire, or came with us 'wooding'. My father had been initiated into camp life as a young cavalry soldier in Africa during the Boer War, so he was very much at home. Most of the time we had sunny weather, and I have a vivid memory of him wearing one of our sun bonnets as he sat and prepared vegetables for lunch in the hot sunshine.

There were many comings and goings, and most Bobs managed at least a few days with us. On clear nights we slept under the stars, and sometimes were awakened by hedgehogs snuffling and snorting around our beds. In the morning there were puddles of dew on our groundsheets! We had various expeditions into the country, especially to Chanctonbury ring, when we toiled up the hill to the beautiful group of trees, devastated later by gales, and then dabbled in the dew pond.

One day it was very windy. Biddy had collected her breakfast of puffed rice and was on her way to her tent, but the wind blew the rice away, much to the delight of a group of chicken which followed close on her footsteps, happily gobbling up the unexpected feast. I have vivid memories, too, of our brother, Jack, wrestling with his tent which was about to take off! There were many magical moments: watching shooting stars, finding a warm hen's egg in the field, singing around the camp fire in the evening and just being together.

Sadly, the time came when we had to return home. We packed up tents and all the paraphernalia we had brought with us, ready to pile into the lorry when it came to collect us. All very fit and happy, but reluctant to leave such a heavenly place.

Although the Thirties saw the worst depression of this century, Biddy Clark remembers happy holidays and outings when she was young.

In the early Thirties my father had a motorbike and sidecar, and somehow he managed to pack the family in for outings or a holiday at Winchester. Our holidays in Winchester were memorable for the walks over the downs. We made posies of the wild flowers and collected bunches of harebells and scabious. We went to the water meadows and caught fish, and paddled in the river Itchen. We bought humbugs and lardy cakes at the Butter-cross, and a treat would be an ice cream from the Wall's 'Stop me and buy one' tricycle. The cheapest ice cream was the penny snofruit in its triangular tube -- the last bit always tasted of cardboard and the juice dribbled down your arm!

As I grew older, the Guide Camps were the excitement of the year. We learned so much and the Guiders were a great influence in our lives.

In 1938 I went on my first Youth Hostel holiday with my sister. There was a wonderful sense of freedom in those days, and the cost of staying at the Y. H. A. was well within our means.

Our Saturday outings were varied. We would take a bus and for 2d could get to the heart of London. Entrance to the Tate Gallery and Museums was free, and we had a milk shake at a milk bar. Or we could catch a train from Clapham Junction and spend a day at Box Hill, or walk over to Mickleham.

Before the Second World War the Diaghelev Ballet came to Covent Garden, and all our money was saved up for tickets in the 'gods'. It was a wonderful season, never to be forgotten.

My parents gave their children much freedom and, apart from saying 'Don't go near the gypsies', they trusted us to be sensible.

*A traditional Joey Lyons Tea Shop, with well-known
gilded shop sign. Service was conducted to a high standard and at a
reasonable cost in this first real attempt at mass catering in genial surroundings.*

The Hon. Mrs. Clay explains how holidays for Baden-Powell's family naturally included camping.

Five, six, or seven of us, with two or three dogs, travelled in Jamroll and our chauffeur Bear drove Jaus (the second Rolls Royce) and pulled Eccles the caravan, with anyone there wasn't room for in Jamroll. We toured the country in the summer holidays, with the camping gear, tents and all we needed. My parents took us camping every year during that period. The purpose of our tours was usually directed by a scout or guide rally or camp. At one time we went to Kent because my father was to be presented with the freedom of the city of Canterbury. That day was a very exciting one; going to the enormous Guildhall for the presentation. Afterwards there was a great march past and rally for about three thousand scouts and guides with bands from the surrounding area of Canterbury. It was a very fine sight.

Jam Roll with Jaus towing Eccles, the caravan.

We had various other stops on the way and in that area afterwards. My parents usually arranged with a friend beforehand that we would camp in one of his fields. So we set up all our tents and my father, who was the chief cook, would set to work to line out his kitchen. He chose the spot and lined it with a white rope to keep out invaders. He got the fire going and there was always a kettle on for those that needed it. He was the chief cook, ably helped by Bear, who was also an excellent cook. Bear had another great talent -- he was expert at catching rabbits and dealing with them accordingly. So we had gorgeous rabbit stews.

I wrote in my diary at one of these camps: 'We spent the whole day making the most marvellous gadgets. We made tables and plate racks and towel rails; every sort of gadget to make our lives more comfortable and hygienic.' My father was a great helper in this way and my mother was also extremely nobby, though she was hopeless at tying knots. She used to be good at doing up parcels but she wasn't good at making gadgets. We had to do that.

The Baden-Powell family.

We loved these camping holidays and the purpose of them from my father's point of view (as he emphasised for scout and guide camps) was the fact that you learned to live comfortably and hygienically, easily and safely in any circumstances. You learned to manage necessary things like eating, sleeping, and dry, warm shelter, so that we could make do with what we had, or make what we needed. In my later life many of these things learned from my father and mother have stood me in very good stead; I don't think I could possibly have done them if it hadn't been for these camping adventures during those three or four years of the early Thirties.

These camping trips were usually based on one particular date and place. So our holidays often included visits to various things such as factories, museums and suchlike. One year we went to the Morris factory for making cars at Oxford, and a Bournville factory near Birmingham for making chocolate. The people who showed you round said "You can eat as many chocolates as you like", but by the end of the trip you never wanted to see a chocolate again! We went to see beauty spots like the Cheddar caves and Wookey Hole in the Mendips; to museums and Whipsnade Zoo in the wilds of Bedfordshire; we toured Suffolk and Norfolk one year and saw the film-making studios at Elstree. We sailed on the Broads for the first time in our lives and went over the famous Framlingham Castle; and we visited Cambridge and were taken round some of the beautiful colleges and great museums there. So these camps always included something that would be useful and intriguing and educational to us, and very, very enjoyable.

There were various trips to London. We usually stayed at the Rubens Hotel in Buckingham Palace Road, almost next door to the Scouts office and Girl Guide headquarters, so it was very convenient and the people got to know us well. My parents took us to various places such as the Tower of London and to the Record Office, also to Kew Gardens and Madame Tussauds. We went to the White City to see greyhound racing for the first time -- we were so amused at these dogs racing round and round; they must have known that hare wasn't a real one! We went over the London Docks and we also went to Hampton Court, never dreaming that years later my mother would live there in one of the grace and favour apartments.

Dick Cunningham was fortunate in that he was able to enjoy holidays abroad as well as in Scotland and England with his parents and sisters during the Thirties.

The knowledge I picked up from travel set me apart from my fellow schoolboys, particularly in primary and the first few years of secondary school. The children at Hillhead High School were fee-paying and middle class, yet in 1931 I was the only boy in my class of forty or so who had been south of the border. Even more significantly, I had spent three summer holidays in France, two in Brittany and one in Normandy, with a week in Paris. I was taken on charabanc tours by my parents to many places of interest, mainly historical such as the Bayeux tapestry and the palace of Versailles.

After the collapse of the pound sterling in 1931, summer holidays had to be spent in Britain, usually for a month or six weeks at a time. My parents tried to take us to further spots on the coast -- the Fifeshire coast, Oban (twice), Blackwaterfoot (twice), Girvan (where my mother was born but a mistake, nevertheless) and, when we grew older, to England, Scarborough and Lyme Regis. We always, having no car, undertook many bus tours and so visited many different corners of the country.

During the Easter holidays we went for a fortnight to a place on the Clyde coast, Bute, Arran or Cowal, and once to Peebles.

We were joined for a week each year by a bachelor friend of my father from Camberley and, when we were old enough to cycle, he used to bring his cycle with him, together with a one inch to the mile contour map of the area. We took our cycles and, after much plotting over the map, we would essay forth most mornings if it wasn't too wet. This detailed reading of contour maps stood me in good stead when I joined the army and when, afterwards, I battled with historians.

I was one of the fifty-two Scouts of the First Glasgow Troop who visited Iceland for a fortnight in 1933. We stayed a few days in Reykjavik, then toured the volcanic terrain extensively viewing mountains, deep craters, large waterfalls, geysers, the site of the first European parliament, and bathed in pools heated by hot springs. On the Vestmann Islands we saw a large dried cod factory, and off them many spouting whales and glorious sunsets. Thus my knowledge grew.

In January 1936 Ian, the elder son of a professor, took me aside one Sunday School after a Boys' Club meeting and astonished me by asking if I would like to visit the Berlin Olympic Games. I immediately said "Yes", and was told the details. A director of Siemens in Berlin wanted his sixteen year old son to visit Britain but, as Hitler allowed Germans to take only the equivalent of 10 shillings out of the country, the only way he could achieve this was by exchange. So I would visit Germany for July and August that year and his elder son, Heinz, would come to us in 1937. My parents were, at first, taken aback, but when the financial implications had been worked out including some pocket money, and putting Heinz up for six weeks the following year it appeared within their means. Another point in my favour was that I had to write German in the Lower Leaving Certificate paper in two months' time, and two months speaking German in a family would obviously greatly enhance my prospects of passing Higher German (my third language) the following year. So my mother corresponded with Frau Dr. Müller in Charlottenburg, Berlin, and it was all arranged.

Apart from the return boat trip -- two nights each way tossing over the Dogger Bank and being too seasick to eat -- it was a fascinating holiday. Three weeks on Sylt, mornings on the beach, afternoons playing tennis or listening to Wimbledon, in Germany, on the radio, evenings learning to play skat, with a whole day cruise to Heligoland (then a customs free port) and a walk around the top of that island.

Back in Berlin, Heinz and I visited all the places of historical or architectural significance. In a museum I saw the most beautiful artifact I have ever seen, the head of Queen Nefertiti. Then, of course, the Olympics: opening and closing ceremonies, two weeks of athletics in between, some swimming, water polo, hockey, soccer and equestrianism. I watched the 50km walk go along the edge of a wood, two blocks from our house, and was moved on by the police for standing close to a German commentator's microphone and yelling "Come on Great Britain" as Harold Whitlock walked past on his way to victory. All in all the greatest sporting event I have ever attended. I also saw the airship *Hindenburg* flying low over the city in celebration.

We spent a day at Potsdam, travelling there and back along the newly built race track, the Avus, in a seven-seater Mercedes tourer and achieving, very comfortably, over 100mph, the first time I had been in a car at that speed. We saw over the buildings built or used by Frederick the Great, one of my heroes. It wasn't until some time later that I learned that he could not speak German, and that is why the Prussian court and important families used French for the next two centuries. I saw Hitler at close range on several occasions as he passed along a main road near our house, often standing up in his open car to acknowledge the crowd's plaudits. I had several interesting conversations with S.S. officers in charge of their troops lining the routes.

Being as interested in trains as in aircraft, cars and ships, I paid a small extra fee to travel on the speedy two-carriage diesel train, *The Flying Hamburger*, back to Hamburg on the way home. It also exceeded 100mph and had a large speedometer in the carriage to indicate its speed.

In 1937 we took my German friend, Heinz, for a summer holiday in Girvan. I cycled both ways and clocked the fastest speed I ever travelled on the hill down to Turnberry. This experience persuaded me to join a fellow University classics student, Bob Carson, two years my senior, in a cycling trip round the north of Scotland, towards the end of March 1939. For economy's sake, we decided to join the YMCA and use its youth hostels as our overnight stopping points. So off we set up Loch Lomond, across the Moor of Rannoch, through Glencoe and, cheating a bit, used the Ballachulish ferry instead of cycling round Loch Leven. We spent the night in the hostel at the foot of Ben Nevis but forbore to climb it.

The next day was the most strenuous of the tour, up the length of the Caledonian Canal from Fort William to Inverness. It was as much the undulating road as the journey's length which tired us so, and Bob was very envious of my three-speed gear. We lunched at Fort Augustus and, on reaching Inverness, agreed to cheat once again and seek the solace of a Bed and Breakfast. A taxi driver took us to his landlady, who treated us most splendidly, throwing in supper as well for our 2/6d each. Our next target was Granton-on-Spey, where we were to stay with a classmate of Bob's, whose father was a Bank Manager there. In passing through one of the towns en route we saw the poster 'Hitler invades Memel', and knew the next world war was even nearer.

1937. Dick Cunningham on his bicycle during his north of Scotland tour in March. Photo by Bob Carson.

We set off the next day, but it began to snow. As we had the steepest climb of the tour ahead of us over the Pass of Killiekrankie, we cheated again when we reached Aviemore, loaded ourselves and our bikes on to the next train, and went on to the next hostel at Fylie. From there to Comrie and on home to Glasgow.

C. R. Davison (Bob), who now lives at Wiveliscombe in Somerset, and his two brothers and sister were fortunate that the family had a holiday bungalow at Lancing, on the Sussex coast.

Our whole family spent three weeks in Lancing at Easter and six weeks for the summer holidays. These holidays began when I was twelve years old. My parents always invited one or two of my and my sister's school friends. I often remember the fun we all had playing on a lake on the shore side of the shingle beach which we called 'the backwater'.

My father bought us a two-seater canoe, which had air-tight compartments; this made it very safe because you could sit in it and fill it with water without sinking. Apart from the canoe, we made rafts out of driftwood and had battles in the middle of the lake. On one occasion, my friend Paul rammed my raft with his. Mine broke up and, in trying to save myself a drenching, I jumped onto his raft. It couldn't bear the added weight, and sank! We were very popular with my mother when we returned home wet through and covered in mud! We were all good swimmers. My uncle, an expert swimmer, came home on leave from Egypt and said, "I'm going to teach you all to swim, and there's 2/6d for the one who learns the fastest." I was swimming after ten minutes! Of course, during the six weeks summer holidays we spent much of our time in the sea.

Bob Davison (right) and Paul -- Lancing 'Backwater'.

Shrimping was another favourite pastime. At the age of twelve I thought up a grandiose scheme: we could catch fish, hire one of the beach huts, put a stove in it and sell fish and chips to the other holiday-makers on the beach! Needless to say, this never got beyond the 'pipe dreams' stage! Incidentally, I remember my grandfather at that time taking me into a fish and chip shop and asking for "Fish and chips for 4d"!

Bob Davison (far left) on Lancing beach.

We had a maid called Lily at our Buckinghamshire home and we always took her to Lancing with us. She looked after us all very well. My wife and I still keep in touch with Lily. Only last year she was saying how much she enjoyed Lancing, especially the last evening of every holiday when we all went to the Variety show at Worthing pier Pavilion. This final outing became quite a ritual. Among other delights, Lily said that even queuing up for the bathroom was fun!??

On one holiday I spent a long time learning to drive. My mother had her own little car, an Austin Seven. When I was thirteen she taught me to drive in our large garden; then she let me play with it on my own for hours on end. I used to speed up and down the drive, and spend ages reversing in and out of the garage. I remember taking one of the corners in the drive so fast that I went round on two wheels. This taught me a valuable lesson!

Four years later, having passed my driving test, I spent most of one holiday teaching my girl friend to drive. One day my father, knowing what time we would be coming home, hid among the trees by the gate. As we turned in, he sprang out in front of us and ran up the drive waving a red flag. My girl friend was so demoralised she put her foot down hard. There were no dual controls, and by the time I could stop the car we had ploughed through a flower bed and embedded ourselves in the potatoes!

Christmas holidays were spent at our home at Princes Risborough. We were within easy reach of London, and one of my father's ideas of a Christmas treat for us was dinner at the Strand

Palace Hotel. We always had the same meal: rump steak, chips and creamed spinach (interesting for a schoolboy!), followed by a sweet called 'Mont Blanc'. This was a mountain of ice cream and preserved chestnuts, topped with whipped cream and violets. It was supposed to be for four persons, but we shared it between us!

For Christmas day we always invited relations and friends, so about twenty of us sat down to Christmas dinner. At that time we had a charlady called Minnie. When we'd finished the first course, my father would suddenly shout, "Who cooked the turkey? Minnie Ha-Ha!" Then everyone would take up the cry, "Who cooked the turkey? Minnie Ha-Ha -- we want Minnie!" Eventually Minnie would throw up the hatch leading to the kitchen, put her head through it and acknowledge the ovation. Christmas party games included Charades, Postman's Knock, This is my friend's seat, Sardines and Bobbie Bingo.

My maternal grandparents always came to stay with us at Christmas, and my grandfather was usually late in coming down to breakfast. When he came into the dining room, my father put down his knife and fork and said, "Heads up, heads up: here's the Governor". This was followed by a respectful silence until grandfather started his breakfast. Incidentally, grandfather always walked the twelve miles round trip to his own home to feed his chickens while with us.

Nina Armour was living in Germany for much of the Thirties but is now at Chesham in Buckinghamshire. She has happy memories of Christmas in Germany but the holiday in France she had been looking forward to had an abrupt ending.

I was to spend one more Christmas in Wickersdorf. Looking back, Christmases in Germany made a deep and lasting impression on me. The German hymn:-

'Stille Nacht, Heilige Nacht' (Silent night, Holy night) sums it all up for me and portrays the feeling of wonder, whereas our English Christmases were 'merry' and 'bright' on a cold and frosty morning.

The preparations for Christmas Eve in Wickersdorf began with the ordering of a suitable tree from the village forester. It would be specially cut for us. It reached the ceiling and was wide and bushy. All the preparations were made by my mother, who decorated the tree, and the first I saw of it was after dark on Christmas Eve, when I was at last allowed into the room, where the grown-ups were already assembled. The door opened and there stood the tree in the glowing room, the gentle flickering of real candles giving the feeling of shimmering life. The glass balls and tinsel gleamed and a scent of pine was in the air. Under the branches stood exciting looking presents awaiting my attention. A great feeling of warmth and wonder accompanied this evening celebration, and outside there would be deep snow and frosty trees. Snow usually fell in November and was looked forward to by us all, as everyone enjoyed either sledging, skiing or skating, and building snowmen of course. The atmosphere was dryer than in England and we didn't seem to get so wet there. The snow went on until February or March, by which time we were glad to be rid of it and looked forward to the joys of spring and summer.

My memories of our holiday in Brittany are vague after so many years, but they were memorable in that I set off with my mother and 'aunt' Lydia from a normal carefree England, as far as I was concerned, and came back two weeks later, into war.

It was August 1939 and I was thirteen. I was home from boarding school (Christ's Hospital, Hertford) and looking forward to our holiday in France. I wrote in my School Girl Diary of that year, on Friday, 18th August: 'Packed and got ready for journey'.

Saturday, 19th August: Started off to France early. Had a lovely crossing but I felt sick part of the time. Got to St. Malo, went up a lock and arrived late at Le Val André. Of what we actually did there is only a brief record, e.g. 'Bathed, lovely and warm. Went for a walk to cliffs and climbed up and down. Had a lovely time. Mummy bought another bathing costume.' Diaries have little space for descriptive passages!

The bathing at Le Val André was good. I remember a vast sandy bay where the sea retreated to the horizon. If we wanted to bathe at low tide it meant a long walk there and back. Round the corner, on the north side of the bay, were rocks and cliffs reminiscent of Cornwall.

We were staying at a family pension. The rooms were clean, but not memorable. The food was interesting and I remember eating globe artichokes for the first time. Also, I was allowed to pick up chicken bones at table! My mother used to think up errands so that I would practise my French. This I disliked!

We visited various little French towns, going there by bus. One of these was famous for meringues. Every shop seemed to have them, in all colours of the rainbow. I don't remember whether they came up to expectations when we sampled them!

We spent a considerable amount of time in shoe shops, and I found this a bore. I could not appreciate then why grown ups took this business so seriously. I bought myself a pair of bedroom slippers for the equivalent of 1/3d. I remember them clearly -- they were green mules with white lambs wool trimming, and I wore them for a long time.

I think we had planned to stay in France for three weeks, but towards the end of the second week there was a sudden change in the little town. Deck chairs disappeared from the beach; lorries with soldiers arrived and were loading up beds from the hotels. My mother decided that it was time to buy a French newspaper. The entry in my diary for 1st September reads: 'The war broke out between Hitler and Poland.'

We packed quickly and managed somehow to reach St. Malo by car, in order to catch the last boat. Many people had had the same idea and I remember sitting for hours in some public lounge with bunks and leather seats. It was night and some people were sleeping. I ached all over with utter weariness. After what seemed an endless wait, my mother and Lydia came to take me to bed in a cabin lent by one of the ship's senior officers. Bunk beds were made up for us with snow white sheets; a fan was blowing pleasantly and I remember the utter bliss of this quiet resting place, where we spent the remainder of the night, all worries about the future temporarily forgotten in sleep.

Southampton Docks, in the grey morning light, looked unusual. Dotted around in the sky were strange elephantine heads, looking benignly down in a protective attitude. I liked our barrage balloons!

We returned to our London flat at Alexandra Road, St. John's Wood, London on 2nd September. War was declared next morning and I went back to school in Hertford, which had been hastily opened to receive any who needed shelter. My mother had made arrangements to work for the Ministry of Information in the event of war. She was expecting to be moved out of London, but this did not happen. She spent all the war years in London, living in the same flat until it was burnt down in 1940.

Trains, steamers, buses and coaches were all used by Ian MacLachlan's family for transport.

Our village was served by a branch railway line, connecting us with Oban to the north and Stirling to the south (L.M.S.). I remember we had Whist Drive excursions. Once we joined the main line the Whist Drive began as we travelled to Stirling. The prizes were always free rail tickets. These excursions were very popular. Once there was an excursion to Wembley: 10 shillings return.

There was a local bus service, but to reach Fort William we had to cross by the ferry at Ballachulish Narrows. This boat took a limited number of cars; otherwise one had to travel the long way round Loch Leven and up the other side. A special steamer would arrive for the Fort William Highland Games and this was very popular.

Our holidays were spent with our aunt and uncle in Edinburgh. They had a tiny tenement flat but always found room for us. Other outings were by coach as we followed the shinty team. Shinty is a form of hockey, played by men. The shinty stick, or caman, is three-sided and all sides are used to hit the ball, unlike hockey. The stick can also be raised above the head. Shinty is still played weekly in the Highlands and Glasgow. Oban Highland Games was always a good outing, too.

Joan MacLachlan has happy memories of holidays in the Thirties.

We never had a car but travelled by bicycles, trams, trains and later buses. Holidays after our father's death were always spent with two aunts, one lived in Brigg, the other near Newark. Our days were idyllic in the country. My brother Raymond and I still reminisce about those lazy, hazy days of summer, and we also discuss them with our cousins.

We picked primroses, made them into bunches, and got 4d a bunch for them in Newark market. In the summer we picked blackberries and they went to the market along with any mushrooms we found.

Our aunt kept bees and we had lashings of honey and new bread -- wonderful! But I think our mother must have missed us: we were too young and selfish to notice, I suppose.

My brother Bernard just spent his holidays with an uncle who was a gamekeeper to Lord Swinton, near Leeds. My mother would go to her sister's at Brigg.

Eddie Boyle celebrated holidays in various ways in Scotland.

Christmas Day, Scotland, 1930, 6.30am. The first trains and buses have left with miners, steelworkers, shipbuilders and factory workers. Two hours later, shops and offices are opening and for the natives it is business as usual -- well, not for all the natives, for the children are on holiday. Father Christmas may have visited some, but for most, father is at work (if not unemployed) and won't be home until after dark.

Hogmanay, 31st December, at Glasgow Cross: thousands of revellers are congregating to welcome the New Year with the fond hope that 1931 will see a revival of their fortunes. All over the land, men, women and children are first footing, carrying black bun and a lump of coal, traditional symbols of food and warmth.

1st January 1931: Scotland is on holiday, well, not all of Scotland, for bus and train drivers are transporting swarms of football

211

fans to the local Derbies - Rangers v Celtic in Glasgow, where up to 120,000 spectators are expected; Hearts v Hibernian in Edinburgh, and Dundee v Dundee United.

July and August are still the holiday months, especially the last fortnight in July; the Glasgow Fair and the popular resorts were Ayr, Saltcoats, Large, Dunoon and Rothsay on the Firth of Clyde. We children, in these salubrious watering holes, indulged in 'tolet' spotting from early April. 'Tolets' were neither ornithological nor aquatic rarities but notices in the window of every second house proclaiming rooms to let for the summer. 'Room and kitchen to let'; 'Two rooms and kitchen to let'. Where the natives ate and slept we never wondered. What we did wonder was why any sane holidaymaker would come to Saltcoats, which was hardly blessed with balmy summers. They were so often forced into promenade shelters to stare gloomily at the sullen sea. We smiled indulgently at visiting children making pies and castles and entering into the annual sand building competition; we, who never set foot on the sands and preferred to spend our time at the Saltpans Bathing Station, a tidal pool whose temperature averaged 54 degrees F. throughout the season.

Ivy Green describes a special holiday she enjoyed in 1931.

When I was ten years old, it was decided that we could afford two weeks' holiday in Margate, staying with friends of my aunt to save money. I and my parents arrived, amongst coach loads of jolly, singing 'Beanfeasters', and when I found that our apartments were opposite the entrance to Dreamland, expectations mounted. I and some friends, who were staying locally also, couldn't wait to get inside. We whirled, white-knuckled, round the Scenic Railway, drifted peacefully in waterborne tubs through dark caverns adorned with fairy lights and elfin tableaux, rode precariously round the miniature railway and shrieked through the Haunted House. In the Arcade we caught flying ping-pong balls in nets, flung balls into grinning, gaping mouths, held our breath at Housey-housey, and spurred on large wheels to stop at our film-star name. There were lovely prizes: furry toys, tea sets, fancy dishes, bird-shaped egg cups, etc. I have some still!

On 'Competition Evening', we cheered the brave contestants trying to eat jelly with knitting needles and groaned when the gooey mess fell on to the table. We watched gleefully the bold people (usually males) who tried to catch eggs dropped from the Arcade roof without breaking them -- in what a state they ended up! But we applauded their courage.

During the day we chased along the promenade seeking Lobby Lud and the *News Chronicle* prize (£2), built moated sand castles and sand boats (designed by my seaman father), paddled, swam and relaxed on the jetty to the strains of Jessie Weldon's Ladies' Band, while we enjoyed the delight of plump, golden newspaper-wrapped chips. We spent an afternoon with never to be forgotten Uncle Mac, sitting on Broadstairs beach in the sun, which always seemed to shine.

Then there was the open coach trip to Potter & Moore's lavender fields at Wingham, and echo of *Nellie Dean* and other old songs drifted across the fields as we returned with the scent of lavender in our nostrils, carefree and content.

1931 -- few cars, no televisions, videos or computers. Nevertheless, that two week holiday by the sea gave me pleasure and happiness which I will always remember.

Mrs. Betty Forsyth was one of the minority who were able to go on holiday each year during the Thirties.

We were fortunate to have relatives in the Lake District, so spent many happy holidays there. However, most of my friends went to rented self-catering cottages within twenty or thirty miles of home, usually in the country or at the seaside. These were mostly professional people. I know now that very many people had no holidays at all and had never been outside their own city.

One annual outing I remember especially was a Sunday School trip by train to a local reservoir and country park. The journey took all of fifteen minutes, but it was a great adventure and eagerly anticipated all year.

Occasionally as a family we would have a day out, often by train sometimes by car, to some pleasant town perhaps twenty miles away. There we would enjoy the rare treat of a meal out -- usually a real Scottish high tea.

Alison Hudson describes holidays when she was living in Galashiels.

On holiday we enjoyed days out to Edinburgh, where we visited the castle, the zoo and museum, and had lunch at Patrick Thomson's, a well known large store. In summer we enjoyed picnics by the river Tweed, long country walks after Sunday School and visits to the park, where the band would be playing.

We went to the Baptist Church and Sunday School, where we had a happy time. There was a summer picnic, Christmas party, soirées where there was a prize giving for regular attendance and written exams about the Bible. I usually had parts in little plays and sketches. I was very shy but did enjoy taking part.

Mrs. Lilian Olsen has vivid memories of the outings she enjoyed during the Thirties.

Our holidays were very few and far between, but our outings were a planned exodus every Sunday at 10am sharp. We piled the old bone-shakers of prams not only with kids but also with pots and pans, kettle, teapot, a bit of coal, potatoes, mince and onions. A stairful of people would head down to Dalry station, a small sub-railway station. We lugged the prams up about forty steps, some of us pulling and some of us pushing, on to the platform to await the old Puffin Billy steam train that would take us to Davidson Mains, about a twenty-five minute journey.

First we had to unload the kids, then the prams were all loaded into the guards van. Kids travelled free, adults one and a half pence. On reaching Davidson Main, all passengers alighted: the train terminated there. Somehow we all joined up snake-like to begin the mile and a half trek down a pothole ridden farm track. It was hard going trying to keep the prams out of the pot holes. We were high up and the track kept leading down: the view was wonderful on a sunny day -- Cramond Island and all her sister islands shone like jewels on the Forth; also the rail Forth Bridge glittered.

Cramond itself is on the sea (Firth of Forth). There was plenty of sand but a lot of boulders, from which we harvested bukkies (whelks) and mussels. Once a fire was going we didn't mind the smoke from damp driftwood getting in our eyes. We filled our pots with water from a public tap and cooked our mince and 'tattie' dinner. For tea we cooked the mussels. We all carried our plain pin in our lapel for scooping out the bukkies.

There was plenty of entertainment, home made: sing songs, spoons, accordions, penny whistles; many a good gig we had while the mothers gossiped or knitted socks. We teenagers would weigh up the talent, or boldly chat them up. Dads played pitch and toss, and if we were lucky enough to be chosen as a look out we earned ourselves a penny. The police had a habit of sneaking up and arresting the men, as gambling out of doors was frowned upon.

If the tide was out, we walked to Cramond Island, but woe betide you if you misjudged the tide coming in; it meant you either had to spend hours on the island until the tide went out again, or a boat would rescue you. There was a lot of wild vegetation and flowers. Our favourite was the rambling rose, and being 'townies' we loved to take some back, more often than not our thumbs were bandaged up with a not-too-clean piece of rag, as though the roses made us pay the price of a prick.

Scruffy, happy and dirty, sand mixing with our runny noses,

we retraced our steps back up the farm road much slower than when we came down it, with many stops to empty the never ending sand still clinging inside our shoes. Not much puff left, it took two of us to push the pram up the hill, what with the added weight of a pan full of salt water and mussels and an extra sleeping kid. We were weary, sore but happy, and shouted cheerful "Cheerios. See you next Sunday" as we parted to go our own ways."

The farm road has now been widened and tarmacked, buses use it to take tourists to Cramond, which now sports a promenade. The view is still there, but unfortunately the wild vegetation has disappeared and there is now a notice on the foreshore saying, *'No Camping Or Fires'*. But that's progress!

7. RECREATION

The shorter working week in the Thirties, with a half-day on Saturday, meant there was more time for people to pursue leisure activities, and although many were out of work, those fortunate enough to have employment enjoyed a higher standard of living than in the Twenties. This provided some money to spend on leisure activities. Commercialism soon made the most of the opportunities.

The cinemas, now showing 'talkies' in colour, continued to attract large audiences. In 1933 Odeon Cinemas was formed by Oscar Deutsch, a former Birmingham scrap metal merchant. They were very luxurious compared to earlier 'picture palaces', with comfortable seats, large screens and canned music instead of an organist, pianist or small orchestra. Charlie Chaplin was still popular, although he preferred silent roles. *City Lights* was shown in 1931 and *Modern Times* in 1936. Among other popular films were *Gay Divorcée* and *Top Hat* with Ginger Rogers and Fred Astaire; *Showboat;* Walt Disney's *Snow White and the Seven Dwarfs* which had taken three years and two million drawings to complete; and *Gone with the Wind*. *The Private Life of Henry VIII* produced by Alexander Korda in 1933, with Charles Laughton, was one of

A scene from 'Plant in the Sun', with Paul Robeson and, on the right, Alfie Bass.

Vivien Leigh

the most profitable of British films. Successful plays were usually filmed and shown in cinemas. Actors preferred the latter as it was better paid and meant less memorising. The Unity Theatre produced plays like *'Waiting for Lefty'* and *'Plant in the Sun'*, which had Communist sympathies. The Diaghelev Ballet returned to London after the war, and in 1934 Colonel de Basil introduced the *Ballet Russe de Monte Carlo*. People were prepared to queue for a long time outside Covent Garden and theatres to get cheap seats.

By 1939 there were only 50,000 television sets, as they were still expensive and reception was uncertain, but improvements were to lead to a gradual decrease in cinema attendances. The Derby, the Cup Final and the University Boat Race were all popular when shown on T.V. Again there was the comfort of watching at home, and it was possible to see the whole event instead of just the beginning and end, as with the boat race.

Winston Churchill at the premier of Charlie Chaplain's 'City Lights' in London's Dominion Theatre, 1931.

217

The quality of radio broadcasts had much improved, so that music enthusiasts could listen at home to concerts from the Queens Hall if they wished. It was also cheaper! The B.B.C. took over the Promenade Concerts and as well as helping a Mozart and Haydn revival introduced British composers like Sir Arnold Bax, Frederick Delius, Constant Lambert and William Walton. When the Royal Command Variety performance was broadcast it emptied music halls, theatres and cinemas all over the country, and the B.B.C. agreed to pay a large sum to charity. Later the B.B.C. broadcast half hour fortnightly excerpts from shows as trailers, and that helped to reverse the trend. New large public houses to serve motorists were built on the suburban fringes of London and other cities, offering much more comfortable surroundings, with dining rooms and lounge bars, but even so much less money was being spent on drink than in the early years of the century, and it was rare to see drunken men outside public houses. Women were also making use of the facilities, though rarely unaccompanied by a male. The large increase in the use of cars and other means of transport also meant that roadside pubs and restaurants could look forward to increased custom.

Youth Hostels were strictly reserved for those who arrived on foot or bicycle, but they provided very cheap overnight accommodation, with the choice of a cooked breakfast and evening meal, or facilities for cooking their own food. It opened up a whole new way of life for many youngsters, who could not afford hotels, and were to be seen trudging the countryside with their rucksacks on their backs or packed on the back of bicycles. Some also took their own tents and sleeping bags.

It was during the Thirties that Keep Fit as well as Health and Beauty became popular. Dances were well patronised, particularly in Scotland, and many large dance halls were built in the larger towns. In 1937 'The Lambeth Walk' was broadcast and the swaggering step could be seen everywhere. 'Knees up Mother Brown', and 'Under the spreading Chestnut Tree' were other favourites. Then 1939 brought jitterbugging to fast swing music from the U.S.A., but this was not popular with the upper classes. All-in wrestling was fashionable for a short while, but was generally considered vulgar and brutal. Boxing was mostly restricted to the industrial areas, although some heavy weight boxers became popular.

Football was still enjoyed by many, but the growth of football pools was the great social phenomenon of the Thirties; Littlewoods, Vernons, Shermans at Cardiff and others. By

1936 between five and seven million people were sending in weekly forecasts and about £800,000 was subscribed each week. The possibility of winning a fortune gave excitement to those whose lives lacked glamour and who had little hope of making a fortune in any other way.

Totalizators introduced on most race courses encouraged small bets on horse racing, and there was also betting on greyhound racing. New large ice rinks were opened at Richmond, Golders Green and Hammersmith, and people learned to waltz and tango on ice; they were also able to watch exhibition dancing from the galleries. In 1933 during the England v Australia battle for the Ashes, body-line bowling reared its ugly head for the first time. The ball was pitched short on the leg side so that it rose towards the batsman's body. This led to much ill feeling and Australia lost the Ashes. However, although he was Australian, Don Bradman became very popular when he scored 334 runs in a match and he was many a small boy's hero.

For many people there were opportunities for the entertainment of their choice and at prices they could afford.

Jim Finlayson describes an unusual form of entertainment.

There was much gloom during the depression of the Thirties, but also the amazing resilience of the man in the street. One of the brave efforts was the Empire Exhibition in Bellhouston Park, Glasgow, just a few years before the outbreak of the Second World War.

One serious exhibit in the Palace of Engineering was a massive propeller shaft for a ship. A hole was bored through the entire length of the shaft. Far from being overwhelmed by this marvel, my friend and I had joy in waiting for a bevy of girls to pass the far end of the shaft, then whistling softly through the hole. The fun was to see the puzzled expression on the young ladies' faces at this mysterious whistle, then wait for their arrival at our end of the shaft. We then had a ready made excuse to speak to them. I often wondered whether the minxes were well aware of our ploy and went along with the deception. However, it was one example of the endless ability of the human spirit to overcome the dreary days.

Dr. William Graham Jardine, BSc, MSc, PhD, ScD, FGS, has had a very distinguished career, including that of lecturer in the Department of Geology at Glasgow University from 1956-66 and Senior Lecturer 1966-1978, but he still remembers with pleasure the fun he had during his childhood.

The exhibition that was Child's Play was first published in 'Scottish Local History' (July 1988); extracts are included below:

The Empire Exhibition held from May to September 1938, in Bellhouston Park, Glasgow, was anathema to my father. It had spoiled his Park: he was its Superintendent! However, my brother, aged thirteen, and I, aged eleven, living in the 'Parkie's' house on Paisley Road West just opposite to White City dog-racing track, saw the Exhibition through quite different eyes.

I was luckier than John. I hadn't yet sat the 'Quallie' exam, so I went twice a day to Craigton School, about three quarters of a mile from home, rather than to the more distant Bellhouston academy -- not yet elevated to the status of Senior Secondary School. There was no time to visit the Exhibition on the way to school in the morning, and there was no point in coming home through it at mid-day because that would mean having to pay for entry. Why pay, or why even have a season ticket, when you lived where we lived? There was no public entrance opposite the White City, but there was what nowadays would be called a 'trades entrance'. I was well known to the friendly man in dark green uniform, who guarded the big wooden gates that separated the park house from the Exhibition. So a quick trip by this route on the way to afternoon school was common once or twice per week.

The direct route to school passed the Crêche first. To us this was a mysterious, unknown place, in fact one of the very few pavilions in the whole Exhibition that we never penetrated in the summer of 1938. Its main attraction, in any case, was an outdoor maze, constructed of strong wire mesh mounted on tubular metal, and reaching a height of about six feet. After the Exhibition closed in September 1938, and for a few months to come, it was an ideal site for chases. The secret lay-out was quickly mastered, but it was not the knowledge of which way to go that was the key to success when being pursued or in pursuit. It was the mastery of the art of scrambling up the wire mesh, leaning over the top and doing a frontal 'fosbury flop' that was useful and at the same time exciting.

Before the Exhibition opened there was one building -- the tearoom owned by Ross's Dairies -- that had not only paid its way but had already made a profit by providing daily meals for the hundreds of workmen employed in construction throughout the Exhibition site. In contrast, after the opening, there was at least one stand in the Palace of Industry (West) that probably was suffering a loss, by inadvertently providing food for hungry children on a rather more irregular basis! Nowadays free samples and special offers are commonplace, but in those days free samples in the form of inch square pieces of meat loaf and the like were a rarity. I suppose they were intended for would-be customers, but I can assure you than some of the recipients of the stand holder's generosity had neither the intention nor the wherewithal to be customers. As but one illustration of what was a regular occurrence, there was a memorable occasion when all but one of the sample morsels had been taken by those who might reasonably claim to be prospective buyers. Suddenly a small hand was thrust through the row of 'wifies' who apparently were unable to decide who should have the treasured prize. To this day, I am uncertain whether it was my brother or I who was greeted with the cry, "Y wee divvil!", but I know it was a tasty bite.

A pavilion exhibiting products of the steel industry doesn't sound a particularly interesting place to children, one of whom was not yet a teenager and the other only just that. It wasn't; yet the Beardmore's-Colville's pavilion was haunted by us more than any other building on the Exhibition site. The explanation lies in the plan of the building. It was shaped like a flattened inverted Y. The arms of the Y contained what we considered boring exhibits, but the leg of the Y provided an irresistible attraction in the form of a cinema where free films could be seen. The fun of seeing these films increased as the months went on, but this was not because the programme improved: in fact, I don't think it ever changed. The difference was that at first there was no restriction on the admission of children, but after a while the management decided that all children must be accompanied by an adult. We felt the restriction really should have been phrased the other way round! -- but it presented a new and exciting challenge. For us, the game now became that of attaching yourself to an adult, couple, but at the same time so as not to give the couple the embarrassment of being thought to own you!

The films were all commercials in black and white, some of them straight and others humorous. In one, concerned with the by-products of coal, a confident gentleman declared at the beginning of the film that he could manage quite nicely without need for such substances and, if he couldn't, he would eat his hat. In the course of the film, all the everyday items he encountered vanished just as he was about to use them. Defeated and frustrated, he was about to eat his hat, but it vanished also!

'Two Frightened Ladies' was the title of my favourite film. In it two ladies were viewing the interior of a house that had been unoccupied for some time and which they were considering buying. The main scenes were enacted in the kitchen and bathroom. The ancient bath was stained and rusty, and the taps dripped incurably -- to the accompaniment of creepy music. The ladies were depressed and frightened out of their wits until, opportunely, there appeared a small figure in dazzling white, with a prototype 'Glasgow smiles' face, short legs and pointed feet. The scene moved to the kitchen as he danced up and down a music score and sang words (and a tune) that are indelibly recorded in my memory:

> 'Meet Mister Therm for really hot, hot water;
> I think you really oughter
> Meet Mister Therm.
> Mister Therm is burning to se-erve you.
> If your kitchen worries, and un-ne-erves you.
> Meet Mister Therm for really hot, hot water.
> I think you really oughter meet Mister Therm.'

Beardmore's Cinema was not far from the Amusement Park, another favourite haunt of entertainment-seeking youngsters. The scenic railway, dodgems, thrill ride (under which you could occasionally find coins dropped from the pockets of unsuspecting clients who had been upended in the course of their enjoyment) and other expensive delights were beyond our normal financial resources. Lots of amusement, however, could be had by watching the laughing sailor outside the Crazy House until *your* sides were splitting too, or by listening to the persuasive patter of a manager who wished to lure you into his den of entertainment, be it *'Savage West Africa'* or *'The Giraffe-Necked Women'*. Our favourites were *'The Cingalese Theatre'* and the booth of *'The Great Carmo'*.

The Great Carmo was a magnificent man -- well, at any rate, until you saw him without his high-heeled boots and in civvies, walking arm in arm with his wife through the park 'after the show' -- in a white uniform and bejewelled turban like headdress. His chief assistant, Miss Ria Rita (who bore a striking resemblance to his wife, we thought) was a charming figure of not over concealed femininity. She was his stooge on the stage inside the booth, except for the act where the manager, disguised as a member of the audience, allowed himself to have his pocket watch appropriated and replaced by a lemon hooked on to his back. (I know how this trick was done because on one occasion when the manager was absent I, as the youngest and therefore presumably the most naive member of the audience, was invited to be the stooge instead.) There was also a junior assistant, the delightful Mademoiselle Nina who, we were assured, had come directly from France and therefore understood not a word of English. The last part of this statement probably was quite true; the only time I ever heard her speak was in a tramcar, when she said in a good Glasgow accent "A penny-haul please". Mind you, she did look as if she was younger than fourteen!

Performances in the Cingalese Theatre were hazier in my memory. The patter of its managers was really my brother's favourite rather than mine, but an outstanding item on the programme was undoubtedly the one featuring the beheading (and re-heading) of a dusky damsel. As the story outside the theatre went -- and who could resist or forget such an exciting item? -- "When the head is removed from the body it will talk to you, amuse you and entertain you". It did! The mystery of the East was embodied in the spell that this particular show and its performers cast upon us. One of the stars was the Gully-Gully man, a kind of Sri-Lankan equivalent of the African witch doctor. It was he and his compatriots who inspired us, together with a twelve year old pal, to found a secret society with a name that we felt had a flavour of the Orient. (Although I remember the name perfectly well, I can't possibly say what it was, of course, because it's hush hush!).

Mention of this society brings memories of what was perhaps the smallest individual pavilion in the whole Exhibition. It stood near the largest building, the Palace of Engineering, and was owned by and was an advertisement for what is now one of the largest multinational petroleum companies - ESSO. The sides of the square building were about twenty feet or less in length. Downstairs the building contained the normal features of an exhibition stand. Upstairs padded seating lined all four walls, which were of glass above the backs of the seating. I don't suppose we visited this building many times in the course of the summer of 1938. Boys of our age were only too conspicuous entering such a small building, and we could not linger upstairs either, although at that time Vandals were a race of the past and vandalism was a crime of the future. When we did go upstairs we just sat there and did nothing other than blissfully possess the place. As far as we were concerned, this was the headquarters of our secret society.

The Empire Exhibition of 1938 was certainly not anathema to us. It was much more like nirvana!

The August Bank Holiday Fair was the highlight of the year for Kathleen Stirzaker and her family.

Every year we had the August Bank Holiday Fair. It was the <u>first</u> Monday in the month then. All the people from miles around came to join in the fun. They had a greasy pole, the men tried to climb to get the leg of pork tied to the top. There were races for children in the morning, and in the afternoon for grown-ups; egg and spoon races, sack races, three-legged races for all ages, with a lot of cheering and shouting going on. There was also a men's walking race that was usually won by a very short man. They had coconut shies and roll the penny booths. There was a band playing most of the day and they had a large marquee where they sold teas of strawberries and cream.

Games of the Thirties are still played today; hop scotch, skipping, rounders, football and cricket, but we also had the Yo-Yo. Some children (and adults) were very clever at it, but it didn't catch on for long. Indoor games were ludo, snakes and ladders, chess and draughts and quoits -- rings you threw on a board like a dart board, but with hooks. There were also jigsaws and playing cards.

Ruth Meyer and her family provided their own entertainment with others in the area.

At Easter we rolled our gaily coloured eggs down any convenient slope, sometimes down the back road and once we went to the old cemetery at Kilmadock and climbed on to the top of the ruined vault and rolled them down the moss-covered roof. Dad always painted the eggs and drew funny faces on them.

Hallowe'en was a night we children all looked forward to. A day or two beforehand, Dad would hollow out a big turnip or 'neep', as they were called, cut slits for eyes, nose and mouth, put a candle inside, light it and make a string handle. Then, with our masks bought at Jeanie Brock's shop, we were all set for our night's guising. We, with the Wilsons, MacIntoshes and others, traipsed all over the estate and down to Kilmadock, a cluster of houses by the river Teith knocking on folks' doors. They'd ask us in and we'd sing a ditty, such as 'See the spider on the wall, dear friends, that's all'; we were rewarded with nuts and perhaps an orange and, if we were very lucky, a penny. Then on to the next house for a repeat performance. Usually there was a brilliant moon and with out lanterns it was great fun. Sometimes the boys took their bikes and the girls rode on the carriers.

At home we ducked for apples, kneeling over the back of a chair with a fork handle in our mouths, trying to spear the lovely red apples bobbing about in water in a dish on the floor.

Guy Fawkes was the next night we looked forward to. We had fireworks and, best of all, we loved to run round the two houses with Davie from next door, in the dark with sparklers in our hands, bumping into each other in our excitement. We'd go in opposite directions and meet in the middle.

Christmas followed on Guy Fawkes as perhaps the biggest event in our calendar. We usually had a party and Mam invited all of our friends. We had crackers but no tree. We played such games as Pokey, putting the tail on the donkey, and musical chairs without music! Mother did the singing.

At New Year we always went to stay with our friends, the McInnes', in Edinburgh, catching the bus outside the lodge gates. They lived in a flat right at the top of a tenement next to the railway, near the Hay Market. Isa, the daughter, was unmarried and looked after her father. We slept three in a bed, Isa, Doris and I, in a small room called the Priest's room, but it was really only a large cupboard. The grown-ups saw the New Year in, sitting quietly listening to the bells pealing out all over Edinburgh. We children heard them, too, lying in bed waiting for Isa to come so that we could talk with her.

On New Year's day we all went to the large Conference meeting held either in the Wolston Hall or New Gallery Room. About a hundred and fifty people attended them, and Dad and Mam had the opportunity to meet a lot of their old friends from other meetings. Doris and I sat up in the balcony, with Willie and Davie Taylor, as we got older. In the interval we sat at long trestle tables while waitresses served us tea, sandwiches and cakes. After tea Dad took us to the nearby museum before going back for the night meeting.

Jessie Lintern and her young brother appreciated the generous hospitality of neighbouring farmers in Scotland.

My brother and I greatly enjoyed the friendliness of the members of my father's church in Colmonell. We were frequently invited to farms for supper, spending the evening playing board and card games such as Rummy and Newmarket, singing old familiar Scottish songs around the piano, or joining the men folk at carpet bowls in the barn. Hospitality was generous and plates were piled high with farm fare. On our first visit to one farm, my shy eleven year old brother was so overcome by the quantity heaped on his plate that he let it slip, blushing scarlet as a large bun rolled across the table and disappeared in the direction of the collie dog slumbering on the hearth rug. He was saved from confusion by the son of the house, who called across the table, "Never mind, Jimmy. It's a' richt. Ah've got ma foot on it". He became my brother's friend for life, and the pair squabbled affably at the Kirk door each Sunday over the relative merits of Ayr United and the Dumfries team -- Queen of the South!

As most of the farmers by then had a car, we were always given a run home rather than having to walk several miles in the dark. Almost every Saturday and frequently during school holidays I visited one particular farm, collecting eggs, carrying teas out to the haymakers and harvesters, helping to wind a hayrick on to the flat bed of the rick-lifters, and treading down the stooks of oats as they were tossed up on to the car. I would urge the patient Clydesdale on along the field and back to the stack yard, where the stooks were transferred to complete the building of a stack, which eventually received the attention of the threshing machine on its annual visit. On a winter evening I was often taken by these friends to see a film in the Girvan cinema -- a treat indeed!

Whist drives, followed by a dance, were popular ways of fund raising in those days. The village hall fortunately was a sturdy stone building, housing a reading room, a library and billiard table, but there was also ample scope for concerts, travelling film shows and dances. Then the hall would reverberate to the sounds of violin, dulcimer, accordion and drums, and the shrieks which go with Scottish dancing! Concerts and plays were presented by members of the 'Rural' i.e. the Scottish Women's Rural Institute, or by concert parties from neighbouring parishes, with a dance to follow.

The village had a grass tennis court, sloping towards one end with quite a dip in the corner. To my cousins and me, spick and span in our 'whites', it could well have been Wimbledon! Later, a bowling green was constructed just outside the village, a great asset to the community. The highlight of the winter would undoubtedly be when, after a succession of days of severe frost, the men folk could prepare their curling rink in the flooded flat fields by the river. They used besoms (twig brooms) to sweep the surface of the ice and their shouts of triumph and "Soop 'em up" (Sweep them up i.e. the curling stones) came echoing across the valley. Boredom was not part of our vocabulary in the Thirties!

Audrey Butler describes some of the entertainments and outings she enjoyed in Yorkshire during the Thirties.

Around the end of November we began thinking of Christmas. As well as tinsel, decorating the tree and writing notes to Santa Claus, we invariably had the first snows and frosts. Sometimes it was so bitterly cold we had fires in the bedrooms. We loved the snow and built big snow men and went sledging on the hilly slopes. When indoors we had coloured paper and cut out and glued pieces to make paper chains, with which the rooms were festooned.

After Christmas came first footing -- the letting of the New Year in, when a dark man would knock at the door and come in around midnight, thus letting the New Year in. It had to be a dark 'letter-in', so my father was out of it, as he was fair. But one

Christmas we just had not got anyone dark to let in the New Year, so my mother blacked my father's face and he wore black gloves: the New Year was officially let in and all was well.

We had two very big attics in the house, and my father rigged up a swing for the children. Some new people had come to live in the village, a little boy much younger than me, but he had two sisters about my age; we became great friends and had some happy times in the attics. One Christmas I had a pair of roller skates and we took turns playing on them. Another Christmas I had a little scooter.

With the coming of Spring and the lighter evenings we played outside after tea, until almost dark. We played hopscotch and skipping. I also had a long drawer and we used to sit in it and paddle, pretending it was a canoe. We wore a band round our heads with a feather sticking up at the back, pretending we were Red Indians.

At that time few people owned cars, but my father had friends who had one, and sometimes we went out with them for a run. Occasionally we went in a charabanc (which we pronounced Sharra-Bang). I remember vividly one such outing. We went 'over the tops' towards Lancashire and stopped at a then famous pub called Nont Sarahs. The men went into the pub for a pint, bringing out to their wives a glass of port or sherry, and fizzy pop for the children. They also brought us packets of potato crisps, with little screws of navy blue paper inside containing salt: this was the first time I had ever seen potato crisps.

Suddenly the sky clouded over and huge drops of rain began to fall. As it was sunny when we set off the canvas top of the 'charra' had been drawn back. The men came rushing out and drew the canvas top closed, so we munched our crisps in the dry.

Brai Harper spent much of his spare time enjoying the attractions that living by the sea provided.

Living on the very edge of the sea at Bexhill, we spent much of our time in it. Our 'beach season' began at Easter and went on to October. We had two canoes, a single and a double, and we won cups in the annual regatta. Our big canoe was called Stella Maris, whereas others were called Buggsy or Bimbo, which shows how ignorant they were. Quite often the whole family went down to the beach for the day, with a picnic lunch, and we swam and canoed and sunbathed until teatime. There were no browner boys than us in the whole of Bexhill.

Apart from cycling eight miles per day to and from school, in the holidays we explored country lanes and nearby villages and, according to season, collected conkers or blackberries. In those days there was little traffic: only the better-off folk had cars.

In the winter, it was roller skating and we had two miles of promenade to swoop about on in the evenings, when the prom was empty. Once the swimming pool was emptied we moved into it to play hockey on roller skates, with walking sticks and a tennis ball. It was a high speed and skilful game, because you could bounce the ball off the wall and pick it up again beyond your opponent. Around 9pm I skated back along the West Parade in the crisp air, with the sea down below, only its white teeth showing in the dark.

On average, we went to the 'pictures' once a week. The films were mainly biographies, costume dramas from the classics, or historical themes. Many were to do with the Empire, which still existed, so we saw Errol Flynn leading British troops in orderly columns through the Khyber Pass, being shot down by the Parthians. Kay Francis was doing Florence Nightingale's rounds in the Crimea, and poor Anna Neagle never knew whether she was Nell Gwynn or Queen Victoria or Nurse Cavell. Then there was Sanders of the River; Clive of India; Nata Hari and Henry VIII. All very informative and instructive. Films were safe for children in those days: no sadistic violence or explicit sex. It was all very well mannered and middle class.

Indoors, in bad weather (which seemed rare indeed), we had our model soldiers, Hornby railway and a big Meccano set which got bigger every Christmas. So it was a case of the Red Indians up on Mantel Cliff being attacked by a mixture of Arabs, cowboys and Coldstream Guards from Sideboard Plateau. The attackers had been brought by train, under Armchair Tunnel, to be lifted to the plateau by Meccano crane. There was probably a Lott's Bricks for somewhere as well. We got so lost in these adventures, crawling around on the dining room floor, that when Mum appeared in the doorway to say that it was bedtime, we had to re-tune our minds as though she had come from outer space -- but, of course, at that time outer space was still to be discovered.

Later, we started collecting gramophone records, mostly of American artistes -- Crosby, Ellington, Artie Shaw, Benny Goodman, Tommy Dorsey, Fats Waller and all. One of the Dorsey crooners was a young unknown called Sinatra!

An annual family outing was to the White Rock Pavilion, in Hastings, to hear *Messiah* sung by Heddle Nash, Jennifer Vivian, Norma Proctor or Isobel Baillie, and periodically we all went to the new De La Warr Pavilion in Bexhill for concerts or plays. I got Paul Robeson's autograph there.

Entertainment for Anna Cunningham was mostly home-made.
As far as recreation was concerned, most of it centred around
home, extended family and church. My mother, in particular,
wished me to have the advantages denied to her, so I was given
lessons in elocution, piano, Highland and tap dancing, which all
bit into my free time. There was no such thing as shyness allowed
and we were expected to perform before family and friends with
a recitation, tune on the piano, song or dance. At a family wedding I sang *'Animal crackers in my soup'*.

Many social activities were connected with the church, in my
case Hamilton Church of Scotland, and I belonged to the church
Brownies and to the junior choir. Every Tuesday evening we re-
hearsed and in March we performed an operetta, later changed
to a variety concert, under the leadership of the organist.

During the week, recreational activities varied according to the
season. In winter we could only have a short time playing outside
because of the early nightfall. Like all small girls, I played with
dolls, my favourite being Margaret Rose, named after the princess. I also had a doll's pram and cot, and one of my uncles made
me a doll's house, with which I often played. We also collected
stamps and played games such as table tennis, ludo, snakes and
ladders and, from an early age, card games. I played patience,
rummy, Newmarket (with butter beans as money) and three
handed whist.

Being an only child, I was often taken to the cinema by my
parents. I had a friend whose father was manager of the Port
Glasgow Picture House and the two of us often sneaked in free
to shows. I saw most of the Shirley Temple films like *Stowaway,
Wee Willie Winkie, Little Princess*; musicals like Deanna Durban's
100 Men and a Girl, and Nelson Eddy and Jeanette McDonald's
Girl of the Golden West, Robert Taylor in *A Yank at Oxford*, and others such as *Gunga Din* with Cary Grant, Victor McLachlan and
Douglas Fairbanks; *Marco Polo* with Cary Grant, *Romeo and Juliet*
with Leslie Howard and I think Norma Shearer and *The Four
Feathers*. I hid under the seat when the branding took place! As
I was tall for my age, I was unable to get into the cinema for half
price over the allotted age, and was often challenged when I was
legitimately eligible. A matinée, accompanied by a poke of
sweets and followed by a high tea of pie and chips, tea, toast and
a fine selection of cakes in Mackays Tearoom in Greenock: what
more had life to offer?

I was taken once a year to a pantomime in Glasgow. This was
a very special treat, looked forward to for months previously. I
remember most vividly the dame played by comedians like Dave

Willis and Harry Morgan, and the audience participation when one part of the audience tried to out-sing the other.

In summer I played outside in the evenings and, as we were part of a council housing estate, there were plenty of young people with whom I could play. We played rounders and guessing games, when one person stood at the kerb and the rest of us a short distance away. The person who was 'it' gave initials like F.A. for Fred Astaire, and the first person to guess rightly shouted out the answer and ran over to the other side of the road. If he or she beat the questioner, then it was their turn to give the initials. Before the days of pop stars, film personalities were the heroes and heroines. A glorious game was devised whereby we divided into two teams and played an extended game of hide and seek in the gardens and hills behind the houses. I think it was called 'Halleleevoy'. It could take all night and frequently resulted in our being late home after the time set by our parents. I had roller skates, but was strictly forbidden to use them on main roads, which prohibition I ignored and got away with it until the day I crashed into the magnificent car of a shipowner and damaged both myself and the car. I didn't have a bicycle, mainly because we lived halfway up a mountain.

Lord and Lady Baden-Powell greatly enjoyed the theatre and riding, and encouraged a similar love in their children, Peter, Heather and Betty.

We lived only about thirty miles from London, so it was quite easy to get up for the day. Quite often, also, we would stay the night at the Rubens Hotel. Whenever we went to London we nearly always attended a matinée, or occasionally an evening show. Mum and Dad both loved the theatre, so they took us whenever we were free to go. In the early days it was pantomime, *Peter Pan* and *Where the Rainbow Ends*. Later we thoroughly enjoyed plays such as '*Fresh Fields*' with Ellis Jeffreys, Lily Raynor and Lilian Braithwaite -- that was so amusing, and then there was '*Laburnum Grove*' with J. B. Priesley and his lovely northern accent, and Gertrude Lawrence singing in '*Nymph Errant*'. Another one which interested me very much was a play called '*Saturday's Children*'. I don't remember anything about it but the person in it, the main girl, was acted by Dorothy Hyson, who was at school with me, so I felt terribly proud, especially when we went round afterwards and saw her in her dressing room. She was the daughter of another famous actress called Dorothy Dickson, and she took on the mantle of being the leading lady in plays. A delightful young woman and very, very attractive to look at.

Other plays that we went to were well known ones like '*Richard of Bordeaux*' with John Gielgud in the part, and '*Rose without a*

Thorn', which was a play about King Henry VIII's beloved wife Catherine, who was later beheaded for allegedly misbehaving. That was a wonderful play and I wept buckets over that one. So we thoroughly enjoyed our outings to plays, and my father always wanted to take us to the scout plays, because at that time the scouts put on a pantomime every year. It was just before the time they started the *Gang Shows*. My father was a tremendous supporter of that: we went every year. He was always keen on acting himself, as he thought acting in the theatre brought out a great deal of character. It made us observant of other people so that we could use our knowledge in portraying a character, and of course the stage craft and the fact that it was a combined operation meant that it needed the co-operation of every member, from the largest part-holder to the most humble electrician or stage builder or remover. Everyone had to do their part to the utmost of their ability to make the whole thing a success, so he encouraged very much the fact that scouts and guides should put on these performances of pantomimes and gang shows, plays and concerts of all kinds.

As well as the theatre, we enjoyed visits to the cinema and Bertram Mills Circus and Lord John Sanger's Circus, and the London Zoo. Among the films we enjoyed were *Thunder Below*, with Tallulah Bankhead; *Last Year*, with Janet Gaytnor, also *Lester Brown* with Jack Buchanan, *Cavalcade, Prince of Arcadia* (Carl Buisson), *F.P.I.* (Conrad Veidt), *Facing the Music* (Stanley Lupino) and of course *The Good Companions* with John Gielgud and Jessie Matthews. In 1934 it was *Heads we go* with Frank Lawton; *Friday the Thirteenth: Morning Glory* with Katherine Hepburn; *The Girl from Maxims* (Leslie Henson and Frances Day); *Up to the Neck* (Ralph Lynn); *Son of Songs* (Marlene Dietrich); *Channel Crossing* (Matheson Lang) and *Voltaire* with George Arliss. So with films as well as plays we had plenty of entertainment.

231

Lord Baden Powell and family at the theatre.

In addition to tennis we also enjoyed card games, and pencil and paper games were very popular, as were the more lively ones of murder, giants and sardines, or 'kick-a-peg' outdoors. We also did a lot of Country Dancing (Cecil Sharpe's collection) as Mum was very keen on it and started a club in the village.

However, riding was our biggest occupation and in the winter we went riding almost every day, and hunting about once a week. We looked after the horses ourselves, with occasional help from a gardener. We cleaned the harness and saddlery and mucked out the stables and groomed the horses. In summer we used to lead them to other pastures, on long leading reins on the verges of roads and commons, which would take us the whole afternoon. We would sometimes arrange to meet other friends and ride together, and we went to Gymkhanas and Pony Club meets etc.

I think we had a wireless, but I can't even visualise where it was and have no recollection of listening to it, and of course there was no television yet, although my father did appear on experimental television several times.

On the whole we made our own amusements, all very lively and innocent, and did not rely on being entertained by others.

Mrs. Juliana Ray describes some of the games and entertainments she enjoyed during the Thirties.

As I was eleven years younger than my brother Bandi, it was almost as though I were an only child, so I loved being able to play with my cousins and other children. Sometimes we played at my father's timber yard -- a large site alongside a main railway station. There was a narrow gauge track within the yard and when this was not in use we sat on the wagonettes and rolled ourselves backwards and forwards along the line. It was great fun.

There was a small flower garden round the office building and in one corner we had a sandpit, so when we tired of riding the wagonettes we built a sand castle, carrying water in our small buckets to fill the moat around it.

However, my greatest treat was to visit Auntie Manci and Uncle Feri, who because they had no children of their own were like second parents to Bandi and me. They had a beautiful house and grounds built on the hillside opposite the cogwheel railway that went up the Buda mountains.

Every Sunday afternoon we had a 'family' day at different houses, and although we children played in the nursery we were allowed to join the grown-ups when we wanted. We shared in the delicious teas -- savouries and cakes. Grandpapushka (Grandpa), who was a barrister, used to entertain us with stories of some of his court cases. He had a natural humility and was loved and respected by all as head of the large family.

One day we heard that he had been given an honourary title by the Regent, in appreciation of his services to the courts of justice (similar to our CBE). This meant that his title would be something like Honourable Sir, but he preferred to keep quiet about it and only their servants and some waiters at the Barristers' Chamber used it.

My parents were very hospitable and loved entertaining. The Charleston craze was over by the time I was old enough to join the guests, the ladies dressed in long evening gowns and the men with black ties. After a delicious buffet and conversation, they played games, including bridge.

Again my favourite guests were Auntie Manci and Uncle Feri; they would 'phone and say they were coming over that night and bringing their supper along with them. They were so close to Shari mama and my father, and I enjoyed their company even more than the fascinating food they supplied. However, this all changed after Germany invaded Austria. My parents perceived the dangers for Hungarian Jews and they and Aunt Manci and Uncle Feri decided to give up their spacious accommodation and moved to smaller homes. The social life came to an end and instead they did voluntary work for a charity organisation. Shari mama still worked in my father's office in the mornings, but in the afternoons visited slum areas. I heard horrific tales of poverty and the terrors of concentration camps built in Germany and Austria for the Jews. So just at the age when I was looking forward to wearing fashionable gowns and going to the theatre and dances, my parents' social life was reduced to almost nothing. Yet

Shari mama made sure that I was not entirely deprived of it. I was bought a season ticket to the Opera House and went fortnightly with my cousin Nushi. She also arranged for me and other friends to have dancing lessons.

Jack Solkhon remembers some of the things he enjoyed during the Thirties.

We used to collect cigarette cards and swop duplicates to complete a set. They were also used for games and one that we played in the school playground was called 'Four you knock 'em down'. This was played by flicking a card with the fingers and aiming at a row of cards four feet away, the cards being set up in pairs leaning against each other. A more enterprising boy might shout 'Five' to corner the business!

Alas, this came to a dead-stop when the Headmaster found what was going on. He was a religious man and condemned us for gambling!

We had sixpence a week pocket money, which was concealed at the bottom of an egg cup full of sweets left by our bedside on a Friday night, whilst we were sleeping. With limited funds we used to shop around for the cheapest sweets, Tiger Nuts a farthing ($\frac{1}{4}$d) an ounce: Liquorice Wood $\frac{1}{4}$d a stick; Aniseed Balls $\frac{1}{4}$d each; Locust Beans $\frac{1}{2}$d an ounce; and Liquorice Shakes $\frac{1}{2}$d each.

In spite of her busy life, Joan Dobson found time to enjoy the theatre as well as concerts and the cinema.

My contacts with Bobs and the Solkhon family had widened my horizons considerably. I remember the Russian Ballet at Covent Garden, 'The Fire Bird' and 'Petrushka'. An early performance of Walton's 'Facade' is a lasting memory. Could it have been narrated by Edith Sitwell? I recall only the dancing of Robert Helpman. Before this my mother had taken me, when much younger, to orchestral concerts and smaller performances by quintets, trios, etc. in the Wigmore and Aeolian Halls. Opera had been her favourite, but never ballet, which became mine. Lighter musicals of the time were by Ivor Novello and Noel Coward, and who could resist Jack Buchanan singing 'Goodnight Vienna'!?

Dennis Thompson enjoyed the cinema in the Thirties.

During the Thirties the cinema really came into its own, following the movie craze at that time on the other side of the Atlantic. Up to 1936 I lived at Chiswick, West London, and a year or two prior to that the largest cinema in London -- the Commodore -- opened just across the borough border in Hammersmith, with the showing of the original *'Show Boat'* film starring Paul Robeson. The next and larger cinema to open was the Odeon in Hammersmith Broadway about a year later. However, that place of entertainment was soon eclipsed in size by the opening of the country's largest cinema in Kilburn, North London, with seats for about four thousand.

It is almost unbelievable when I recall that in those days my mother and I used to go to the Commodore at midday on Saturdays and for the 6d admission each we enjoyed the following entertainment. From midday until 1pm you sat (very quietly) and listened to Joseph Muscant and his orchestra doing a live radio broadcast for the B.B.C. from the stage. After that we saw screened the main film, news reel, and forthcoming attractions. In the interval Harry Davidson played the organ. Finally, there would be nearly an hour long stage show, usually one of the top bands of that era. I realise now how fortunate I was -- though it would mean nothing to the rock and rollers, soul and heavy metal fans of today -- as I was able to see most of the leading bands of that day, such as Jack Payne, Jack Hylton, Harry Roy, Roy Fox, not to mention big bands from America: Louis Armstrong, Cab Calloway, Duke Ellington, Guy Lombardo and his Royal Canadians.

Andrew J. Blair was fortunate in having local cinemas and dance halls in Greenock.

Practically everyone went to the pictures fairly regularly: a few very regularly. Dancing, at public dance halls mainly, was also popular. Theatre, if at all, was almost entirely variety. Occasional amateur choral or orchestral concerts were reasonably supported.

Every game and every sport (except posh recreations like polo) were available at reasonable costs. But reasonable costs were not within the reach of many. Working men were spectators at a lot of football matches.

The films and other forms of recreation that Betty Forsyth enjoyed.

I loved the cinema and eagerly awaited each new film starring Nelson Eddy and Jeanette Macdonald, or Fred Astaire and Ginger Rogers.

We had little opportunity to go to the theatre, apart from the music hall type of variety show, which did not much appeal to me. Having strict elderly parents, I was not allowed to go to dances, greatly to my disgust!

Organised games did not appeal to me, but I loved cycling, and my girlfriend and I used to go for long runs every weekend on roads that were, by today's standards, almost free of traffic and other dangers. That was certainly a pleasure denied to today's children and young people with so much traffic, and the always present fear of attack.

We also enjoyed ice skating after the local ice rink opened in the mid-Thirties, and we followed the fortunes of the local ice hockey team with great enthusiasm. Ice hockey had a huge following in Scotland in those days -- never regained after the war.

It was unheard of for women to go into public houses, and alcohol was offered to guests only at New Year.

I can't remember how much pocket money I received, but it seemed to be enough to buy chocolate at one old penny per bar, or a wide selection of children's sweets from the 'penny tray'. I read comics and children's annuals avidly, but their titles elude me completely. I was given a copy of Arthur Mee's *Children's Encyclopedia*, which I found fascinating in parts and boring in others. I still have all ten volumes and refer to them occasionally to settle arguments. I used to rush home from school to listen to Henry Hall and his B.B.C. Dance Orchestra. I loved all the big bands: my favourite singers were Bing Crosby, Deanna Durbin, Jeanette Macdonald, Nelson Eddy and Paul Robeson. We listened to the radio, but apart from the above I have no recollections of any programme. T.V. was something I had hardly heard of and found almost beyond comprehension.

Joan MacLachlan and her brother Raymond enjoyed various inexpensive entertainments.

The Mental Hospital where my brother Bernard worked was enormous, but a kindly place. There were vast grounds and lawns, and every week there were cricket matches: the male patients loved to watch the games.

As children we were able to go and watch, too. There were some great games; the sun always seemed to shine and there was a buffet. We children could have sausage rolls and slab cake and mugs of tea. We enjoyed those days: our mother came with us.

We knew all the card games: Pelmanism, Rummy, Old Maid, Patience, and in the early Thirties this is how we spent the evenings when friends joined us.

I played tennis and swam; my brothers both played cricket. We all enjoyed football matches and the boys liked the speedway.

I was fond of the cinema and an occasional visit to the theatre, especially when I was at college. Dances I never went to until the Forties, but Raymond and I spent much time at Trent Bridge cricket matches -- 6d admission, 1d for a card of the match. We never dared move or we would get a poke in the back from a

Panama-hatted gentleman with a walking stick. Trent Bridge was our paradise in the days of Larwood and Voce, Jack Hobbs and Sutcliffe, Don Bradman and the rest. We were never bored -- the days were too short.

There were various forms of recreation available for Ian MacLachlan.

It is just a hundred years since my grandfather chaired a meeting, hoping to form a Shinty (a Highland form of hockey) Club in the village. Each generation of MacLachlans had a share in the success of the team: it was my turn in the Thirties. We all lived for shinty and the women supporters took it all very seriously. We travelled throughout Argyll and as far north as Inverness.

After my brother was killed in 1933 my mother was agitated in case I was hurt in what was a physical game. So reluctantly I resigned and was made a member of the committee.

Dances were held in the Drill Hall. They were very popular: Eightsome Reels, Strip the Willow and Dashing White Sergeant were the favourites. Accordions always featured largely at dances.

There was a cinema several miles away at Kinlochleven and this was very well attended in the Thirties, as the 'talkies' came in.

Most of us walked the hills for recreation. We were not mountaineers, just hill walkers. Quite a bit of deer stalking went on, too: it would be called poaching today!

My family had a boat, shared with the uncles, and everyone fished, fish being a staple part of the diet. The anglers fished the rivers, hoping for trout and salmon.

Whist drives were held, too, and the Women's Rural Institute (W.R.I.) provided the ladies with relaxation and entertainment. There was also a guide company run by one of the ladies from the neighbouring village.

Some of the entertainments enjoyed by George Topping during the Thirties.

My mother, like many others, was keen to keep me off the streets so I took up golf, which my dad had played, on the local course in 1932 at 2/6d a year. This rose to 5 shillings by 1939, by which time my handicap had dropped to single figures. Tennis was popular, and miners' bowling greens and tennis courts were opened at a small cost.

Lanarkshire Scots generally went south (better weather) for holidays. I liked the Isle of Man and in 1939 Cunningham (Young

Men's) Holiday Camp cost 42 shillings a week, all in, and the fare by the Isle of Man Steam Packet Co. was 12/6d.

The interest Lilian Smith's father had in politics influenced some of her family's recreational activities.

We lived in a cul de sac, so we could play outdoor games like skipping, marbles, and hop scotch in the street. Indoors we played draughts, Ludo, shove halfpenny, and snakes and ladders.

Occasionally we went to the cinema to see Shirley Temple with a young aunt who was dotty about her. I was fourteen before I was taken to a theatre by an older friend. Paul Robeson was the lead in a play about downtrodden workers -- I think it was at Unity Theatre. It must have been communistically inspired, but politics meant nothing to me then. Dad helped out at weekends at the local working men's club: this was a family club where we had concerts and dancing. Vera Lynn sang there at the start of her career.

Anne Docherty spent her teenage years in Glasgow, but now lives in Australia.

I realise how fortunate I was to live in Glasgow in my youth. Housing was terrible, with 90% having no baths and three families on each landing of a tenement sharing one toilet. Yet in spite of the poverty we had many cultural opportunities. My friends and I were able to attend the theatre for 9d (gallery, of course) and saw all Bernard Shaw's plays, Margaret Rawlings in Strunberg's play *The Father*, and Yvonne Arnaud. It cost slightly more to see Jack Buchanan and Jessie Matthews. Also we saw Robert Helpman dance *Bollero*, but had to pay 3/6d for the privilege of watching Pavlova in her last appearance at the Royal. I think Barbarolli made his debut in Glasgow, with the Glasgow Orchestra.

To save money we walked to the city and did not buy a programme. We were not afraid of walking back along the gas-lit streets: there was no fear of being mugged. Perhaps we were more honest, although money was very scarce, or it could have been the fear of Banlerine Prison.

Sometimes during the weekends we went for a walk from Milngavie, round Blanefield and Craigdhu. There were no soft drinks, but high tea when we arrived home.

Visits to the cinema were the main form of entertainment as far as Jill Clarke was concerned.

Most people went often to the cinema. Seen now the films shown then would seem simple and unsophisticated, but in the Thirties, they were very popular. Good mostly prevailed: bad girls almost invariably got their just deserts. Many people had a fairly drab existence and to see the glamorous lives film stars seemed to lead was attractive. We all copied their clothes and hair styles, and had film stars as pin-ups on our walls.

Apart from a pantomime at Christmas most children did not go to the theatre. I remember my mother going: people wore evening clothes in those days. Mother came in to say goodnight to me wearing her long evening dress.

My grandmother had bridge afternoons. I can remember her having her ladies to tea, and they had dainty little sandwiches and cups of tea halfway through. I used to hope some of the sandwiches would be left over! On the whole I don't think people entertained very much -- and when they did, it was much more formal.

A variety of games and entertainment were enjoyed by Eddie Boyle and his friends.

Like many British boys, we played all the seasonal games: cigarette cards, I spy, kick the can, release, rounders, cricket (of a kind), conkers, marbles and football, mostly on the streets. Girls had their dolls, shops, skipping ropes, ball games and 'peever' (hop scotch). While no-one grudges the present generation their videos and P.C.'s, it is a great pity they do not have the best of both worlds. Street games were exciting, exhilarating, engendered sportsmanship, discipline, cooperation and were infinitely more healthy than 'couch potatoing'. Lack of money and resources forced children to use ingenuity and imagination in the invention of street games. As well as collecting the full set of cigarette cards by pestering relations and friends, and even gentlemen in the street, "Please Sir, have you any cigarette cards?", and the thrill when he reached for his pocket. We were obliged to say "Thanks" and either lift our school cap or salute if we were bareheaded; indeed, this applied to any adult whom we met in the street.

There were card games. Cards were two-faced, a picture on one side and the reading on the other, what was called 'face' and 'blank'. You chose one, covered it with your hand, and your adversary called "Six a face", "Ten a blank", with a limit stake previously agreed. One ingenious lad invented a game which he called the 'brush hunt' for the dry, dusty weather. Borrowing his mother's besom, he made off while the hunters covered their eyes, as in I Spy. After a count of one hundred, they set off in pursuit and it required the skill of an aborigine to track him through tenement back doors, closes and across patches of grass.

There was always something to do whatever the time of year: any combination of the popular games in spring; in summer, making kites from brown paper and hoops cadged from the local grocer as he opened the wooden barrels of butter, catching minnows, sticklebacks and eels in the burn: autumn for chestnuts, blackberries and mushrooms; winter for sledges and slides. How we booed the janitor when he appeared with his pail of sand or salt! Also, it must be admitted, mischievous ploys on the neighbours: ring and run with doorbells, or tying handles of adjacent doorknobs and summoning the tenants with a knock or a ring.

Equally popular was the cinema. In two of the three cinemas there were twice weekly matinées, Wednesday after school at 4.15pm and Saturday. Wednesday's was the more exciting with boys and girls, penny in pocket, impatiently doing nature study or handwork and straining for the bell at 4pm. Pupils from three schools spewed into the streets and went helter-skelter for Tom Mix or Pearl White, and joined in the conducted community singing until the cinema darkened, to prolonged cheering. Some of the patrons gained entrance without paying. Nothing illegal. Jam jars in those days carried a penny deposit on return to the grocer and were accepted by the Countess and the Casino. Some mothers would not trust their offspring with a jam jar, especially on the mad Wednesday stampede. A clever advertising campaign by a local soap company provided further free entry. Cowan's Cleanser came in a diced green and white wrapper, which was as good as a penny at the Countess. Many mums refused to buy Cowan's because it was not kind to their hands. With typical childish perversity, those who had neither jar nor wrapper considered the others as unfairly privileged, and it was not uncommon to trade our picture penny or a *Rover* or *Film Fun* for a jar or a soap wrapper. Although every child in town appeared to be at the pictures every Saturday afternoon, the Countess had further temptation in that if you paid three ha'pence (1½d) on Saturday, you were given a ticket for the Wednesday show.

8. RADIO, TELEVISION, MUSIC, BOOKS.

During the Thirties, radio improved tremendously, as primitive 'cat's whiskers' were replaced by accumulators and then valves. Programmes, too, became more sophisticated. However, its success caused problems for live shows. When the Royal Command Variety show was broadcast in 1937 it emptied music halls, theatres and cinemas all over the country. In response to protests, the B.B.C. donated a large sum to charity and agreed in future to broadcast fortnightly excerpts (trailers) from shows for half an hour.

This proved a very helpful form of advertising. In 1937 *Me and my Girl* at Chelsea Palace was about to close when the B.B.C. broadcast an extract, including *Doing the Lambeth Walk,* sung by Lupino Lane. The song and accompanying dance, a jerky swagger and the 'Oi' with appropriate gesture, became very popular and revived interest in the show. It was a welcome change from foxtrots, rumbas and tangos. *Knees up Mother Brown*, and *Under the Spreading Chestnut Tree* followed. In 1939 jitterbugging to fast swing music arrived from the states, but mostly the upper class disapproved.

One great advantage of radio was that the ordinary musical man in the street, who could not afford to go to concerts, could now listen to classical music performed by top orchestras from the Queen's Hall, London, and elsewhere. For the less high brow there were the many popular dance bands like Jack Payne's. Television made its first shaky appearance in the Thirties and I was able to watch the coronation of George VI at a friend's house. It seemed little short of a miracle to me at the time! But it was expensive and black and white T.V. could not compare with the coloured sets we enjoy nowadays.

Books were still avidly read by many children and adults during the Thirties: the media had not yet dimmed this interest. With new technology, books were better illustrated, and had the advantage of colourful jackets, first introduced in 1928, to brighten up bookshop windows. Some of them are known today, like *Love on the Dole* by Walter Greenwood, a

working man who describes the effects of long term unem-
ployment; Sir Arthur Conan Doyle's *Sherlock Holmes;* D. H.
Lawrence's *Lady Chatterley's Lover; For whom the Bell Tolls* by
Ernest Hemingway; and George Orwell's *Keep the Aspidistra
Flying* and *Coming up for Air.* For poetry lovers there was the
Oxford Book Modern Verse, compiled by W. B. Yeats. Newspapers were also improved by the invention of photo-journal-
ism which developed from the miniature Leica camera, which
could take snapshots of unsuspecting people. Magazines like
Picture Post and *Lilliput* took advantage of this technique. For
children, as well as the much loved comics and Christmas
albums like *Tiger Tim,* there was the well balanced *Children's
Newspaper.* For those who could not afford to buy books and
papers, there was always the local lending library.

**Radio had come into its own during the Thirties, when televi-
sion had its beginnings, and Molly Campbell was able to enjoy
both.**

'Children's Hour', of nostalgic memory, was a highlight of the
Thirties: Toytown, Uncle Mac, Larry the Lamb and Mr. Growser.
In time I grew out of that and changed to listening to Henry Hall
and Jack Payne's bands. I remember that my father preferred
'Children's Hour' and we had many arguments about what was
suitable for me to listen to! Later 'In Town Tonight' became very
popular on a Saturday night. It was a kind of magazine programme, introduced by one of Eric Coates' Marches. One offering I remember clearly was that of a man who lived on grass. Yes!
He cut his lawn and dined off the clippings!

A friend had a television set and I was invited to watch the
coronation of George VI in 1936. The picture was fuzzy and kept
disappearing; it could hardly be called black and white - more
shades of grey mist.

**During the Thirties it was the radio that provided music for
Jill Clarke and many others.**

There were no transistors in those days, so when there was music
being played on the radio we listened. Dance bands like Henry
Hall and Jack Payne were popular, and people who had a piano
played sheet music of popular songs. Gramophone records were
also played quite a lot, but they had to be wound up very often.

Most people had radios, but not everyone. I remember one of
my mother's friends coming round to listen to the Boat Race with
her husband, as they did not possess a radio. The Boat Race was
quite an event in London: we all supported Oxford or Cambridge
and wore the appropriate colour. Families were beginning to lis-

ten to popular programmes -- I was allowed to listen to one called
'*Monday Night at Eight*' and '*In Town Tonight*' on a Saturday, when
interesting people would come to the studio to talk. My mother,
with others, said that it was destroying the art of conversation. I
wonder what her generation would think of T.V. meals and the
way we all sit round the set nowadays! I don't remember watching T.V. until after the Second World War.

**Entertainment for Pauline Thompson's family in their York-
shire village was provided by radio and gramophone.**

Our early radios were run by a wet accumulator, which was
recharged every so often, either by an electrical shop or at the
local garage. Other than the gramophone, this was our only
source of music. The popular songs of those days have always
been a joy to us and often we would sing along with the radio. '*If
you were the only girl in the world*'; '*Daisy, Daisy, give me your answer
do*'; '*Tiptoe through the tulips*', etc. How well they have lasted!

**Anne Lebeau is now living in British Columbia but spent her
early years in England at Godmanchester.**

The Thirties may have been the last period of calm before the
gradually accelerating swing of the pendulum towards a very
different society from that in which I grew up.

Others will tell of seaside holidays, life in the country or city,
schooldays and job opportunities, work and play. I would like to
write about the popular music of our times, for the simple reason
that, looking back, it is apparent that it was an oasis in time, soon
to change and perhaps never to be repeated.

First I should say that one of my biggest disappointments in
those years was to find that I had no real appreciation of classical
music. Some ballet music and some of the more romantic of the
classics I enjoyed, but never was I to have the pleasure that a real
appreciation of the classics obviously brings to others.

However, dancing I loved and the popular music of the Thirties
was made for dancing...

It is said that rhythm and blues were born in New Orleans --
one reason why I have always wanted to visit that city. By the
Thirties, this music had spread all around the globe and had been
adopted by European bands and recording artists as their own.
So English boys and girls with home made crystal radio sets were
tuning into the smooth rhythm of '*Whispering*', Roy Fox's signa-
ture tune, and to the lush tones of Jack Payne's '*Say It With Music*'.

The extraordinary thing is that I, and probably many, many
others of my generation, remember literally hundreds of those
songs, can still recall almost every word of the lyrics, and remem-

ber the emotion they prompted. I say 'emotion', because almost all of our popular songs were romantic. Layton and Johnson's *'You're the Cream in my Coffee'* is one of the earliest I remember. One of the last was Bing Crosby's dreamy little number *'I don't Want to Walk without You, Baby'* -- a record which I owned and played every morning while dressing, nearly driving my poor mother crazy in the process.

There were a few fun numbers, though. Remember the inimitable Gracie Fields' *'Biggest Aspidistra in the World'*? and Jack Hulbert's *'The Flies Crawled up the Window'*? Then George Formby broke onto the scene with his catchy *'When I'm cleaning Windows'*. Bing had a few novelty numbers too, starting out with something I seem to recall as *'Mississippi Mud'*, in which he did some respectable scat singing; and much later there was the marvellous, rhythmic *'Small Fry'*. Another winner which would be fun to stage was *'The Waiter and the Porter and the Upstairs Maid'*.

But it was the romantic, ah, the romantic numbers over which we swooned in our teenage dreams. Bing again, crooning to Dixie Lee (we read -- I had a scrap book of Bing, Dixie and the family) at the Coconut Grove with heartbreakers like *'I surrender, Dear'*. Then the Gershwins with their brilliant love songs, sometimes with extremely clever lyrics. *'How Deep is the Ocean'* for instance, consists of nothing but questions answering questions:

> *'How many times a day do I think of you?*
> *Well, how many roses are sprinkled with dew?'*

--really beautiful song. *'Embraceable You'* is eminently playable and singable -- an actor's song. *'Nevertheless'*, another with clever lyrics (*'Maybe I'll live a life of regret and maybe I'll give much more than I get...'*) can't be bettered, although the lyrics are not as good as some. *'The Best Things in Life are Free'* was another in the same cheerful vein. Both songs, it might be added, included an almost mandatory love interest.

'These Foolish Things' I first heard being played by a piano tuner visiting our school. The song, written by an English peer, has sophisticated wording which probably came naturally to His Nibs but was exciting new territory to a fifteen year old in a country boarding school.

> *'A cigarette that bears a lipstick's traces;*
> *An airline ticket to romantic places;*
> *And still my heart has wings,*
> *These foolish things remind me of you...'*

and *'You came, you saw, you conquered me...'* - shades of Caesar's Gaul and a classical education!

244

One last song I'll mention, for it's another with clever lyrics: *'Smoke Gets in Your Eyes'*.

> *'When laughing friends deride*
> *Tears I cannot hide,*
> *I still smile and say,*
> *ÒWhen a lovely flame dies,*
> *Smoke gets in your eyesÒ'*

The result of all this barrage of romanticism? When you add it to the sugary sentimentality of the average Hollywood movie of the time, it probably did have quite an effect on us impressionable teenagers. I don't believe, though, that it did any lasting harm. It probably tended to feed expectations of matrimonial perfection never, of course, to be attained. But on the whole there was a gentility and a sensitivity about most of the popular songs of those days that has since been totally lost.

Lilian Smith remembers some of the popular songs of the Thirties.

We had a piano at home, but we were not musical so could not play it. Fortunately we had friends who could, so we were able to have singsongs. I remember *'Oh, my darling Clementine'*, *'Ramona'*, *'Moonlight and Roses'*, *'Home, sweet home'*, *'The old rugged cross'* -- these were some of my parents favourites.

We had a wireless set. This had an accumulator, which had to be taken to the hardware shop to be topped up with distilled water every now and again. This was one of my chores. Later we had a radio that plugged into the mains. On Saturday nights we listened to *'In town tonight'*; *'Lovely violets' Lovely violets'* was the theme tune. In those days very few people had T.V. sets and I never saw any programmes during the Thirties.

Bob Jones developed his early musical interests and is an accomplished pianist.

One of the early popular songs I remember is *'The Ogo Pogo'*. It goes like this:-

> *'I'm looking for the Ogo Pogo,*
> *The funny little Ogo Pogo;*
> *His mother is an earwig,*
> *His father was a whale -*
> *I'm going to put a little bit of salt on his tail.*
>
> *Oh, I'm looking for the Ogo Pogo*
> *For to put him in the Lord Mayor's show*

> *The Lord Mayor of London,*
> *The Lord Mayor of London,*
> *The Lord Mayor of London wants to put him in*
> *The Lord Mayor's show.'*

There was also *'The Frothblowers' Anthem.'*

> *'Oh, the more we are together,*
> *Together, together,*
> *Oh, the more we are together,*
> *The happier we shall be,*
> *For your friends are my friends,*
> *And my friends are your friends,*
> *And the more we are together,*
> *The happier we shall be.'*

Another song I remember is:

> *'Oh, there ain's no sense*
> *Sitting on a fence*
> *All by yourself in the moonlight.*

'Like her husband Rob, Muriel Jones, enjoyed music from the early years, and still has a lovely voice, so he enjoys accompanying her (and others) on the piano.

I remember at a children's party my friend's elder brother was very keen to teach us how to do the Charleston and this dance, with its syncopated music, was very popular indeed.

During the summer, when we visited the seaside, there were many concert parties and pierrot troupes along the promenade. These were extremely well supported, in fact we nearly always had to book our seats in advance. I was fortunate in having a good singing voice, even as a child, and an accurate idea of time and pitch, so I eagerly presented myself on the stage when children in the audience were invited to do so. Each child would give a recitation, a dance or a song of some sort. The following is a verse of my most successful song:

> *'I passed by your window*
> *When the morning was red,*
> *The dew on the rosebud,*
> *And the lark overhead,*
> *And oh! I sang softly*
> *Though no-one could hear,*
>
> *To wish you 'good morning,*
> *Good morning, my dear.'*

This was considered a fairly serious song, and was always well received and applauded, although I was equally at home with a syncopated little one which went (in part):

> *'Tiptoe, from your pillow,*
> *To the shadow*
> *Of the willow tree,*
> *Come tiptoe, through the tulips,*
> *With me.'*

At home, there was a piece of music on our piano, which depicted a very large black cat, with a huge tail. This piece began as follows:-

> *'Felix keeps on walking,*
> *Keeps on walking still.*
> *With his tail behind him,*
> *You will always find him.'*

Sentimental ballads were also very popular. I remember my mother singing: *'Down in the forest something stirred'*, and also:

> *'What'll I do, when you*
> *Are far away,*
> *And I am blue*
> *What'll I do?'*

Very catchy, swinging and syncopated tunes were all the rage. Part of one such is as follows:-

> *'Every little breeze*
> *Seems to whisper 'Louise',*
> *Each little rose*
> *Tells me it knows*
> *I love you, Louise.'*

And another is about a young lady who has a *'cute personality full of rascality, That's Peggy O'Neale.'*

I remember these years as tranquil and easy going. Children were entirely safe then (I used to ride my little bicycle all over the place with absolutely no fear). It was a good time to look back on, and we used to sign a song which says it all:-

> *'Happy days are here again,*
> *The skies are blue and clear again,*
> *And we can sing this song of cheer again,*
> *Happy days are here again.'*

Meg Matthews also came from a musical family. Her father played the piano and the violin. He and his sister Jane both had good voices, and she had singing lessons. She also enjoyed books.

My grandfather gave my young brother, but not me, the piano our father's brothers and he had practised on as children, and I did not learn to play: something I have regretted since. I enjoyed singing. My mother had a sweet voice and sang many songs to me like:

> *'Where'er you walk,*
> *Cool gales shall fan the glade;*
> *Where'er you sit*
> *The trees shall form a shade...'*

Also *'Blow the wind southerly', 'Sweet Lass of Richmond Hill', 'Bobbie Shafto', 'Bluebells of Scotland', 'God bless the Prince of Wales'* and *'Londonderry Air'*. At kindergarten I enjoyed the Christopher Robin poems and stories, like *'They are changing guards at Buckingham Palace',* and *'The King's Breakfast',* as well as the usual nursery rhymes. We also learned the *Ten Commandments* and the *23rd Psalm.*

I remember my mother had a copy of *Chatterbox* which had been given to her around 1910. I read it for many years, but then I lent it to an old lady who was in her nineties and was in *The Golden Staircase Book of Poetry.* Unfortunately it was never returned.

My grandmother used to read to me books like *Black Beauty* and Dicken's *Little Nell* whilst we were stringing beans on the garden seat in summer time; and mother the Beatrix Potter and Enid Blyton books; also *Alice in Wonderland,* and Grimm's *Fairy Tales.* Soon I was reading myself and enjoying stories from *The Little One's Annual* and a book called *The Little Match Girl.* Classics like *Treasure Island* and *The Water Babies* followed later.

Books, magazines and comics that Eileen Davison enjoyed.

We started off with a comic called *Chicks Own;* then there was *Tiger Tim, Beano, Wizard,* and *The Childrens' Newspaper.* There were annuals such as *Girls' Own, Boys' Own, Felix* and *The Boys' Own Paper.* Books were fairy stories, *The Wide World Magazine, Biggles, The Count of Monte Cristo* and *The Three Musketeers* by Alexander Dumas; also R. L. Stevenson's *Kidnapped* and *Treasure Island,* Rider Haggard's books, *Chums,* and books by Dickens, the Brontes, Jane Austen and Sir Walter Scott. We had a wonderful encyclopedia comprising a book each of *The Fireside Lesson Book, the Fireside*

Story Book (that was practically worn out), and then there were books of poetry, history, artists, animals, and so on.

Molly Campbell appreciated the facilities provided by her local library.

The public library was the best source of books, but books were actually very cheap. My father had hundreds of paper backs, all thrillers. As I remember they cost 1 shilling each. *The William Stories* by Richmal Crompton, and *Anne of Green Gables* by L. M. Montgomery were my favourite reading. These have had a permanent influence on me. At the age of ten, and wanting desperately *'Tiger Tim's Annual'*, I awoke on Christmas morning to find a whole set of Dickens, a special offer from the News Chronicle.

I was not allowed a comic, but was encouraged to read widely. *The Children's Newspaper* was allowed: boys had *'The Boys' Own Paper'*.

9. RELIGION

Although there was a slight increase overall in church attendance during the Thirties, as a percentage of the population it was steadily decreasing.

However, there was a noticeable revival, especially in the Anglican Church, among the intellectuals of Oxford and Cambridge Universities, public schools and elsewhere. The church had some outstanding leaders, of whom William Temple, Archbishop of York, was the foremost. A modern intellectual with a brilliant mind and wealthy background, he could yet identify with the working classes and became president of the Workers Educational Association even before he was ordained. His enthusiasm and sense of humour inspired people of all backgrounds; he was very approachable and unpompous: a great reconciler.

The free churches were also undergoing changes, with Methodist reunion at the beginning of the Thirties. They, too, had a vigorous, outgoing leader in Donald Soper, who was only thirty-three when he was appointed to lead the West London Mission from Kingsway Hall in 1936. Leslie Weatherhead, also a Methodist and an outstanding preacher, was appointed minister at the City Temple, the well known Congregational Church in Holborn. The appointment of C. H. Dodd as Norris Hulse Professor at Cambridge in 1935 gave full national recognition of the contribution the free church could bring to Christianity. Yet in spite of the influence of these and others, membership of the free churches was in decline.

It was the Roman Catholic denomination which expanded during the Thirties. Its sphere spread from the main towns to the new estates being built in many parts of the U.K.

Also, many outstanding people were converted to Roman Catholicism during the Thirties, because they appreciated the authoritativeness of the doctrine, among them Maurice Baring, Ronald Knox, Sheila Kaye Smith, Evelyn Waugh, Graham Greene, and G. K. Chesterton. The latter died in 1936 but his writings such as the Father Brown stories have endeared him to generations of Catholics and non-Catholics alike: his influence has far exceeded that of his contemporaries.

On 1st January 1935 Cardinal Bourne died after more than thirty years as leader of the Catholic Church. He was cold and remote, the antithesis of Cardinal Hinsley, who succeeded him. Hinsley had spent much of his life as a priest in Africa. He was warm and fatherly, willing to have discussions with Archbishop Lang of Canterbury, unheard of before then for Catholics and Anglican leaders to meet. It was Hinsley who asked Ronald Knox, Oxford's Catholic chaplain, to translate the Vulgate Bible into English in 1939; he completed the New Testament in 1941.

Hilaire Belloc was a man of great intelligence but was sixty at the beginning of the decade and well past his prime. His nonsense poems 'Cautionary Tales' (1907) have delighted many children and he wrote a number of historical books and studies. With G. K. Chesterton and his brother Cecil he founded the New Witness. He had Nazi sympathies and despised the Jews, and was able to influence the younger generation of Catholics with his teachings.

Someone who will be remembered by many of those who lived in the Thirties is the Reverend Harold Davidson, rector of Stiffkey in Norfolk. He was accused of immorality and formally defrocked in 1931, though there were many who supported him. Three years later he and his daughter decided to observe a fast, esconsed in separate boxes on Blackpool beach, where they attracted huge crowds before they were arrested. His career ended when he decided to preach from a lion's cage at Skegness: he was savaged by the beast and died of his injuries.

Most people in England were unaware of Hitler's venomous attacks on the Jews, and it was not until after the end of the war that they learned of the millions sent to die in concentration camps or murdered in other ways. Even those of mixed parentage were not free from persecution, nor those who had become Christians, as some of the contributors to this book describe.

For the ordinary family, church going was still the norm, and children dutifully accompanied their parents or went to Sunday School, but the pattern was gradually changing as the ways of the world drew them away.

I was sad when the time came for me to leave Christ's Hospital in July 1929, but was looking forward to being free to attend the Guildhouse and hear Dr. Maude Royden's dynamic preaching every Sunday, instead of just in the holidays.

However, this was not to be. In 1928 Maude Royden embarked on a worldwide tour beginning with three months in America, where she preached almost every day to thousands in many parts of the country. From there she went to New Zealand and Australia, where she received rapturous welcomes and again preached to crowds of enthusiastic people. She went on to Japan, China, Ceylon and India, where she met Mahatma Gandhi. For someone with her disability (both her hips were dislocated at birth) it was an exhausting tour. She returned to England in January 1929 and there was a service of thanksgiving to welcome her back to the Guildhouse in February, but she was far from well.

She was made a Companion of Honour in 1930 and became president of the Society for the Ministry of Women an interdenominational group which sent a memorandum 'Women and the Priesthood' to the Archbishop for consideration at the Lambeth Conference to be held that summer. Their response was 'We cannot encourage in any way those who press for the Priesthood of Women', so they proposed to meet the shortage of priests by ordaining 'auxiliary clergy', men who often had no vocation, whilst they would not even consider the claims of women who had an obvious calling.

Unfortunately, Maude became very ill with a severe nervous collapse and was told by two specialists, Lady Barrett and Lord Moyniham, that she must have a prolonged rest. So she was away for the whole of that year, and though others rallied round to support the Guildhouse, it was not the same. She was back again in 1931, but the finances of the Guildhouse had been affected by her three years' absence.

It was not until her book, A Threefold Cord, was published that her relationship with the Rev. Hudson Shaw and his wife, Effie, was generally known. He suffered from heart trouble and depression, and gave up work at St. Botolphs, Bishopsgate, 1935, when he and his wife moved to a beautiful cottage in Kent. It happened that the house next door became available and Maude and her friend, Evelyn, moved there from Hampstead. By 1936 Maude felt the time had come for her to resign from the Guildhouse, so that she could devote her energies to Peace work. Although her work there ended in December, she went straight to the U.S.A. at the invitation of American pacifists. She preached her last sermon at the Guildhouse in June 1937.

However, I missed her last years there as in April 1931 I moved to Bristol, so again it was only in the holidays that I could hear her at the Guildhouse. Instead I attended services at the Chapel at Colston's School and at Stapleton Parish

Church: they were good, but I missed the penetrating wisdom and encouragement of Maude Royden.

Jessie Lintern was the daughter of a United Free Church minister in Scotland, so it was natural that she was brought up as a Christian.

Before moving to Closeburn, I had always accompanied my father to a large bookshop in Glasgow, where he selected the church and Sunday School prizes for regular attendance. Meanwhile I was allowed to roam through the shelves unhindered, dipping into as many books as possible while hoping to avoid those which might become mine in due course. When his order had finally been completed, he and I had lunch in style at one of Miss Cranston's tea-rooms; waitress in uniform, silver cutlery, choice of menu, all made up a memorable day out. A trip for the same purpose by bus to Dumfries did not seem so exciting!

Grace was always said before meals, and weekends were fully occupied. On Saturday shoes had to be cleaned, Sunday meals prepared in advance to free the lady of the house, while Father remained in his study-- checking his hymn-list and special announcements, revising his address to the children and his notes for the sermon he would provide for the congregation. On Sunday, after breakfast, he held family worship, followed by the church service and then that of the Sunday School. Bible class for the older children took place prior to the evening service in church, after which we returned home for supper and a peaceful hour or two, during which I might slip off upstairs to deal with any unfinished homework!

At Colmonell, my brother was given the task of pumping the organ, for which he received a copper or two and a bag of sweets from the organist, who kept a post office and grocery store three miles away. He was hidden from view by a curtain which shut off the stairs to the pulpit, and there he settled down with his 'Wizard' or 'Hotspur' as his father began the sermon. One memorable Sunday he was so engrossed in the doings of Roy of the Rovers that, oblivious of the sermon's end and the announcement of the final hymn, and that the organist was sitting with hands poised above the keyboard, he failed to put the pump into operation. Silence reigned, until the organist hissed loudly "Blow, Jimmy, blow " The bag of sweets rolled out from under the curtain, my father glared down at his son, and with a mighty surge of air the organ sounded forth!

At the start of my college days I went to look for the nearest United Free Church, and to my delight found that the preacher that day was a dear friend of ours - my father's predecessor at

Colmonell. He announced that in the evening he would be preaching at another church in the area, and I decided to find my way there. The welcome was so warm, the congregation so cheerful and friendly, that I knew this was the right place for me. I was invited to join the choir and to become a Sunday school teacher, in the process of which a wonderful relationship was built up over the next three years between a brilliant student of modern languages and me. We became engaged on my twenty-first birthday and were married two years later in my father's church. Six months of happiness was ended by his service with Bomber Command in the Second World War and his early death over the North Sea. He now lies buried in the cemetery at Esbjerg in Denmark.

According to Betty Forsyth, religion was taken very seriously in Scotland.

As an Anglican (a 'Piskie', short for Episcopalian) I was not subject to quite such a rigorous regime as my friends in the Church of Scotland, but even so we did not play cards on a Sunday and my mother would never have hung out washing. I remember being bitterly disappointed at not being allowed to go to a concert by one of the 'big bands', whose only visit was on a Sunday. My best friend was allowed to go for a walk, but not for a cycle ride.

Church going and Sunday School attendance were taken for granted, and women always wore hats to church.

Andrew J. Blair's view of religion during the Thirties.

The firm grip of the church was just beginning to slip but church-going was still very much the in thing. The Empire Exhibition in Glasgow in 1938 was closed on Sundays. Church of Scotland was the majority denomination but Catholics, Irish and Highland, were prominent and many others made up a measurable minority. Most churches supported Scouts, Guides, the Boys Brigade or other clubs.

Sundays were still kept as special days in Scotland during the Thirties, as Ruth Meyer describes.

We were not allowed to play on Sundays, so if it was fine Doris and I walked into Doune to go to the little meeting there, and at night in the summer sometimes we went back again, or perhaps to the Sunday School. However, in winter Dad held a meeting in the parlour with just ourselves there. We'd sing some hymns whilst I played the organ, then he'd read from the Bible and give us a talk about it. Often after work he cycled the seventeen miles to Alloa and back to help out in the small meeting there.

Now and again we went to the one in Stirling and we were
regularly invited to one of the brothers' houses for the day, so that
usually we were at a meeting somewhere on a Sunday. Occasionally we went to Alloa, changing buses at Stirling. It was
something to look forward to, too, when our friend Martha came
from Deanston, a little mill village not far from home, to tea on a
Sunday. She always brought chocolate éclairs and afterwards we
accompanied her back to the meeting.

**As his father was Presbyterian and his mother Episcopalian,
Ian MacLachlan and his brothers and sisters attended both
churches.**

My mother's family were all Episcopalians, supporting Ballachulish and Glencoa churches. They were all very devout and
the ministers were exceptionally good men. My father's family
were Presbyterian and all attended church. My uncle was the
Precentor: he stood facing the congregation by the minister, and
led the singing. Unlike the Free Church, they had an organ. He
also conducted the Gaelic Male Voice Choir. He was a fine singer
and led them to success in the Rural Choirs Competitions at the
National Mod (like the Welsh Eisteddford).

Everyone knew and sang the Gaelic songs and Ceilidhs (sing
songs) were a feature of village life. My uncle was so keen on
music, he never missed a musical film at the cinema (Caruso, Gili,
Paul Robeson).

As children we went to both churches. Only the Episcopalian
men took Christmas day off and lost a day's pay.

**Eileen Davison is now living in Wiveliscombe, Somerset, but
in the Thirties she was near Oxford and as her parents had
different church backgrounds, they landed up going to Presbyterian services there.**

My father was an anglican and my mother a presbyterian, so we
were reared as anglicans, but we were also brought up in other
non-denominational churches, as presbyterianism was non-existent where we lived. However, during the Thirties my parents
managed to track down a presbyterian church in Oxford, twelve
miles away. We began to attend this church, largely because the
reigning vicar in our local parish church would not allow my
mother to take communion unless she was confirmed. This, my
mother, being a staunch presbyterian, refused. The presbyterian
church at Oxford was not very large and it catered mainly for folk
from the colleges, students and professors, which meant that it
was very interesting for us to see who was who and what was
what. For example the most humble and shabby looking individ-

ual revealed himself as a very learned professor of ancient languages! Then there were the hats -- we all had to wear hats and gloves to church and, as we sat at the back, we could enjoy these to the full. We had some fine learned preachers, who preached very long sermons, which largely went over our heads. One of the notables who attended the church was the novelist John Buchan; he was an elder, and as an elder he had to help serve communion. This was a great thrill for us, as we were all John Buchan fans. He was a small, slight man, who always looked very serious, and I remember wondering how it was he could write such tales of high adventure and romance!

Attending church in Yorkshire meant quite a long walk for Pauline Thompson's family.

The family were Church of England. Every Sunday we walked the one and a half miles to church and the same back. Only in a very hard winter, when the church had to close, were we allowed to go to the Salvation Army hall in our village. This we enjoyed very much, no doubt because of the different style of singing.

Peggy Vanderkar was actively interested in religion during the Thirties.

Biddy and I were in Connie Grant's Sunday School class at East Hill Congregational Church. What *did* we do that was so terrible that we received after class lectures? Giggling, I expect. We often saw the funny side (we thought) of things! Four of us, Audrey Charig, Eileen Rushton, Biddy and myself joined East Hill Church, but we felt that all the interest shown in us before we joined petered out afterwards. However, I enjoyed hearing Dr. Maude Royden at the Guildhouse.

One day Dorothy Zimmerman, one of our gang, ate a whole slab of Ex-Lax chocolate and suffered extremely! She felt really hard done by as, being a Roman Catholic, she had to go to confession and admit to stealing the chocolate from a shelf at home.

When I was about twelve I taught in a Sunday School in a poor district of East Hill. One child asked me if I was eighty years old and another, when asked to do a drawing of Jesus, dressed him up in a suit, complete with hat on head, and carrying a case with the initials J.C. on it. I suppose the epitome of respectability and status! Conditions were improving for these folk, because someone told me that they could move away but did not want to leave the friendly family atmosphere.

Also, Biddy and I helped at a play centre in London. Again they were very poor children and some had been sewn into their clothes for the winter. They were not very keen on the good, nourishing food provided. One small boy called out, "Oi, Bill, like a bit of potater?" He put it on his spoon and flicked it across the table. Custard was also 'Out'.

It was probably at Guides that I received the most important religious training. Dorothy Lovegrove, the Captain, and her sisters Maude and Evelyn, Lieutenants, all had a deep faith which they shared with us. We had great fun at guide camps at Thakeham, where Mr. Harris, the farmer, let us use his land and collect water and milk from the farm. There was a tiny church we attended for parade on Sundays. It had an enormous window sill, like a small room, which always had a vast bowl of flowers on it. This was exceptionally beautiful and I have never forgotten it. It epitomised the whole wonderful experience of living and eating in lovely country surroundings, far away from London streets.

Guides was a great experience. We spent a long time making sure our uniforms were as smart as possible. There were many interesting and exciting activities, and among the fun we learned to be responsible and self-reliant human beings. Very useful attributes when the war descended on us in 1939.

The Salvation Army played a large part in the life of Lilian Smith's family.

Religion was rather a mixed affair in my family. My paternal and maternal grandparents belonged to the Salvation Army; one uncle was the Band Master, so the Citadel was a family meeting place. For reasons I've never known my mother was confirmed Church of England and we children were baptised Church of England too, but this did not stop us from joining in the fun at the Salvation Army band and tambourines.

Bob Davison had the advantage of being brought up by Christian parents.

My earliest memories about religion are of a Nativity Play which we produced at my primary school. As one of the wise men I had to carry the offering of gold the entire length of the village hall, watching my step so that I didn't go too fast or too slow.

Then followed years of regular attendance at chapel. My father supported three Baptist Churches, one in our home village, one in a village six miles away where my maternal grandparents lived, and one fifteen miles distant where were other relatives. He used to take us all to each in turn: we children liked the fifteen mile ride to the more distant one, where we all thought the singing was the best. The services were the normal eleven o'clock ones, complete with a lengthy sermon. We had no choice in the matter; my father said we were going and that was that. Actually,

I don't remember feeling repressed or hard done by, and I don't think it occurred to us to misbehave in church. In fact, looking back, I've always been very grateful to my father for taking us, because it laid such a good foundation. Sunday afternoon was usually spent doing a four mile walk as a family. Tea was followed by hymn singing in the drawing room, with my mother playing the piano, and the day closed with my doing my scripture homework.

The time came for me to leave primary school and I sat an examination for Lord Williams' School, Thame. The headmaster reported to my father: "He's not quite up to the mark, but he knows a lot about Moses!" So I was accepted. I've always been grateful to that headmaster for the way he took Assembly every morning. Through this I acquired an everlasting love for the Collects, and he read from the scriptures beautifully. We had regular scripture lessons.

I remember when I was seventeen I became particularly interested in the church. For some reason, in that year I spent part of my summer holidays with my maternal grandparents. They were very active in the chapel and I attended services with them. I was also sufficiently interested to attend the mid-week meeting. Grandmother was very amused when the villagers pulled her leg, saying "He's more regular than you are."

Don Clark's experience of church during the Thirties in Wales.
We were sent to Sunday School each week and joined the Band of Hope. We enjoyed this because we marched through the village with banners and sang, then had tea and buns when we got back to Sunday School.

While I was working on the farm I never went to church as I had to work on Sundays.

In the valley the miners were so poor that they believed that God had forgotten them, but they were afraid not to believe in Him because the minister preached hell fire and damnation if they didn't!

Like many other children, Brai Harper went unwillingly to church because his parents expected it of their sons, but he has later been able to appreciate the advantages of that forced attendance.
My parents were devout churchgoers and we boys suffered for it. Sunday morning meant black pin-stripe trousers, black jacket and Eton collar, and we marched down the seafront to a fashionable Anglo-Catholic Church in the town. The much nearer church was too ordinary! On this parade, we fervently hoped that our school

chums would not be on the beach to see us in all our finery. In the warm weather it was a form of torture.

At Christmas we went to midnight Mass, and on Good Friday it was the three hour service, although sometimes we got away with only two. These festivals brought drama to the proceedings with their processions, incense, banners and banks of candles, which I suppose interested us, but the kneeling, prayers and the sermons seemed to go on forever. Strangely, we were never sent to Sunday School.

In hindsight, I can see a positive side to the churchy upbringing. I know my Bible better than most people and, from hymns and prayers, I gained an awareness of music, poetry and beautiful prose.

In the village where Lucy lived most people took it for granted that they would attend the church every Sunday, whether Church of England, Methodist or Baptist. There was a Roman Catholic Church in the nearest town.

We were well taught in Religious Education at home and school, including the Prayer Book services and bible stories. We attended church regularly on Sunday mornings for Matins -- and occasionally Holy Communion. The latter was not celebrated as regularly as it is nowadays. Religion was not discussed (neither was sex) but it could be referred to in an objective way, and opinions expressed on various sects or dogmas.

Feelings and emotions of all kinds were not expressed as openly as nowadays, in fact we were positively not encouraged to do so, and it would have been considered bad manners and arrogant. Discussing our complaints and illnesses was not indulged in, or was glossed over. Detachment and a stiff upper lip were expected and mostly adhered to -- young people were not as assertive as they are today.

The Hon. Mrs. Clay shares the beliefs of her parents during the Thirties.

We used to go from Pax Hill to the lovely old church in Bentley. It was a delightful walk across the fields and we always walked to church and back; it was about a half mile through the fields and very often when we had visitors we took them to church.

My parents were not, on the whole, very ardent churchgoers, but they were both very deep believers in God. I think both of them found it a little bit difficult to identify very strongly with the Christian faith only, because they had seen such a lot of wonderful Christian ethics in people of other faiths. They had become very accustomed to meeting such people through the Scout and

Guide movement, and both of them recognised this very universal belief in God and reliance on God's mercy and protection.
There was the idea of duty to God and duty to one's neighbour.
Both my parents recognised that this was the basis of all the great
religions of the world, therefore they thought that the Guide and
Scout promise, and the law would help anyone of any faith and
any age to discover for themselves God's love and God's will.
The activities within Scout and Guide training would give them
opportunities to carry this out, inspired by the example of their
dedicated leaders.

**Jean Gillis is a Londoner, now living in Sutton, Surrey and has
learnt to love and trust the Lord over the years.**

At the beginning of the Thirties, on 17th February, I celebrated
my tenth birthday. I had two younger sisters and brother. We
were a very united family and were taught to respect our parents
and respond to their discipline, something we see sadly lacking
in this day and age!

I was brought up during the hard times following the Armistice
of the First World War. Dad had returned from France, having
served in the forces, but found a scarcity of available work. Finally he accepted a job as a tram conductor, but with Mum and
four children to keep life wasn't too easy: in fact, it was very hard.
If you found you were not able to pay your rent in those days,
you could expect the bailiffs to come and remove your furniture,
and it wasn't too unusual for poor people to have to pay a visit
to the pawnbrokers to alleviate a situation. But through all this,
we were a loving, close-knit family.

Mum and Dad, being musical, went out occasionally on a Saturday evening to earn a little extra money in a small dance band.
This meant that at ten years of age I was left to look after my two
sisters and brother. I well remember how frustrated I became as
the evenings drew on and they were fast asleep, but I just could
not allow myself to do the same. I felt such a sense of responsibility -- I would get out of bed and take a long look out of the
window to see whether Mum and Dad were coming up the road.
As time went on I became concerned for their safety -- it was so
difficult for me to relax and settle down to go to sleep.

On one particular occasion, I had come back from looking out
of the window and lay down on the bed pondering. I was saying
to myself "What's this life all about? Where did it all begin?
Where is it leading? How can there be a forever and forever --
surely it must have had a beginning, but what about the ending?"
Well! As I lay there pondering I heard GOD speak to me quietly
and lovingly in my ear. He said:

"It's *All right*! It's all in my loving hands, and I will show you." Well, I thought, fancy God speaking to me *And He is going to show me!* Whatever am I worrying about, if He is looking after us? So you've no idea how peaceful I became. I breathed a great sigh of relief. What a weight had been lifted from me, and from then on I was at complete peace in these situations and just could not have worried if I had tried.

From that time onwards I was able to wait upon God and knew that He was showing me his love and the power of his loving presence and loving care. I just loved going to Sunday School and reading the Bible, and through those early troubled times I came to know that there was security in this life for me because God was real and, as He promised, through the circumstances of my life God has kept his word and has been showing me the reality of his promise.

Although I didn't realise it at the time, the boy who played the saxophone in that little dance band, whom I had met for the first time when I was ten years old, was to become my husband, although he was seven years older than me and I used to call him 'Uncle Val' (his name being Valentine).

I really felt that God was in charge of my life throughout my schooldays and that faith and security helped me along the road of life even through the hard times, for in 1939 we found that war was upon us and the future could look uncertain, but God's love and comfort sustained us. This has been very precious to me.

David Leach describes the important part religion has played in his life.

When I came to England from Japan in 1920 I first went to the XIV prep. school in Clifton, Bristol; and my boys went there after me. Then I went on to a small public school, Dauntsey's School in Wiltshire, and I was there fore five years. I was a games fiend and played all manner of games: Fives, Tennis, Hockey, and I was captain of Cricket. I didn't do very well at academic subjects and had no art at school.

Religion hit me, but not at school. There we did what was expected in an anglican school: it didn't really touch us. Nevertheless, I had already formed a very clear impression of a love for Jesus, and I did not find this was being met by the church, although we went to church every Sunday and had prayers every morning at nine o'clock. It wasn't until a bit later that my brother Michael went up to Cambridge from the same school. He was at Downing College and he met up with Christians there. The chaplain, Nick Wade, who was the father of Virginia Wade, had met the Oxford Group movement and had a team in the college.

My brother joined it and was very moved. He came home one summer vacation very considerably changed. The family all said to him "Mick, what's happened to you? You are very different -- it's almost possible to live with you these days. You do all the washing up in the kitchen, among other things." It was very apparent that something very special had happened to him. So he described this Christian experience with the Oxford Group movement. The leader was a Lutheran minister, and an American: he was having quite a considerable impact. It was very simple, mostly Baptist, Methodist and Evangelical Anglicans -- the Catholics disapproved in some ways, though strangely enough in later years there's been a very strong Catholic following of the movement on the Continent.

I became very interested in it: We believe in the guidance of God and the Holy Spirit being available to you and to me as we listen to Him. Quiet times of meditation and listening are very important. It upholds very high moral standards, based on Jesus's sermon on the Mount: absolute honesty, absolute purity, absolute love and absolute unselfishness. So I continue with them because I find this idea of listening and meditating, preferably at an uninterrupted time in the early morning, coupled with the assurance of God's love, does lead one into all sorts of situations and expectations in one's life, through the Holy Spirit. I have seen wonderful changes taking place in people just as it did in my brother.

However, the long and the short of it is that I said to Mick, "If this has done some good to you, no doubt it could do some good to me. I am going up to Stoke-on-Trent next September and I shall be on my own." So he found some addresses and I contacted these people in Stoke. They took me to a house party, which was a great gathering and I thought, 'this is wonderful. This is terrific. This is really authentic Christianity'. That was with anglican churches. Then my wife, Elizabeth, became a Catholic, and so for a period I became a Catholic because I thought, 'We've got the boys to bring up and it would be better if we brought them up together'. But I didn't really find it right for me, much as I admired lots and lots of Catholics. The Oxford Group movement influenced me very strongly.

Pottery took most of my time, but apart from that most of my thinking went into the religious side of life, and very, very often I wonder whether the preoccupation with pottery was right. I believe in the second best being the enemy of the best and if, in fact, our religious convictions are the deepest level of our life -- which I think it should be for all of us -- then everything should spring out of that. I wouldn't say that my pottery activity has necessarily been inspired by that. I've had a problem in my life of balancing my involvement in pottery with what I feel in a way is nearer what I think the Lord would want me to do with my life. I can't help thinking that the world is in desperate need of a renewal of faith: this generation hasn't much faith compared with our forefathers. I think there has got to be a revival, and it is beginning to take place -- the charismatic movement, the whole of the evangelical movement, and the fact that we have a new Archbishop of Canterbury is going to have a very profound effect on the evangelical side of the church. There are lots of things happening, and happening in different churches.

Over the last hundred years western civilisation has seen great technological development: now we've got to get our spiritual side developed, and the next move for western civilisation is going to be the real acceptance of the faith -- which I don't think is going to be Catholic or Protestant, or whatever -- we're going to get back to Jesus. We are not going to be so institutionalised that the Protestants are going to think the Catholics are alien to them, and the Catholics to the Protestants. We're going to get back to the source of all that Jesus said, "That you all may be one". Not uniformity, but unity. The magnet is the same magnet that is attracting you as is attracting me -- really the foundation is the New Testament.

Mrs. Mary Horseman was among those who joined the Oxford Group Movement.

My 'aunt' (father's cousin) was in the Oxford Group and I went to a meeting with her. I was feeling very apprehensive about Oxford and realised that here was an anchor, so I joined, and belonged most of the time I was at Oxford. This involved a meeting in a college every day before breakfast with the college group, and sometimes elsewhere with the girls from other colleges. Then at 1.30pm every day we met at St. Mary's (University Church) in the school room for a general meeting of all the Group in Oxford.

We were fine until the heads of the Group in London began interfering. We got more and more frustrated and eventually there was a mass walk out.

I suppose it was the Group's influence, but I practically spent no money on myself the whole time I was at Oxford. The 'indiscipline' of today's students horrifies me -- I didn't go to a cinema or theatre, and as for spending all that money on pubs ...! I am horrified now, though not quite as much as I would have been then.

Margaret Beavis is now living at Hove, Sussex, but spent much of her life in London. She describes how she became a Christian.

At boarding school I was often frustrated, but also had much fun. Sport was the only thing I was good at. Oh, those terrible Sundays, compulsory this and compulsory that, but the Bible class (Crusaders) which we had to attend, led me to Christ. Having been quite a rebel, I became a Christian.

We senior boarders, fed up with so much compulsory Sunday observances, decided that, if we had to go to Crusaders (held in our school hall on Sunday afternoons), we would have some fun and break it up! We did! We made the forms at the back of the hall tip up and we slid on to the floor amid much merriment. Then one day something happened to me. I had always thought of myself as a Christian, having said my prayers, gone to church fairly regularly, and lived a fairly decent life, but one evening lantern slides of Pilgrim's Progress were shown by the late Hudson Pope. As Pilgrim lost his heavy burden of sin at the cross of Jesus, I knew God was speaking to me. I was a sinner and I needed the Lord to be my very own personal saviour. I asked Him to come into my heart by his Holy Spirit, and I know He did: I was a new person.

Everything then became new. I was a new person, truly born again. The laughing ridicule of my fellow senior boarders in the days that followed did not deter me. I had a joy and a peace that is not easy to describe: it was just wonderful. Since that day in 1934 I have failed my Saviour and Lord many times, but He has never left me or let me down. He has been with me through storm and sunshine, joys and sorrows, all through these years, and I love Him more with every day that passes. It doesn't mean that in an instant all my problems were solved, but He is with us in them all. What a glorious life it is now, walking and talking to Him, my very own Saviour. I recommend Him to all.!

The Rev. William Wood had a life changing experience in 1930.

I had emigrated to Australia during the Twenties and was working for a sheep farmer. One day I was enveloped in dazzling light, and was overwhelmed by the love of Jesus. Before then I had known of him, but not experienced him personally. I knew I wanted to be ordained a priest and wondered how to give my employer such sudden notice. When I returned to the sheep station the owner asked me if I could find work elsewhere. For two years he had been looking for a book-keeper and now someone had applied and he did not want to lose him. So in 1930 I was able to leave and go to the theological college. I became a Bush Brother under the name of Brother Bill, and was able to visit many outlying farms to take Communion and help in any way I could. This let me into divine healing and there were many miracles, so my Bishop agreed that I should return to England to find out what was happening in the Ministry of Healing there.

I arrived in 1937 and met the Rev. John Maillard, who had a Prayer Healing Fellowship with centres in London, Brighton and Milton Abbey. He invited me to join him at the latter Home of Healing. John Maillard had worked with the layman, James Moore Hickson, as his chaplain. In 1882, when James was about fourteen, it became apparent that he had a special gift of healing. First a small cousin was healed of acute neuralgia when James was praying for her and heard the Lord say, "Lay your hands on her face." She was healed immediately, as was her sister a few days later from St. Vitus'dance.

When a London doctor, a relative, saw the miraculous healing of a young officer in the British army when James prayed for him, he said: "You have no right to be doing anything else, with such a gift of the Spirit." From then on he devoted himself full-time to preaching the gospel and healing the sick.

He was soon invited to visit America and a worldwide ministry followed. John Maillard looked after the work in England whilst James More Hickson was away and later developed his own ministry. I worked with him at Milton Abbey for some time, then for the Guild of Health. Eventually John Maillard suggested I should begin my own Healing Mission in London, using his centre in Dawson Place, Bayswater, which he let me have for a peppercorn rent for the first year. The London Healing Mission was formed to help bring the healing ministry back into the church; it has been doing that ever since 1949 and is continuing to do so.

Alfred Ridpath was born of Jewish parents, but, because of the fear of persecution, they did not tell Alfred of his background for many years. They much resented the fact that he became a Christian.

Because of the general poverty in Liverpool, my sister had been fostered by a Canadian family. She became a Christian and in 1933 returned to England to seek to convert her family. That year I attended evangelistic tent meetings with her at Queens Drive, Liverpool, and had a conversion experience. This profoundly affected my life from that time on. My heavy drinking, godless parents put out both my Christian sister and myself, so to help her I gave up my seafaring career and found a job in engineering ashore. I found that evangelical fellowship and evangelism abounded in Liverpool in the Thirties, and there were conversions nearly every week, vividly revealing to me that 'where sin abounded, grace did much more abound.'

I was very acutely politically and socially conscious of the widespread irregularities of our society, having been quite communistically orientated since before leaving school. Seeing corruption and exploitation the world over, I always resented our class society. As far as we know we were the first team to bring communist teaching to Havannah, Cuba, a time when Fidello Castro was influenced by our indoctrination methods. However, I now recognised that more than anything people needed conversion to Jesus Christ, and that before the people could rightly relate to each other they must first relate to God, recognising the wisdom of the Lord's words to 'seek first the kingdom of God and all else would be added'.

It was in 1939 that my sister and I had a double wedding ceremony at our Liverpool Assembly -- total cost £12.10s. My weekly wage as a married man was £2.2s, and we rented a two-up two-down house at 35 shillings a week. The approach of war didn't worry folk very much -- everyone thought that it would be over in a few weeks, or maybe months.

Margaret Willis, a Jewish Christian describes life in Germany in the Thirties.

I had read Hitler's book, *Mein Kampf*, and when he was voted premier of Germany on 31st January 1933 I knew what his attitude to the Jews would be. Fortunately, I had been brought up in a Jewish Christian home. I had known from my early youth that my father had left his orthodox Jewish family in Vienna and become a believer in Jesus the Messiah. He was now engaged in Jewish evangelism and had many contacts with different churches. I myself had become a believer and follower of Jesus Christ. There were many people in Germany who did not know they were Jewish or of Jewish descent, and many more had no faith whatsoever. Their discoveries were a shock to them.

In August 1933 my father returned from a preaching tour absolutely devastated. The Gestapo had ordered the minister to prevent my father from entering the pulpit. He was to have preached on Jewish evangelism during a missionary weekend. This was the first sign of the coming conflict between Church and State. In the past the church collection on the first Sunday in August had been given to Jewish missions, in memory of the destruction of Jerusalem. That had come to an abrupt end. Furthermore, from now on my father had to appear once a month before the Gestapo in Cologne to give an account of his work.

The conflict between Church and State (Kirchenkampf) widened as time went on.

In September 1933 my father was given notice by the Trustees of the Mission, but we were allowed to stay on in the house. I moved to a small room under the eaves; my mother having two rooms available took in students, as we were very close to the university. In December we closed in even further, as a Jewish Christian pastor who had been serving as a padre to several hospitals had been dismissed, losing with it his accommodation. He spent Christmas 1933 with us and soon afterwards moved in and lived with us for quite a long time. Pastor F. died in the ghetto of Warsaw building the ghetto wall. [See book *Excluded from the Land of the Living* by Prolingheuer]. Many discussions took place on theological themes. I got to know Romans chapters 9-11 from every angle. The encroachment of the powers of the State on the Church and the role both were playing in society were discussed at length, too. Can the Church keep silent much longer? Will they not stand with their Jewish brethren in the faith in their sufferings? We expected much from the Synod in Barmer, 29-31 May 1934: Declaration of the Confessional Church. They did speak out against the State, but as to their suffering brethren they kept silent. The Aryan-Paragraph, which had closed all the professions to Jews (medical and legal, teachers, artists, journalists, etc.), had silently been accepted by the Church. We knew this was unbiblical, but we were powerless.

One after another of our Jewish and Jewish-Christian acquaintances disappeared: one took his small son and went to the Argentines; another crossed the green frontier into Holland; another committed suicide. In 1935 my parents received a written invitation to emigrate, but they declined the offer. 'You can't transplant an old tree', and 'Our responsibility is here', was their answer. My eldest sister married a Dutchman and was living in Holland. My eldest brother with his young bride was on his way to Brazil when the 'Nurnberg laws' were made public at the Nazi rally in September 1935. They set out who could marry whom. With all the Nazi propaganda that had gone before, they came as no surprise: we had anticipated them and had experienced the outcome. It does not bear thinking of the distress they must have caused in relationships where they led to divorce, desertion, neglect or plain cruelty. In my parents case -- my mother was a German and my father a Jew -- the 'Nurnberg laws' brought them closer together and I myself added a new dimension to an understanding of what the church of Christ really is -- a union in the Spirit of Jew and Gentile, as we read in Ephesians 2.15-18: 'His purpose was to create in himself a new man out of the two, thus making peace ....' With all the Nazi propaganda banded about I really learned to seek and to apply the comfort of the Scriptures. The Nazi slogans said: 'The Jews are our misfortune': the Bible says, 'You will be a blessing'; 'I will bless those who bless you', Genesis 12:3; 'Let God be true, and every man a liar', Romans 3:4.

I also went out on cycle rides together with Hilda L. whom I had met at the 'Paulusbund', an organisation for non-Aryan Christians, fostered by the Gestapo. We met once a month for cultural activities.

On Sunday, 6th March 1936, on my way to a special exhibition, I was stopped from crossing the Rhine bridge by a large crowd that had gathered at the bridgehead, waiting for something to happen. I heard a rumbling drawing nearer and, sure enough, the first armoured tank, followed by an endless stream of tanks, rolled into Cologne. I was disturbed to the core. This was a flagrant violation of the undertaking to keep the Rheinland demilitarised. How would it all end? This would mean war! Looking towards the river I saw Hitler turning to the right and left acknowledging the adulation of the people, who were standing many rows deep along the banks of the river Rhein. I was disgusted with this display of idolatry, combined with military strength. How would it all end? I asked again. Then I heard God speaking to me. It was the same word that was once given to Abraham in Genesis 12.1: 'Leave your country, your people and your father's household and go to the land I will show you.'

I did not speak to anyone of this experience. Neither did I know that one of our Jewish Christian friends would be giving my name to 'World Friends', as the organisation was called. But I received a letter from a young couple in England asking me to correspond with them. They wanted to brush up their German, so letters went to and fro for many months and years. It was through their invitation that I went to England on 3rd August 1939.

It was because of the Christlike behaviour of a soldier that the Rev. Alan Sax wanted to know more about Jesus.

During my time in the army I met a young insignificant private soldier, who was kind and thoughtful. On one occasion I asked him "Why are you so kind to me?" His reply astounded me. "It's because you are a Jew". "What difference does that make?" I asked. His reply surprised me even more. "It's because my Saviour was a Jew and He died on the cross to save me". This was the first time I had been told why Jesus had died. Because of this man's life, by the time I had left the army I was on the threshold of becoming a Christian. I emphasise here that at that time I knew nothing about doctrine, but I saw what the fruit of a Christian life should be.

Some little time afterwards, sitting with my father just prior to going to the synagogue, I told him that I was thinking of becoming a Christian. He burst into tears, probably thinking that I was going to become a Gentile and divorce myself from everything he held holy. I left him and went to the Sabbath eve service, after which I said to the Rabbi; "I'm going to become a Christian" and added the words "Stop me".

"If you can lead a better life as a Christian, become a Christian, but I do not need Jesus as a mediator between God and myself." It took me three years to realise that I did.

Quite sometime afterwards, I was working in a Jewish hospital, caring for boys who had come from the concentration camps of Europe. Some had seen their parents put into ovens while they were still alive, some had the ashes of their parents with them. They hated Christ and blamed him for all the atrocities that had been put on their parents and themselves. Yet in this place, where I knew no Christians in or out of the institution, I became a Christian. Someone had given me a book, hoping that by reading it I would accept Christ. One evening prior to taking the evening Sabbath service, I took this book from my shelf and read the title, 'The Kingdom of Promise'. I shall never understand why the words were able to place me on to the path where I would enter into eternal life.

I began questioning 'Was Jesus everything that He said He was?' because, if not, all he said was not true. It was then that I accepted Him as my Saviour and Lord. Let me emphasise again that I still knew nothing about doctrine. I wrote to my family, not that I was thinking of becoming a Christian but I said I was a Christian. I could hear my mother weeping. My father told me never to visit them again. I wrote and told them what had happened: the reply came on the reverse of my own envelope and it said, "We don't know you, you never existed". I was then disowned for approximately fifteen years, but eventually they both became Christians before they died.

My small room at the Institute was set on fire; I had to leave their employment because I could not promise that I would not propagate my new-found faith among the inmates. I became unemployed for a long time. Jewish organisations would not employ me, for I had converted to Christ: Christian organisations would not employ me, for they thought I had an instability and because of this I had changed my religion. Ultimately I was in charge of two Community Centres in London. While in one, late at night, sitting with a friend from Nigeria, he gave me the magazine of a Missionary Society to the Jews. I read it and the next morning I telephoned to say that they were wrong. They asked me to call and I did so on a number of occasions. Ultimately they asked if I would join their staff. I refused. On returning home and mentioning to my wife what they had requested, she wept, telling me that she felt this was what God wanted us to do. The General Secretary of the Mission called the next day: I was to appear before the mission's Central Committee and, to my surprise, I was appointed. We continued with the Mission until retirement for more than thirty-two years and now, in retirement, I am chaplain at the local hospital, chaplain at the prison, chairman of a Board of Governors of a school, preaching almost every Sunday and sometimes during the week. I also do a small amount of work among our Jewish friends. It is marvellous what the Lord has done!

For Juliana Ray the early Thirties were happy times, but gradually the Nazis invaded the peace of Hungary as well as other countries in Europe.

The communist revolution of 1919 was short lived, but during this time there were many atrocities committed which embittered the middle and upper classes. After the fall of the communists in the autumn of 1919 the revenge was terrible and anti-semitism flared up because many Jews had taken part in the communist revolution. Any hopes for a new beginning were undermined by the peace treaties of 1920, which the victorious allies forced on the countries that lost the war. Hungary was deprived of about two-thirds of her former territory and population, a large part of her industry and almost all her raw materials.

For several years we went to Lake Balaton for our holidays, where we could sun bathe and swim, or play in the little pine forest. It was there that I had my first experience of anti-semitism. There was a yacht club and a tennis club for holiday-makers, yet my parents and my brother never made use of them. For the first time I learnd that we were not thought good enough because we were Jews. Later on at school and during the persecution it was rubbed in much more forcefully, but this was the beginning. In 1936 or 1937 we met a real Nazi family staying in the same hotel, when we were on holiday in Austria. The children were friendly, but we were amazed to find how enthusiastic they were, giving the Nazi salute whenever they saw a swastika flag on another car. When I told them that we were Jewish they said: "Well, that doesn't matter, you may be different from the others, but the Fuhrer is right in all things so what he says about Jews must be true".

My father was president of the Timber Federation and in 1938 the annual Timber Ball was to be held on the 12th March 1938, and everyone was looking forward to this prestigious occasion. Suddenly preparations were interrupted by a telephone call from Uncle Feri. "Have you heard?" The German army has just marched into Austria and annexed it to Germany." It was the day of the 'Anschluss' -- a tragedy for millions.

Shari mama wanted to stay at home, but my father knew that was not possible and they had to go. Much worse was to follow once war was declared.

10. POLITICS

AND THE OUTBREAK OF THE

SECOND WORLD WAR

Following the Wall Street Crash in the U.S.A. in 1929, the Thirties began with a worldwide recession. Money that the Americans had lent overseas was called in, spreading despondency and unemployment to many countries. This was compounded by the introduction of tariffs by America to protect its farming and industries. Other nations followed suit, effectively blocking world trade. With no markets for their goods, countries found that production retracted, leading to yet more unemployment. In Britain there were three million unemployed, but the position was much worse in Germany, with double that number in 1932, and over twelve million in America.

Unemployed demonstrators in front of Victoria Station,
carrying 'the coffin'.

Labour was the party in power in 1930, but found itself unable to cope with the devastating unemployment that followed the Wall Street Crash. Their leader, Ramsay MacDonald, unable to take the party with him when he proposed cuts in government spending, including unemployment benefits, decided to form a National Government, with representatives from each of the main political parties. Accordingly, in October 1931 he called a General Election, which the National Government won easily, though in fact the Conservative party dominated it. In 1935 Stanley Baldwin, a Conservative, became Prime Minister in his stead.

Some of the Jarrow Crusaders arriving in London.

In England, there was still a high regard for the monarchy, and the Jubilee celebrations of King George V in 1935 enabled the people to show their loyalty and affection. The Prince of Wales was also popular, but after the death of his father his deep affection for Mrs. Wallis Simpson, a twice-married American, and his determination to marry her, caused conflict with church and state, and in December 1936 Edward was forced to abdicate. Divorce was unacceptable to the British people in the Thirties, and he and Mrs. Simpson made their home in France – a devoted couple. Edward's brother, the Duke of York, succeeded him and was crowned King George VI. He was shy and had to fight a stammer, but his wife, Elizabeth, made a very popular queen and was a great support to him.

King George V and Queen Mary with their granddaughter Elizabeth in 1931.

In Britain as a whole there was a great desire for peace - another war was unthinkable – and the people placed much faith in the United Nations. So they closed their eyes to what was happening overseas: the invasion in 1931 of Manchuria by Japan (although she had some cause for complaint against China); the rise of Hitler's Nazi party to power in Germany in 1932, followed by Hitler's announcement in 1935 that Germany was to rearm; and the Italian invasion of Abyssinia that same year. As with any blackmailer, if you do not resist his first demands you later find you are powerless against him. The United Nations and the nations that supported it had neither the will nor the means to take decisive action. When they employed sanctions, it was too little and too late.

Yet there were some that understood the menace that Hitler posed and were willing to speak out against it. In the book *'1936 as recorded by THE SPECTATOR'*, Goronwy Rees reviews 'Hitler', by Conrad Heiden:

> Hitler is a treacherous man. He has, in the past, made many promises and broken many. Those who believed him are dead, tortured or 'defeated. For he understands promises, not as obligations to be kept, but as instruments for deceiving people.

There was also the problem of Communist Russia and what her intentions were. She was to disregard her alliance with

France and instead ally herself to Germany; thus protecting that country from a war on both fronts – until it suited Germany to go back on her agreements once again and attack Russia. Stanley Baldwin was held in much affection whilst he was Prime Minister, but after he retired in 1937 people began to blame him for not warning them of the menace of Nazism.

He was followed by Neville Chamberlain. He believed that Germany's grievances arose from the harsh treatment they received when they lost the First World War, and Hitler would be open to negotiation. So it was that in September 1938 he flew to Munich where he met Hitler, and having signed over the Sudetan Germans to Germany, leaving the Czechoslovakians very vulnerable to attack in the future, he returned to great applause. He waved a piece of paper as he alighted from his 'plane saying 'Peace in our time'. How he had misjudged Hitler!

In March 1939 Hitler moved his troops into Czechoslovakia. When they recognised Hitler's perfidy, France and Britain guaranteed the borders of the other countries of Eastern Europe. Hitler thought that once again he could take over another country with no active response from the French and British, but when he attacked Poland in September 1939 Chamberlain was forced to declare war on Germany. It was anticipated that there would be massive air attacks on London and elsewhere, so many children had already been evacuated to safer places.

Chamberlain was not the right person to lead a country at war, and in May 1940 Winston Churchill became Prime Minister. For years Churchill had been urging the country to re-arm, as he recognised Germany's desire to seek revenge for her defeat in the First World War and Hitler's desire for power. Churchill was a great orator and his speeches did much to inspire the nation. On May 13th he told the House of Commons that he could only offer them 'blood, toil, tears and sweat'. Two days later Reynaud, the French Prime Minister, telephoned Churchill to say they had lost the battle – and the will to fight. By May 20th the Germans had reached the Channel. There followed the miracle of Dunkirk when British ships of all shapes and sizes made the journey across the Channel and between them rescued 338,226 men. Britain and the Commonwealth were alone.

For much of the Thirties Winston Churchill was a voice crying in the wilderness. People were suspicious of him, for having begun as a Conservative he switched to the Liberals, only to return to the Conservatives in the early Twenties. By

1930 he had already held various Cabinet posts: Home Secretary in a pre-war Liberal government, First Lord of the Admiralty during the First World War and Chancellor of the Exchequer in Baldwin's government 1924-29. He had also written some outstanding books, including a five volume history of the First World War, and was a very successful writer. He undoubtedly had great gifts, but his early perception of the dangers of Nazism and demands for rearmament to counter them, met with little sympathy in a country counselling peace. He was out of step with public opinion.

In 1932, even before Hitler came to power, he was warning:

> Equal status is not what Germany is seeking. All those bands of sturdy Teutonic youths, marching through the streets and roads of Germany, with the light of desire in their eyes to suffer for the fatherland, are not looking for status. They are looking for weapons and when they have the weapons, believe me they will then ask for the return of lost territories and lost colonies.

Churchill was convinced that the next war would be won in the air and already during the Twenties, when he was Chancellor of the Exchequer, he had reduced expenditure on the army. His sympathy was with the cavalry, and he allowed the tank programme to be downgraded -- the tank which was to prove such a devastating weapon (together with air power) during the Second World War. He protested powerfully against appeasement policies, first when the government made no response to the incorporation of Austria into Germany in March 1938 and later when Chamberlain abandoned Czechoslovakia in September 1938 - the Munich agreement. At last, when Germany seized the rest of Czechoslovakia in March 1939, people realised that Churchill's warnings had been justified. Hitler wrongly assumed that the allies wanted peace at any price and would not withstand him, so he prepared for the conquest of Poland. But Britain had an agreement to go to the assistance of Poland if she was attacked, and on 3rd September 1939 declared war on Germany. Churchill was made First Lord of the Admiralty, as he was in the First World War, then when Chamberlain resigned in May 1940 he became Prime Minister.

Ted Chaplin's involvement in politics began when he was quite young.

I remember a mock General Election at Colston's School in the summer term of 1929, which resulted nationally in Ramsay MacDonald forming his second Labour government, with a small majority over the Conservatives. I supported the Liberals who, together with the Conservatives, outnumbered the Labour members. My interest in politics started then, when I was twelve and a half years old. It was a boarding school, so we did not take part in the campaigning amongst voters, but we read the literature put out by the parties and made speeches from soap boxes to our fellow school boys, who enjoyed heckling and jeering. I was not the Liberal candidate but I did made a couple of speeches.

I remember getting involved in the so-called 'Peace Ballot' organised by the League of Nations Union. This was a house to house canvas of all households throughout Britain, asking questions about disarmament. It resulted in strong support for collective security by all means short of war, but there was some support even for war. I supported disarmament at that time, despite the quite obvious threats from Hitler and Mussolini.

There was a General Election in 1935 which was won by the Conservatives under Stanley Baldwin, who in the campaign had not pressed for rearmament. I took no part in that election -- I was eighteen but had no vote -- but felt I would have voted for Baldwin. Churchill pressed for rearmament, but he was not supported by the majority of Conservatives. My father, finally back from India, strongly favoured Churchill - principally because he spoke out in favour of policies designed to keep India within the British Empire.

It was about the end of 1935 that I read an English translation of Marx's *Das Kapital*. I just could not swallow the arguments for dialectical materialism. I found the book boring, and reading it helped to shape my political loyalty towards being an anti-Marxist. It was also about that time I had a very long talk with the national organiser of the Social Credit Party, who happened to live near my home. He told me the Social Credit Party had won power in an election for the government of Alberta and he was organising a campaign to apply its policy in Britain. The central theme of the party was to give all adults in Britain free credit to buy whatever they liked, provided it was British, up to, I think, £5 a week. As my wage then was under £2 a week, that policy might have resulted in securing my vote, if I had had one, but the political ruse was easily seen through and I doubt if the Social Credit Party would have gained much support. There was a plan to call the party 'The Green Shirts'. Mosley had founded the British Union of Fascists some time before and they were known as 'The Black Shirts'. A friend of mine joined them. He and I went to Paris for a holiday in the summer of 1936, when the Spanish Civil War was on. We found all the talk in the cafés was about it. I felt neutral, but as a Fascist my friend was pro-Franco. Although not a Fascist, I felt I could not support the Spanish Republican Government because the Communists sided with it. However, another friend of mine from schooldays joined the International

Brigade, fighting for the Spanish Republicans: he was killed. It was a time of political turmoil. My principal feeling was that we must maintain peace without getting involved in the war. I was glad I was not personally involved.

*Police with drawn truncheons clear the way for a
car carrying Fascist officers, October 1936.*

At the end of 1936, there was a test of Baldwin's political competence when the King, Edward VIII, announced that he intended marrying an American divorcée, Mrs. Wallis Simpson. Baldwin decided he had to be firm and told the King he must give up all thought of marrying Mrs. Simpson, or abdicate. I, and the nation, followed all this in the newspapers. I noticed the issue became one for levity and in my workplace there were a lot of jokes about it – mostly very coarse. It was a relief to me and most people, I think, when the King abdicated. Practically everyone listened to his abdication speech on the wireless: it was an emotional one, which gained him some popular sympathy.

Baldwin's reputation soared for his handling of the abdication issue, whilst Churchill, who had supported the idea of a morganatic marriage of the King and Mrs. Simpson (in which event she would not have become Queen) suffered a loss of prestige. My father continued to admire Churchill, but it was Baldwin who remained in power. He retired after the Coronation of George VI. Consequently it was Neville Chamberlain who followed him as Prime Minister. Although I had followed these events closely, I did not feel I knew much about Chamberlain. It was not until I left for a job in Singapore in August 1938 that Chamberlain's work impressed itself on me. The Munich crisis occurred whilst I was on the P & O ship *Ranchi*. Chamberlain believed in his own ability to keep Hitler from unsettling the tenuous peace of Europe and went to see Hitler several times about his demand for territòry in Czechoslovakia, peopled by Sudetan Germans. After several meetings Hitler secured his objective and Chamberlain and he signed a paper saying the Germans and British" ... agree never to go to war with one another again" Chamberlain appeared at 10 Downing Street with a copy which he waved to the photographers saying, "I believe this means peace in our time"

On the *Ranchi* we all discussed this and I was amongst those who felt ashamed of Chamberlain's actions. When we reached Singapore, I found that my British colleagues there were furious at the course of events. It seemed inevitable that war would come, and so it was. I joined the volunteer artillery to help protect Singapore from the Japanese, who had already taken French Indo-China.

The Thirties for me ended in a series of disheartening events. I tried to join up in Britain after war broke out in September 1939, but the authorities would not allow that. They felt people like me would be more use in Singapore. I was still there when the Thirties ended. Indeed, I was still in the Far East in August 1945, because I became a P.O.W. of the Japanese until their surrender. By then I felt I had fully grown up, and I married the girl I had left behind in England in 1938.

John Magee describes the growth and effect of Hitler's Germany.

In 1931 when Hitler's name had become well known in England, many thought very lightly of the 'Nasties'. Indeed, some praised his efforts to attain full employment when we were failing to do so. Others excused his treatment of the Jews by pointing to the strangle-hold which Jews had on German commerce and other things, but were still uneasy about Hitler's excesses. Some realised that the autobahns he was building were for strategic purposes and that industry was secretly being geared for armaments production. Idealists pointed out that we were all losers in the First World War, that war as a political instrument was out of date, and that no-one but a lunatic would ever start another. We all hoped that way, but how wrong we were! Churchill warned us of our peril if we did not rearm, but Hitler was not the only one to shout 'warmonger' at him. Contempt for Hitler was changed to fear and a sense of helplessness. Many Germans were ignorant of Hitler's intentions and of the atrocities of the concentration camps. I was present at a meeting where an enthusiastic Nazi tried to persuade us that Hitler's intentions were pacific. He told us a story which he was sure would convince us. A little girl was being sent to bed and came down in her nightie to bid the company goodnight. She raised her little arm, said 'Heil Hitler', and departed. We were not impressed!

In this decade Low's cartoons in the Manchester Guardian were a brilliant appraisal of the growing power and menace of Hitler. Even when the Hitler-Mussolini axis came into being people were still blaming the Treaty of Versailles for humiliating Germany and calling for an understanding of that country. Little did they realise how much more draconian the Kaiser's terms would have been had he won the war. Chamberlain tried to deal with Hitler as a rational statesman and became the greatest dupe in history. In a way it was a relief when this phoney situation came to an abrupt end and our war preparations began in earnest. Gas masks and air raid shelters followed the threatening news, and plans for the evacuation of children were completed. It was as if the nation had woken from a dream. When evacuation came there were few emotional scenes when the children departed. Again, wishful thinking expected a short war and a quick resumption of normal life.

The first air raid warning in Hull was really a false alarm, but it occurred during a thunder storm. From my window I watched with both fascination and fear as masses of flaming material were blown across the sky, thinking they must be some new method of destruction. In fact they were the barrage balloons that had been struck by lightning, this being inevitable as they were such efficient lightening conductors.

Our school's first evacuation was to Bridlington, which turned out to be more dangerous than Hull, as we suffered daylight raids there, while Hull was free from trouble. The thirty boys I was billeted with in an hotel were remarkably cheerful, although they were not very well fed on 8/6d per week. A teacher of French was with us and we listened to French broadcasts, which kept us more up to date with the news than the B.B.C. As the Germans pushed southwards from Paris, the French broadcasts became weaker and weaker, and in the end it sounded as if the Marseillaise were being played on a portable gramophone.

So the Thirties ended at the period of Britain's greatest danger. Its towns were blacked out, its heart-rending shipping losses mounting disastrously, and yet with its citizens endeavouring to live lives as normal as possible and treating 'Lord Haw-haw', with his menacing German broadcasts, as a joke. Churchill became Prime Minister and from then on we really knew where we were.

Professor W. E. Burcham found that Hitler's rise to power and preparations for war spread their shadows over the peaceful life at Cambridge.

The later years of the decade were different, because even in the sheltered life of Cambridge I could not be ignorant of world affairs. I was aware that many of my contemporaries had a strong sympathy with communist ideals, and some of them belonged to the Society for Cultural Relations with the Soviet Union. Both Donald Maclean and Alan Nunn May were at Trinity Hall and I knew the latter well as a very able fellow physicist. Then before long the escalation of Nazi oppression in Germany brought us many distinguished refugees whose lives had been disrupted and who sought whatever help we could give them. I was fortunate in having interesting work to do in the Cavendish Laboratory, at first under Rutherford, but none of us could disregard the tensions that events not under our control were generating. I found at that time that my contact with college was decreasing and that I was making new friends in the Laboratory, where perhaps half a dozen people of my own age started research each year. We were all growing rapidly in independence and in confidence, though not in wealth, and despite the news we could not believe that Europe was in sight of a Second World War, like the First World War that we dimly remembered in our earliest years. And when some of us had acquired a second-hand car, it seemed proper to use these vehicles to motor around the continent to see what was going on. I made two journeys of this sort in the twelve months of peace after the Munich agreement. But soon senior academics from Cambridge began to be called away to confidential meetings in London and in August 1939, when the shape of things to come could be seen, there was for most of us a termination of the pleasant life that I have tried to describe, and a commencement of new undertakings in the Government service.

Life in Cambridge for most of the Thirties, and in other universities as well, I am sure, was a life of unhurried enjoyment. What we did was done because it interested us and we grew as individuals rather than as a member of a team or task force. In the Cavendish Laboratory particularly the spirit of Rutherford counselled us to remember that '*physics is fun*' and warned us against trying to be too complicated. It was a life-style that prepared us well for many different types of war service, but one which itself could not survive unchanged into the Forties. That we were able to be of some use in that decade (in my case in radar work) is, in my opinion, in no small measure due to the apprenticeship that we had served as we grew up in university in the Thirties.

Mrs. Eileen Davison describes how, before the Second World War, Germans came to visit the factory, and took many photographs with high-powered cameras.

In the months before the outbreak of war, we had many visitors to the Cement Works where my father and I worked. They were very interested in the machinery, and they also visited our factories, asking many questions. Mainly they were Germans, and there were batches of teachers and students as well as men, all armed with very sophisticated cameras. Some friends of my parents took in two of these teachers as paying guests and they went all over the place, taking photographs. We became friendly with them. One of them was called Liselotte Jackstein: she was an East German, short and square, with masses of blonde hair swept back into a bun -- very dour and uncompromising. The other, her friend, was called Annie Schaper, an Austrian and a most beautiful young woman, tall and slender, with very black long hair coiled on her head, and lovely eyes: she was a very gentle person. Liselotte was a physical instructress at a school and she taught us how to swim in the local river, with the aid of support mats made by herself of reeds lashed together!

Hitler was just coming into power then and she was most enthusiastic about him. Her fiancé was a member of his Black Guard, who went everywhere with him. She said how much he was doing for the young people of Germany. She painted a wonderful picture to us of camps in the Black Forest, of torchlight marches through the night, and so on: it sounded wonderful to me, and fired my imagination! She very badly wanted me to go out there with her and join in, but my mother was very suspicious and wouldn't let me go. She thought there was something fishy about it, particularly as Liselotte had told us that her father, who had been head postmaster of Dusseldorf, had been dismissed his post and sent in ignominy to a tiny hamlet on the Silesian boarder because he would not say 'Heil Hitler' instead of good morning. "Stupid old man" said Liselotte contemptuously.

Also, mother had intercepted a letter written in German to a friend of Liselotte's, which had been posted by mistake to her. Mother knew a bit of German. Our names were mentioned very frequently. Liselotte never knew how much German mother knew and was visibly agitated by this letter falling into her hands. I was very glad my mother refused to let me return with them to Germany, as I know I would have been overcome with the glamour of it all, and who knows perhaps encouraged to stay and help perpetuate the master race! Anyway, Liselotte was always harking back to the First World War, and how the German's couldn't understand how we had won it as we were such an idle people, and were not industrious like them! She did enjoy the countryside, however, saying it was like a wonderful garden, and that all the verges in Germany had been tilled and tidied up, and crops grown on them: wild flowers were not allowed!

Another character who came to our house was a scientist by the name of Herr Moebius: he also was very busy with his camera, not photographing the scenery or people, but all kinds of factories and installations. He was like Liselotte, short and squat, very earnest, with a cropped head. He came home with my father one day for lunch and afterwards we played tennis on our home-made court, which was full of potholes, which meant that the balls never went where you expected them to go, and shot off in all directions. The sight of Herr Moebius rushing round in a pair of voluminous plus-fours, mopping his brow and trying to hit the ball, will be with me forever. My sister and I spent the whole time trying not to laugh. When at the end of the game he tried to emulate a tall young man who leapt over the net (by charging it like a bull at a gate and landing in the middle of it) we dropped our racquets and fled into the house, where we could have a good laugh without offending him!

I wonder where all these folk are now and whether they survived the war, particularly Annie Schaper, the beautiful Austrian, who was a Jewess I believe. Well, Oxfordshire was not the only county to get German visitors: it was remarked upon what a lot of Germans we were getting as a country and I expect, like the Oxfordshire visitors, they all had cameras! When war broke out, my mother was triumphant. "There you are!" she said! "I always knew they were up to no good, visiting our country in such numbers with those cameras – getting ready to take us over! We're so gullible and easy going!"

Hitler continued to become more powerful and popular, particularly with the young folk, with his massed rallies and fiery enthusiasm for a new Germany. In 1939 he marched into what was called the Sudetenland. This land was really part of Czechoslovakia, where there was a great number of Germans living, and he later marched into the whole of Czechoslovakia. By that time our government, under the leadership of Mr. Chamberlain, was very perturbed and Mr. Chamberlain went to see Hitler to have talks with him about this move. He returned to England, beaming, saying that Hitler had no ulterior motives: that was all he was going to annexe. Naturally, we were all jubilant and very much relieved.

However, this jubilation was short lived. My sister and I were on a walking holiday with friends, staying at a Youth Hostel in Argyllshire, when it was announced that Hitler had broken his promises and had marched into Poland, and that we were at war!

What a shock we all had: we cut short our holiday by a week and joined a train packed with young people and soldiers rushing home and to army bases. I think everyone thought invasion was imminent and that we should return to our stations. My parents and young brother had been spending their holiday apart from us and we arrived home first to find relations in command, cutting up pieces of black material to make blackout blinds for the windows. We felt they were being very bossy in our house and resented them, though they did a good job, but we were thankful when our parents returned. Also it seemed as though the invasion would not be taking place at once, and the relations returned to their own home!

Of course, we were totally unprepared as a country: underarmed, and undermanned. However, we all set to with a will, shot out of our easy going ways by the horror of what Hitler had done so far and what he might do. Appalled by the strength of his armed forces, when we were so weak militarily, I shall always remember hearing on the wireless the news of Hitler's take-over of Poland: how gallantly the Poles fought, and how we just had to stand by, unable to lift a finger in their defence.

On 10th May 1940 Chamberlain was forced to resign and Winston Churchill was summoned to Buckingham Palace, where he accepted the King's commission to form a government of national unity. I know he had his faults, but he was certainly the man for the hour, and I don't know of anyone else who could have encouraged us all as he did. To hear his sombre tones saying that he could offer nothing but 'blood, toil, tears and sweat' was an uplifting and wonderful experience, and we felt we could do anything.

We were put on strict rations: anyone with metal railings or old metal saucepans gave them to be melted down into arms. Gardens were dug up, a 'Dig for Victory' campaign was started, and vegetables grown where there had been lawns and flower beds. Air raid shelters were constructed in gardens, and for those for whom this was impossible details were given as to how to strengthen a table!

At the office we had extra duties, as my boss became commander of the local Home Guard platoon. He had retired from the army as captain and he and an ex-Brigadier had the time of their lives sorting out the motley company of men who volunteered. Volunteers ranged from an illiterate dustman to a gentleman farmer, lorry drivers, plumbers and white collar workers; they all joined up (those who hadn't been called up into the services). Weekends were spent on manoeuvres. My boss was also in charge of the petrol ration the men were allowed, so there was plenty of form-filling to be done. Weapons ranged from rifles and old pistols to hay forks and knives: anything they could get their hands on, including home-made bombs known as Molotov cocktails! Everyone was issued with a uniform: 'Dad's Army', as seen on T.V. was not at all far fetched. They were so proud, and we were so proud of them too. If put to the test, I'm sure they would have acquitted themselves well.

Later on, my sister and I joined the W.R.N.S. and, later still, there was conscription for everyone of all sexes except the elderly, either into the armed forces, the land army, or munitions factories. Those who were in reserved occupations worked also as air raid wardens and fire fighters. But that's another story.

Dennis Thompson ruminates on the events leading up the Second World War.

The people were just recovering from losing a horrific number of menfolk in the First World War, and the country was getting back on to its feet after the effects of the post-war recession and the unrest that led to the General Strike in 1926. Life, I am sure, appeared to be very peaceful, but unfortunately it blinkered the awareness of the threats that were on the horizon Ñostrich syndrome: it will not happen to us or, if it does, it will go away. Of course, as is the wont with all governments, the people were not told the whole story, and if the German threat did get into the press there were many who shouted 'scaremonger'. But the government and most military leaders of the day, as history has shown, were to blame for our unpreparedness for the Second World War.

It was not until the outbreak of the Second World War that Lucy and most of the younger generation took any interest in politics.

My parents, like most adults in the Thirties, concerned themselves only superficially with politics. They were Conservatives, though many people in the south west were Liberals at that time or, in the Dockyards, Labour. We young people took no personal interest at all but went along with the opinions of our elders, with little understanding. It was not a topic of conversation, other than on very broad issues about those at the top in Parliament.

The Munich crisis and then the onset of the Second World War changed everyone's awareness and concern. World politics became the issue, rather than party politics. The outbreak of war changed the very social structure and way of life of all of us, whoever we were, whatever our background or occupation.

Joan MacLachlan's mother had very definite ideas about politics!

We were brought up to be future Conservatives, poor as we were! We must work for what we wanted and do without what we couldn't afford. (She wasn't pleased when I wanted to buy a single bedroom suite on hire purchase. It was limed oak and cost £26. I paid £2 a month for it: it was beautiful!).

I once asked her what Labour stood for. She was quite definite: 'They take the money off the rich and give it to the poor, then we will all be poor.'

There was unrest in Europe and we used to talk about it warily. In the spring of 1939 my brother Raymond left school at seventeen and obtained a job as an insurance clerk, a post he held until he retired. My college loan was repaid and at last my dear mother had an easier time. But it wasn't to last. In the July I went home with lots of goodies from the school open day and found her at the foot of the stairs, suffering from a stroke. She died that evening. Her own doctor was on holiday and when I eventually went to see him and told him, the tears rolled down his cheeks. He simply said, "Poor soul. She wore herself out fighting against the odds."

When war was declared, I was in church. On the way home I met my old school friend with her mother. She told me the news and then added: "Your mother's lucky: she'll miss all this" True words!

My brother Bernard was an army reservist and was called up at once into the Medical Corps. Decisions had to be made quickly, so my sister-in-law moved into our home with their two small children, our home being nearer my brother's work, should he return safely from the army. It worked well: we were all good friends.

I remember nothing of those last three months of the Thirties --it's just a blank. We had to make blackout curtains and be fitted with gas masks. Later we had to have a huge table shelter as there were children in the house.

Don Clark heard about politics from his parents.

My father cut other people's hair on a Sunday and they would discuss politics and the possibility of war. My mother would come in and say what she had read in the Bible and who would win if there were a war. Men from the village went to fight in the Spanish Civil War – probably to escape from their hopeless situation in the coal mining valley.

Communism was very strong in the pits and I remember my older brother joining the Communist party, but I was too involved in farming to have much political awareness.

Not surprisingly it was the Labour party that won support in Ian MacLachlan's village.

Labour was the popular party amongst men who worked hard for low wages.

We were aware of the fact that things were not going well in Europe and followed developments on the radio. When war was declared the Territorials assembled in the Drill Hall and men were dispatched to their units. Most belonged to the Argyll and Sutherland Highlanders.

Like other teenagers, Betty Forsyth was not much interested in politics during the Thirties.

In 1938, at the age of sixteen, I was amongst those naive enough to believe Neville Chamberlain when he returned from Munich proclaiming 'peace in our time' and waving the paper signed by Hitler.

Even though I worked in a newspaper office, I'm afraid I took very little interest in world affairs and viewed the onset of war with some trepidation, but also some excitement, which proved to be justified as time went on and the area was flooded with troops. This made life much more exciting for a seventeen year old girl!

We took the blackout, sandbags, torches, etc. in our stride, but it was rather shattering when all the cinemas were closed for the first week or so of war!

Undertones of war affected Lilian Smith's family some time before the outbreak of the Second World War.

By 1937 my parents were getting worried about what was happening in Germany and the madman Hitler, as my dad called him. About the same time we had a new girl in our class; she was a German Jew visiting her English relatives, supposedly on holiday. She never went back and so became the only survivor in her family: she was a lovely girl, well liked by all.

At the end of 1938 and early 1939 schools were making arrangements for evacuation. My younger sister had forms to fill in, but Mother decided we would all stay together in the event of war. Air raid shelters were being dug in gardens and we were issued with gas masks. Two of my brother's friends were Territorials and they were getting edgy. I remember the Sunday morning Britain declared war on Germany: my mother burst into tears, thinking no doubt of her brothers killed in the First World War and the fact that she had a son who was nearly eighteen.

The possibility of another war was a very menacing prospect for Jill Clarke's family.

As long as I can remember war was deemed inevitable. Most of my generation had parents who had had brothers or fathers killed in the First World War -- it still seemed quite close to us. The teachers at my school were all maiden ladies who had never married, and many of them had lost fiancés in the war. We all thought it very romantic -- somehow the horror of the First World War did not seem as terrible as it does today. It was all patriotic and rather glamorous -- older people, of course, viewed it with horror.

I remember hearing the grown-ups discussing Mussolini's rise to power, and then Hitler's, but until the end of the Thirties it seemed very unreal. In 1938 when the Munich crisis was being played out, we all suddenly realised the impending horror. We were measured for gas masks, and planned for evacuation from the bombing, and suddenly I was very afraid.

The Second World War made a big impact on the Yorkshire village of South Heindley where Pauline Thompson lived.

At the age of fifteen I did not have any political views, but I can remember how sad I felt when war was declared: the family was glad that my brother was only thirteen years old, so too young to be called up. Soon any available ground and also large houses were used to accommodate the troops whilst they were being trained. Not many families in our village escaped having a member in one of the services. Miners were not exempt in the first years of the war, though they were later.

Evacuees began to arrive in the village when the bombing raids commenced in London. Children were as young as three years old; they were so quiet at first – strange places, faces, and no doubt missing their mothers and wondering what was ahead of them.

The outbreak of the Second World War, as it affected Barclay Hankin.

I had completed my degree and had returned to the H. Q. of the Post Office Engineering Department, near St. Paul's Cathedral. Prior to the outbreak of war, I was on holiday in a remote hamlet called Carsaig, on the southern coast of the Isle of Mull. There was little more than a quay, two or three cottages and the main house where my godmother lived. 'Carsaig House' was later used for part of a famous film starring Wendy Hiller, called '*I know where I'm going*'. During the build up to the Second World War an incongruous red telephone box had recently been installed near the quay: this was part of a national scheme to link up the

It was Sunday, 3rd September. We were warned to listen on the wireless at llam to the Prime Minister, Neville Chamberlain. There was a fearful silence as Big Ben struck eleven. Mr. Chamberlain explained that he had sent an ultimatum to Hitler, but had had no reply. "As a result", he said gravely, "a state of war now exists between our nation and Nazi Germany". At about this moment, we heard the sirens going in Whitehall for an air raid! We all feared such an eventuality and wondered if gas attacks would start! The 'All clear' went soon after. We debated whether this was a genuine air raid, or a psychological ploy to shake the nation into active realisation that war was upon us! That evening, soon after dark, we heard loud shouts outside. "Put that light out!" A small chink in the blackout was showing and the local air raid warden was assuming his duties determinedly on the first night of war, even on the Isle of Mull!

On Monday morning I went to the new phone box and called my office to see if I should return from leave immediately. "Oh no", they said, "We are in a state of chaos; there is not much you can do. Come back in ten days." London was beginning evacuations and huge demands were being made on the Post Office Engineering Dept. for thousands of new lines and private wires for Defence services.

Air raids on London had been expected, but nothing happened until Saturday, 7th September 1940. Four of us went to the theatre that night at the Criterion, Piccadilly Circus. The play was Terence Rattigan's 'French without Tears'. The stage and auditorium were below ground, so we had heard nothing untoward.

We came out at about 10.15pm and were astonished to notice a bright red glow in the sky to the East. Ack-ack guns were pounding away noisily, searchlights were weaving, and fire engines were rushing around all over the place, ringing their bells madly. It was obvious that the blitz had begun, and we must get home as soon as possible. There were complications, however. My friend Harry was already in the army and had to get back to his unit in south London before his pass expired. His girlfriend, who was a stranger to London, was staying with friends in Hampstead Garden Suburb, and my mother and I lived in Shepherds Bush. We agreed to split up. My mother would go straight home; Harry would make his way back to his unit as best he could; I would take the girl home to Hampstead and then return to Shepherds Bush.

The girl and I managed to get by tube to Golders Green. Ack-ack shells were exploding in the sky, and an occasional tinkle of metal on the pavement reminded us it was dangerous. At the same time, I knew her friends would be extremely worried. I asked what she would like to do, to chance it and walk home, or wait in the comparative shelter of the tube station, with no idea how long the raid would last. She chose the former, and we set off for Hampstead Garden Suburb. When we got nearer it became clear that, in the dark, she did not know the address or recognise the house! All she could remember was that it was near a pillar box! We managed to find it somehow, and I returned as quickly as I could to Golders Green, and just caught the last train south.

The Underground was disrupted by the danger of flooding. We were turned out at Warren Street and told, 'No more trains in any direction!' It was well after midnight by this time. There was nothing for it but to walk to Oxford Street and set course west, on foot, for Shepherds Bush. I knew my mother would be worried, so I walked as fast as I could with many others struggling homewards. Ack-ack guns were still blazing away, and a succession of fire engines came tearing down Oxford Street and Bayswater, going east, again ringing their bells continuously. London had a scheme to use appliances from the centre of the fires and replace them with others from the suburbs. It was a little alarming, but in a strange way both exciting and exhilarating.

At about 1.30am I finally got home. My mother had been ordered into a brick air raid shelter in Uxbridge Road and could not get out until things quietened down, so she was delayed and equally worried as to how I was getting on, or whether I would reach home first and be concerned on her behalf. The red glow had been caused by docks and warehouses on fire in the East End, near the river. In a fairly dramatic way, we had shared part of the first night of the blitz. Fire engines don't have those nice bells any more!

Molly Campbell's family had to face up to the problems of blackout when war became a reality in 1939.

On the whole we were not much concerned with politics during the Thirties, but eventually the menace of Hitler began to penetrate our small world. An exchange visit for boys of the school was arranged with a German school, and when the German boys came they refused to discuss Hitler at all. They were well disciplined and wore strange clothes, but spoke good English. Afterwards we wondered if the exchange was entirely innocent. In 1939 when Chamberlain made his historic dash to see Hitler many people really believed in 'Peace in our time'. When war was finally declared we expected immediate annihilation, but the decade ended with the phoney war.

Our house, with its large windows, needed a great deal of blackout material. My mother got on with it with her usual efficiency. By that time I was working in a bank in Oxford Street. Our windows were all taped in a criss-cross design to protect the glass against bomb blast, as were the windows in the buses. At first there was much apprehension about, but there was also a lot of humour and good neighbourliness.

The outbreak of war in September 1939 was to cause disruption to many lives, as it did to that of Mary Horseman.

In the summer of 1939 Arthur came to Budleigh Salterton with the family, and I can well remember the end of the holiday when he went off to do war work on the radar chain. I saw him off and my best friend Mary, too, back to her boyfriend. Then I returned to Epsom armed with yards of material to make blackout curtains. No-one knew when we would see each other again.

By then I'd got a job at Nuneaton High School, where I was for a year until Arthur and I were married. We saved sugar from our ration and dried fruit, that was on points, and the baker made the cake for us. We went to Sutton, near my parents' home in Surrey, to look for clothes: my wedding dress was a blue crêpe with matching felt hat, and my sister Peggy's bridesmaid's dress was dark red taffeta. Afterwards we went to Swanage, where Arthur was posted to do research. I seemed to be busy all the time, learning to cook and house keep and do the laundry – all new skills to me.

It was a splendid way to learn, as we were very poor (£250 per annum). Rationing meant I couldn't spend much – I think at that time we spent £1 a week on rent, £1 on food and £1 on fuel. We had a coal fire in our sitting room and a coal range in the kitchen, which heated the water, and also a gas stove. We always had one good meal a day, meat or something of the kind and two vegetables, with pudding; but our evening meal was usually bread and margarine and marmite, with lettuce when we had grown some in our pocket handkerchief sized garden.

With the meat ration at 1 shilling per week we couldn't do many meals with it, but we sometimes got sausages or offal off the ration (or under the counter!). We were lucky if we had one egg each a week, but tinned meat and fish were on points, and so were lots of other things, so we were always juggling to decide which was most important. As we didn't take sugar in tea or coffee, we usually saved that although most people found the ration quite inadequate. So I was able to make jam and marmalade and didn't have to spend points on them.

On Saturdays we went to the British Restaurant. They were opened up everywhere and provided a good two-course meal for 5 shillings: this helped the ration considerably.

We knew a garden where they grew some vegetables, more than the house needed, and each week we called in and stocked up with enough to last a week.

Clothes were rationed soon after war began. Fortunately my mother had started me off with a lot of clothes and also linen, so there was very little we had to buy.

The furniture was quite a problem and we had to scratch around and buy one thing here and another there. By this means we got quite well equipped, even if some of it was a trifle peculiar. Later on conditions got worse.

People had time to make preparations and my father built a brick air-raid shelter in the back garden, complete with bunks and a food store. We were glad of this later in the war.

Some of the children who were evacuated to safer locations at the outbreak of the Second World War were very unhappy, but Graham Jardine found it a most exciting experience. He describes his evacuation from Glasgow to Dumfriesshire.

"You won't be able to do that when you're staying with Mrs. Colquhoun!", said my mother for the umpteenth time. It was the summer of 1939 and 'Mrs. Colquhoun' was the family code-name for the unknown landlady my elder brother and I would be joining somewhere in Dumfriesshire or Galloway in a few week's time, when the Glasgow schools were expected to be 'evaporated' (as schoolboys would have it).

The historic Saturday September the Second dawned and there we were, aged 14 and 12, my secondary education just begun but rapidly approaching crescendo, rattling out of St. Enoch's railway station towards our destination in the south. Like many others, we were to prove very lucky. 'Mrs. Colquhoun' turned out to be a cheery buxom lady, and her husband, whose girth was the direct antithesis of hers, a kind of former evacuee himself as he had found lodgings in the same household during the First World War whilst employed in a nearby munitions factory -- and had stayed on when he married the daughter of the house! The couple had no children of their own, but now, by the flick of a gas mask, their two-bedroomed terrace house in the market town of Annan had become filled to the satisfaction of the local billeting officer and, for many practical purposes, they were the parents of two stirling sons. Indeed, our National Health Service numbers testified to this 'fact', being quite different from those of our real parents, whose National Registration took place at the same time as ours, but in Glasgow.

By 1939, our landlord (the name 'Mr. Colquhoun' never really would have fitted him because he had a most pronounced Cumberland accent) had become a railway linesman and, in addition, he was secretary of the local branch of the National Union of Railwaymen. As far as we were concerned, one major advantage of this was that, to boost the funds of the N.U.R., every Saturday evening Mrs. Colquhoun and he ran a whist drive in one of the many halls that existed in the town at that time. This meant, in days before it was illegal for children younger than sixteen to be left on their own, that John and I had the house to ourselves for a couple of hours. As a bribe towards our good behaviour we were allowed to listen to '*Bandwagon*'. To many who read this, such an item may not sound much of a treat. To us, however, coming from a home provided by the Corporation of the City of Glasgow (since our father was a public park's Superintendent) where the only sources of power were coal and coal gas and therefore electric light and the 'wireless' were unknown 'necessities', to listen to Big Hearted Arthur's 'clean though they're not very clever' jokes was to be in sixth if not seventh heaven.

Mrs. Colquhoun, as well as being an accomplished card player and a superlative cook and baker, was a real dab hand at knitting -- which was just as well! This was not only because she now had an extra four over-lively feet to keep warmly and fully covered, but for another reason of much greater consequence to the nation. The female equivalent of the male 'dig-for-victory'. Dozens of women and girls in the town must have knitted hundreds of socks, mitts and gloves of every shade of khaki, navy-blue and air-force blue within a few weeks of the start of the war. Along with a few other expert wielders of two flashing steel rapiers, it was Mrs. Colquhoun's task to re-knit the most grotesquely-shaped and ridiculously sized socks that I have ever set eyes upon. How some of the patriotic knitters imagined that Hitler would be beaten by soldiers, sailors and airmen with feet and hands the shapes they had knitted defeated me, even if not the Führer. So, on many an evening the house was festooned with socks that had been ripped down, the wool steamed into a semblance of its earlier non-kinky state and, if a pair of youthful hands was not available, the back of the chair would be draped in a hank that was being furiously rewound. The garments that this wool was refashioned into would certainly be fit for victors!

Being evacuated to Annan was as good as having a half-holiday from school every Monday to Friday. The only difference was that the half-holiday was in the morning because the local children used the school buildings then; our schooling began at 1 o'clock. This really was the better part of the bargain, of course, because, throughout the winter months it was always light while we were free to enjoy the outdoors. After dark, in the blackout, there was less fun to be had, except on one occasion when some of us, rather daringly we thought, rapped on the window of a nearby (but not too nearby) house and shouted in what we hoped would be a gruff air raid warden-like voice, "Put out that light!"

The street where we lived was heaven on earth for boys of our age: it had an abandoned, but not too empty, builder's yard located at a corner that it shared with the street where the house with the faulty blackout stood. The most memorable game that resulted from the proximity of the yard was the one that came to be known as '*Moat Road Hockey*'. It consisted of finding yourself a suitable stick from the yard and whacking a tin-can to and fro along the length of the pitch as the fortunes of two teams of two or three a side ebbed and flowed. A major benefit of using a can rather than a ball (in addition to that of a can being less likely to reach window height) was the one that my brother discovered on what came to be regarded as a famous occasion. He was being hard pressed and was retreating towards his own goal when a disastrous mishit onto the road surface shattered his hockey stick. By the luck of it, the accident happened almost opposite the broken down gate of the builder's yard. He had time to rush into the yard, seize another hockey stick and return to the fray in time to clear the ball just as his opponent was about to shoot for goal.

The yard itself may no longer have been in use, but above part of it was a loft in which logs and other scraps of wood were kept by a man who made a living, or at least part of one, by chopping up the logs into small sticks, bundling them and selling them for kindling. Occasionally we helped with this, learning in the process that to complete a tight bundle of wood you don't tie the string as tight as possible round the sticks and just leave it like that. What you do is to tie the string into a loop of pre-determined size, pack in as many sticks as possible and then hammer in the last few sticks somewhere in the middle of the bundle so that the string is really tight. Did I say that we had our schooling in the afternoons?

We made a few (old) pence for our efforts as stick merchants. We also became professional sheep and cattle drovers one Friday. It was market day and we slaved throughout the long morning, trekking back and forth between the pens at the railway station and the two or three auction rings in different parts of the town. At the end of the morning the official drovers delved into their pockets and gave us our hard-won reward. We were so thrilled by the princely sum that I remember to this day that it amounted to four pence three farthings -- between the two of us!

For a few weeks, four-wheeled bogies, made out of old plants and pram wheels, were all the rage. The steep Bruce Street and Battery Brae (the latter not so named because of the bruises we received at its foot) were ideal for these fore-runners of the skate-board. It was fine for evacuees whose foster parents had brought up families of their own and thus had outgrown prams and push-chairs from which to procure the necessary wheels. After a good deal of pestering, our host supplied two pairs of wheels from an undisclosed source and, since he was unable or unwilling to drill the necessary hole in the front axle, we were sent to a blacksmith who had his smiddy about half a mile out of Annan, on the high road to Dumfries. It probably was this event that led to the dis-covery of the spot, a short distance from the smiddy, that we called 'The Haunt'. The hedge-bounded triangular shaped area at the corner of a field, and sitting high above a road and a country lane that joined it, became our den for a while, being suitably hidden from passers-by. From our eyrie we were able to enjoy the celebrated view of the town hall clock and bridge over the River Annan that has appeared in hundreds if not thousands of postcards before and since 1939, and goes by the title *'Annan from the Howes'*.

Annan from the Howes, with clock tower.

The town hall clock, with its four faces, was mainly a friend in need during our morning escapades because it warned us from afar and well in advance that 12 noon, the hour of lunch and time to scrub-up and prepare for school, was approaching. There was one never-to-be-forgotten day, however, when, from very much afar, the clock's animosity rather than its amiability was obvious. This must have been a day in October, because the circumstances that led to 'time being of the essence' began with an innocent foray in search of 'chessies' ('conkers' to the more refined) up the road that lies to the east of the river and passes the estates of Warmanbie and Mount Annan. It was to the trees of these estates that we were directing our attention when we became aware that it was much later than we had expected. The precise time of the moment of realisation is unimportant, although hindsight would suggest it was about 11.30. The remarkable fact is that it was at this point that John decided (and who was I to dispute the case with my elder brother?) that it would be best to proceed in a direction away from Annan, towards the village of Brydekirk where there was a bridge over the river. We could then return on the road on the west side of the river, and cross back again either by the suspension footbridge or by the bridge that carried the main road into Annan. At any rate, it was reckoned that this would be a lot easier than returning by the (much shorter) way we had come. My memory of the result is that it was a long, hot slog carried out in wellies. Much of the time at a run or a jog, the elder brother meanwhile encouraging the younger with the indisputable arithmetical axiom that 'twice the distance is less than the distance itself'. From a long way off we watched the town hall clock, as if mocking our predicament, place its hands on its forehead and slowly move the smaller of them to above its left eye, whilst more rapidly it wiped its larger hand around its face to its left ear, then to its chin and, just as we arrived home, to its right ear. Memory, perhaps in its kindlier way, does not record what Mrs. Colquhoun said on our arrival, or which pool in the River Annan she had been about to have searched. What I do remember, however, is that we gulped down our lunch, washed, changed our clothes, grabbed our schoolbooks and were crossing the High Street at five minutes to one that day, fully four minutes earlier than was our custom!

In our Glasgow home we had plenty of books of our own so we had never discovered the joys of borrowing from a public library. This omission was quickly rectified in our new home town, and so it was that we discovered (as the book jackets said) 'Richmal Crompton's lovable rascal', William. Annan was an ideal place to put yourselves in the shoes of William, Ginger and company. There was at least one empty house with a neglected garden that fitted well the kind of scene where many of William's exploits took place and, remarkably, there was also a boy of my own age from Glasgow who fitted only too nicely our picture of William's deadly enemy, Hubert Lane. What more could you want? The scene was set for a multitude of William-like adventures, which, of course, existed almost entirely in our vivid imaginations rather than in real events.

Many boys must have gone through a 'William the Detective' stage about our age. We had lots of minor adventures of this kind within the town, but it was a lengthier one that remains most clearly in my memory. It started early on Sunday afternoon when we happened to see one of the young Glasgow teachers stride purposefully along High Street, pass the town hall and make towards the bridge over the river. At the rate he was travelling we can hardly have regarded him as 'loitering with intent' and it is not really true either that he was 'behaving in a suspicious manner'. Nevertheless, we decided he would have to be tailed. The details of the chase are tedious. Suffice it to say that 'our man' chose to take neither the road along the side of the river nor the 'low' road to Dumfries. Instead, he made for the Dumfries high road. Even then there was a chance he would fork right and take the Lockerbie road after about 300 yards. But, of course, he didn't, and from that point the high road goes on, and on, and on in an almost straight line for about six miles, so that there is little cover for would-be pursuers. As a result, we were forced to drop back and linger at least 200 yards in his rear.

After about three miles of tailing, the afternoon, and we, were wearing on and, with no sign of a bend in the road in sight, we began to anticipate that there was a distinct risk that our quarry would abandon whatever nefarious assignation he had set out to keep, turn to retrace his steps, and thus confront his pursuers face to face. Not a bit of it! All at once he made a sharp left turn down the road that skirts Kinmount estate to joint the Dumfries low road near the village of Cummertrees. The end came swiftly. It is a mere two and a half miles along the minor road to the village, and the long legs of the agile young suspect strode rapidly along them whilst the shorter limbs of his 'shadows' tottered less steadily in pursuit. Just outside Cummertrees he glanced at his watch, looked back in our direction (horror of horrors, had he spotted us?), leapt onto a bus that had just bowled past us, and sped off towards Annan. It was at this point that the young sleuths really came unstuck. There was no taxi waiting for us to jump into as we gave the command, "Follow that bus!" and, in any case, the budding detectives had neglected the first principle of tailing when they had left home in a penniless state that afternoon. What we did, in fact, was to stand helplessly in the road and chant rather feebly after the rapidly departing vehicle, "You can't take it!" -- singularly inappropriate words, considering our vanquisher's and our own respective relationships with the bus! About an hour, and three miles, later we stumbled back into Annan. At school the next day, the man who so clearly was William's Conqueror smiled sweetly as he asked, "Well boys, did you have an enjoyable walk yesterday?" Perhaps when I tell you that his name was Mr. Forrest you will understand why, even now, I wince every time I see signposted in the countryside, 'Forest Trail, ten miles'.

Mrs. Jessie Lintern's family was living in one of the areas of Scotland where it was considered safe to send evacuees from the more vulnerable parts of the country: a new experience for all.

Before returning to college for my final year, I had arranged to spend most of September with my cousins and their parents, my uncle being head of a primary school in Lanarkshire. This gave me the opportunity to have several additional weeks of teaching practice. I was at Colmonell preparing for this visit when the outbreak of war was announced on 3rd September, and with that came our evacuees. My grandmother as usual was spending the summer with us; Mother's brother and his wife arrived from Surrey; afraid of bomb danger in Glasgow, an uncle brought his two sons for refuge; last, but by no means least, Thomas and Francis were billeted at the manse!

Anxiously clutching a carrier bag containing some margarine, a tin of baked beans and one of evaporated milk, plus a minimum of spare clothing, the apprehensive pair arrived at the manse gate, to be led into our vestibule and then the hall, where they stood aghast. Thomas eventually found his tongue and the following conversation ensued. "Hi, Missis. Is this a palace?" Mother replied in the negative. "Is't a castle, then?" Another negative. "What is't then?" "It's a manse, Thomas." "What's a manse, Missis?" "It's a house where a minister lives," said Mother. "What's a minister -- d'ye mean a priest?" and before Mother could answer, he screamed, "Are you prodies?" grabbed hold of Francis and bolted out of the gate, to be caught in the firm grasp of Mother's brother. Bath-time was the next hurdle: I had to tackle Francis, while Mother struggled with Thomas. Both were sure they were about to be drowned! Well scrubbed and clad in my brother's spare cricket shirts, they obediently knelt by the bed and said their prayers, accepted with some suspicion a goodnight kiss, and we hopefully left them to their slumbers. We had hardly reached the foot of the stairs when a howl was heard from the bedroom. "My Lord, my Lord. I canna sleep withoot my Lord," came the sobbing cry. Mother hurried back upstairs to pacify the boys: it occurred to me that they might possibly be thinking of a crucifix, so I went into our kitchen to examine the contents of the carrier bag more thoroughly. Right at the bottom, among the old worn clothes, were two round circles of scarlet felt, in the centre of which was a figure of Christ. When I took these up to the bedroom, the faces beamed. Thomas seized the emblem of the 'bleeding heart', carefully attached by its hook over a button on his shirt and the other on that of his younger brother, then, arms round each other, they were soon sound asleep. I often thought later of that impoverished mother from a Glasgow slum tenement who, in the stress and upheaval of that wartime parting, had ensured that her sons would have the familiarity and comfort of their faith as they were put to bed in an unknown home among strangers.

Next morning I set off for Lanarkshire, there to enjoy a few weeks of teaching in my uncle's school. I became used to the wail of air-raid sirens, of planes droning overhead and of hearing the sound of the pipes, knowing that another batch of kilted troops was en route for a railway station and the south of England. When I returned to college, it was to find shelters in the basement, sandbags bolstering up doorways, windows criss-crossed with bands of tape, blackout curtains in lecture rooms and bedrooms, and air-raid wardens constantly on parade throughout the area. Glasgow was on the alert!

Brai Harper did not have long to appreciate being employed before the outbreak of the Second World War disrupted his life and that of many others.

At the age of seventeen and a half I was apprenticed as a cub reporter on the local paper. This meant learning to ride a motorbike, and then doing a weekly tour of the nearby villages to collect news from whoever was willing to give it. Sometimes it was rather eccentric rectors, or hall secretaries, or the cobbler or baker. In the summer, I attended village fêtes or concerts in the hall. Back in town for the rest of the week, I attended annual general meetings of the many societies, anniversary celebrations at the Methodist Church (which seemed to happen every month!), and I also inherited the children's corner and the entertainment page. The latter I particularly liked, because it took me round each week to the four cinemas to get details and adverts for their forthcoming attractions. I also had a free pass to see the films. When the fire maroon went off, so did I on my motorbike, listening for the fire engine's bell and trying to get onto its tail. There were never any big fires; just frying pans or gorse bushes or bonfires out of control. In odd moments, I dropped in on the undertakers, who would tip me off on any death which might give a story. It was not too productive to ring the police station or the hospital: they were terribly cagey.

After the 1938 crisis, when Chamberlain assured us of 'peace in our time', my older brother and I joined the R.N.V.R. to ensure that when the peace ended we would be in the Navy. We attended every week at the depot in Newhaven, where we did gun-drill round an obsolete 1916 gun, and had lectures round a similarly obsolete mine, not realising that Hitler had a whole new range of mining tricks for our delight. In 1939, when they felt sure we were really interested, we were issued with our uniforms. On the 6th September we were mobilised to Portsmouth and went on the longest train journey I had had, all the way to Thurso in Caithness, where we embarked for Scapa Flow.

We were berthed in the old battleship *Iron Duke*, a whole big mess-deck of R.N.V.R. rookies, used for the next two months for various working parties, replenishing the stores of the cruisers and destroyers when they returned from operations. I managed to dodge much of the heavy stuff by being appointed to the crew of a small speedboat, which took sailing orders out to tankers and supply ships, at any hour of the day or night in all weathers. After that, I was put into the Captain's office, because I could type and spell. Then *Royal Oak* was sunk not two miles from us, and a few days later the bombers hit the *Iron Duke* and we abandoned ship. A happy boyhood ended with a bang!

11. SCOUTS, GUIDES, CLUBS.

Scouts and Guides, as well as other clubs, continued to flourish during the Thirties. In addition, Youth Hostels added to organised activities, and the Central Council for Recreative Physical Training was formed to encourage more physical exercise, indoor and out, to try to improve the general standard of the nation's health. There was concern because so many young men volunteering for the forces were not fit enough to be accepted.

When war seemed imminent my brother, who had had double pneumonia whilst at school, applied for a commission, having been a member of the Officers Training Corps. He was classified C3 and refused. However, when conscription was introduced he was graded A1, as were many others who had previously been C3. Standards had changed!

Scouts and Guides were able to help the war effort in many ways, and their training proved very useful.

Scouting became a very important part of Brai Harper's life.

The happiness of my boyhood, first and foremost, was due to my parents. They provided a secure, loving but disciplined home, and looking back after sixty years I am amazed at their wisdom in so many things.

The second most important influence was undoubtedly Scouting. When I floated the idea of joining, my mother was rather taken aback. I think she thought I would be meeting rather rough boys and associating with people who were 'not quite our sort', but eventually approval was given, my uniform was bought, and in my large dimpled hat I set out for my first scout meeting. There were other pals from school already in the troop, which helped.

I am sure that my whole outlook on life was changed from then on. I had been in danger of drifting into a smug bourgeois lifestyle, with all its suburban snobbery, but suddenly I was enjoying rough-and-tumble games in a damp smelling old grain loft, which was scout H.Q. There followed all the wonderful adventures of camps and hikes and country-wide games, and the challenge of learning Morse code and semaphore, first aid, campfire cooking, maps and compass bearings, tree recognition and more. There was the camaraderie and the adventure, an opening up of a whole new outlook on nature and on society in general.

Lady Baden-Powell unveiling an engine of the LMS
'Schools Class at Euston. Lord Baden-Powell christened another called
'The Boy Scout'.

Baden-Powell was still alive, and his book *'Scouting for Boys'* was our Bible. We lived by his rules. We wore the big hat and corduroy shorts, and each of us had a staff, marked off in feet and inches. For weekend hikes or camps we had frame rucksacks and carried all our needs, including tents and food. For bigger camps, using the large tents, we had a trek cart which we trundled for miles into the hinterland, usually Ashburnham Park. All cooking was on open fires, with biscuit tin ovens, and we made 'dampers' by twisting dough round sticks and toasting them. The big hat was invaluable for fanning dying embers into life!

We were a very outdoor troop, and our Scoutmaster strongly discouraged the taking of badges which were not what he called 'useful', such as first-aid, lifesaving and swimming. He scorned other troops which covered their arms with badges for music or art or train-spotting, but never went hiking or camping.

Ashburnham Park was a paradise of long bracken, rocky out-crops, wonderful trees, a stream and a pond, across which we built aerial rope-ways. A week's camp was utter bliss, and we made a film there called *'Scouting Out of Doors'*, which I believe is still on the H.Q. rental list, in London.

Scouting took me from my featherbed and put me next to the earth in tents, barns, church porches or belfries, and even the old naval jail at Lewes. I think I became the keenest boy scout ever invented and it has stood me in good stead all my life.

Barclay Hankin describes a scout camp, shortly before the outbreak of the Second World War.

My grandmother lived at Bexhill-on-Sea and I had a close association there. I became linked with the 9th Bexhill Scout Troop, one of the best in the town. I helped to organise a week's summer camp for about twenty boys in superb weather at Arne, near Wareham, Dorset, from 12-20 August 1939. We had found a good site, with the assistance of the Dorset Scout Association, near Shipstall Point, a promontory sticking out into Poole Harbour and within sight of Brownsea Island, where the first scout camp was held. It was an ideal spot, with privacy in a lovely field, surrounded by heath and woods for games, and providing wood for cooking and pioneering. Water was collected from the farm, and it was only about five minutes' walk to Shipstall Point for bathing on a safe, isolated beach. For scouting in those days it really could not be improved upon.

The following is a quote from the notice calling the camp. 'The camp will be according to the H.Q. publication *'Camping Standards'*. The inclusive cost of the expedition will be 12/6d per boy. This low figure is possible through the generosity of St. Andrew's Church. (Our garden fête is to be at St. John's School in July). To help people save, there is a camp bank open now, and deposits are accepted every troop evening. A little pocket money will be useful. It is hoped that every boy will be able to attend, as it is an occasion for the training received during the year to be put into practice. Absence from annual camp definitely retards a boy's progress in the troop....'

I travelled by car and the other scouter accompanied the boys by train to Wareham. A lorry kindly loaned from Bexhill brought the tents and other kit. We reached the field on a glorious Saturday afternoon. We had only been their about half an hour and were busy setting up camp, when a parson appeared in the field and said, "Have you a boy here called Tony Smith (or some such name)?" Yes, we had such a boy. "Could he come to early service tomorrow at eight, please?" The astonishing efficiency of the Roman Catholic communication system surprised us, but we assured him we would do our best to get the boy up and ready! Most of us attended the delightful little Arne Anglican church at 11am on Sunday.

There were four patrols who did their own cooking, based on three patrol meals per day. In addition, cocoa and biscuits round a nightly camp fire was prepared centrally. The menu varied but followed a regular pattern, adjusted if there were an expedition. For Monday 14th August it was as follows:

Breakfast:
    Porridge, boiled eggs, bread and marmalade, tea.
Dinner (12.30):
    Brawn and pressed beef, salad (watercress and lettuce), raisin pudding.
Tea:
    Bread and jam, buns, tea.
Supper:
    Bread and cheese, cocoa.

The Hon. Mrs. Clay has contributed an article from 'Trefoil' (an association for retired Guides) written by Margaret Brightwell just before her unexpected death in 1990; and another by Molly Gange.

One memory of Guide camps is the smell of black shoe polish as we got ready for inspection, and another is the crunching of grass by cows in the early morning. In those days we had 'hard' broad brimmed felt hats and black shoes and stockings.

I dare say the modern uniforms are more comfortable and easier to maintain, though I feel our were more distinctive. Patrols usually slept six to a bell tent. In the daytime, bedding was rolled in ground-sheets and placed round the central pole. Palliasses were filled with straw.

In 1932 in France, I camped with a small group of E.A. (Eclaireuses Aînées), the equivalent of Rangers. In this case, we did not have palliasses, but a layer of straw covered the grass in the ridge tent. The tent was sited in a wood. In England, I believe tents were not pitched under trees. Perhaps because of the climate, the French seemed much less particular about sitting on the ground without a groundsheet or wearing hats. Later, in 1935, we camped as Rangers in a field shared with a guide company. They seemed a rather strange lot, as they had their meals at a table and I believe they burnt coal. They had the nurse to see to first aid, but disappointingly they only suffered a broken metacarpus!

As guide camps take place in August and as in England August tends to be one of the wettest months, there is likely to be a good deal of wet weather. It had been found that by wearing plimsolls without stockings we did not catch cold. At any rate, it worked in my case.

Molly Gange writes:

The Thirties were not affluent years. Our summer holiday to the Swiss International Guide Chalet was a great event, but it was not the holiday but the journey which remains a vivid memory after over fifty years.

Firstly the train connecting the boat broke down. It sat like a broody hen until all hope had passed. We missed the train, we missed the boat, we missed the reserved seats, and Thomas Cook missed us. How anyone could miss twenty-three guides and four harassed adults, I shall never know.

The next boat was at midnight: crowded, with deck space only. It was very chilly, and when we got to Ostend the train was full. At least the sea was calm. Nothing daunted the guiders got us all into the train. As the carriages emptied we settled down, shoes off, feet up, and ties undone. But not for long.

"Arlon, Arlon" -- a burly official made it all too clear, in any language, we had to get out. With our luggage around us on the platform we looked up to see the front half of the train carrying part of our company move rapidly out of sight. It was a frequent service so we were soon reunited on the next station. We behaved as if we had been apart for weeks!

Memory dims a little but my next recollection is of midnight again.

Was it Berne or Bêsle? Had Thomas Cook at last materialised? Or have the Guiders risen to even greater heights of organisation? Anyway there was a large 'Rescue Home for Destitute Girls' and there we spent the night. Two to a bed, some on the floor and it was bliss.

We were up next day at five o'clock into another overcrowded train. Wedged like sardines we stood gazing out of the window. I was longing to see my first sight of the mountains, but I had to be patient a little longer. There was a jolt and we had arrived. For the last hour I had been standing upright and sound asleep.

Miss Enid Dynes, a former Headmistress of Chichester High School for Girls and before that of King's Norton Grammar School for Girls, died on 20th September 1991 and many paid glowing tribute to her great ability, kindness, generosity, sympathy and courage. The diaries of the guide camps she kept during the Twenties and Thirties have been passed to me, and provide happy memories of those days.

Camps at Foxlease were always very special, particularly when we were invited to the house itself, where Guiders from many countries came for training. In the entrance hall was a verse from Longfellow:

> Not chance of birth or place has made us friends
> Being of ten times of different tongues and nations,
> But the endeavour for the selfsame ends
> With the same hopes and fears and aspirations.

There was also a plaque stating:

Her Royal Highness, as President of the Association, also endowed Foxlease with the sum of £6,219 placed at her disposal on the same occasion by the Marys throughout the British empire and these generous gifts:

> As a training centre for guiders from all parts of the world;
> As a recreation and home for those needing rest;
> As a place of camping for those of every race.
> May Foxlease live to develop greater happiness and useful service through goodwill.

Summer Camp at Foxlease.

Wednesday: Leave Bedford 10.25; arrive Foxlease 4.30. Put up tents, have supper and go to bed.

Thursday: Reveillé 8.0; breakfast 9.30, parade 10.30. Inspection, competition making maps of neighbourhood; dinner, design of names; tea, forest walk, supper, camp fire, bed.

Friday: Competition on nature observation in forest; dinner, expedition to Milford by charabanc. Return 6.30; supper, camp fire, bed.

Saturday: Gathering leaves competition; dinner, tea, walk in forest; supper, camp fire, bed.

Sunday: Church; dinner, rest hour free. Tea. Look over Foxlease house and grounds and cow sheds. Supper, camp fire.

Monday: Games; competitions with Farley guides. Dinner; inspection by Miss Warren. Malvern guides look over camp. Sports; supper, camp fire.

Tuesday: Flag raiding and despatch running. Patrol sports competition. Making up poems to tunes. Dinner. Outing to Beaulieu Abbey. Tea; evening free; supper; patrol stunts; bed.

Wednesday: Pack up, strike tents and go home.

Knowing that the guiders who had been training at Foxlease were going home the following day, Miss Behrens very kindly invited us to a camp fire. The patrols at Foxlease including our company, the Fifth Wandsworth, were invited to give items of entertainment. On arrival we were ushered into a magnificent drawing room called Scotland. As we did not know the names of the guiders, we christened them according to the country they represented. We sat down, Miss Cattely taking Miss Behren's place by the fire. We sang a few camp songs and then, with many cries of 'pink''pink' from the audience, the Chaffinches started their entertaining. Miss America, looking very charming in guiders' uniform, came on stage and began singing in that delightful American accent of hers, a song she had made up. As she sang the verses about olden guides, two guiders entered dressed very funnily with crinoline skirts -- everything to make them look old fashioned. They paraded around and were followed by two guiders dressed ready for the war, who entered when Miss America sang 'In 1914 came the war'.

The scene following represented the guides of today and the Chaffinches ended their entertainment with short guide songs, plus cheers from the audience. Much credit is due to Miss America, who made up all the songs sung by the 'pinks' and who led them and the guiders in singing them. One of them was:

> *There are all sorts of girls in this camp of ours,*
> *Some like their books and their study hours;*
> *Some like to dance the very best of all;*
> *Others to follow the tennis ball.*
>
> *All these girls you see here tonight,*
> *Please like them all for they're quite all right;*
> *No matter how different they all may appear,*
> *They're really the same, for we're all girl guides here.*
>
> *Girls there are of every sort,*
> *Some are tall and some are short;*
> *They're as different as can be:*
> *They all look good to me - da, da, da.*
> *Some are dark and some are fair,*
> *There's not one that we can spare,*
> *For big and small*
> *We love them all:*
> *We're all girl guides here.*

There were a few more camp songs and then the Greenfinches came on the stage. Their entertainment consisted of songs, the most popular being a parody of *'Singing Polly Wolly Doodle all the day'*. The chorus was:

> *Fare thee well,*
> *Fare thee well,*
> *Fare thee well my company,*
> *For I'm off to Lyndhurst Road,*
> *For to see my new abode*
> *And it's Foxlease Park for me.*

The next item was dancing by the Chiff Chaffs. They did a few country dances and an elf dance: the latter was encored.

The rooks then completed the patrol items. They were hailed by most of the Fifths with cheers and whispers of 'Isn't Lady Nigeria a sport'. The 'caw caws' acted the building of a nest in guiding. To everyone's amusement, all the rooks entered made up as rooks, holding sticks in their hands. Lady Nigeria led all the songs, which consisted mainly of CAW, CAW, CAW, CAW. First the nest was started by winning the tenderfoot; then the second class. At length the egg was hatched.

The Fifths clapped until their hands were sore, and then they sang a few songs as also did the Morgans. The delightful evening ended with more camp songs.

Jessie Lintern did not have the coveted joy of belonging to Guides in her youth, but that did not prevent her from devoting much of her life to the movement.

My two cousins in Lanarkshire had been first brownies and then guides, and I would have given anything to be one too. Apart from the dozens of guide stories acquired from libraries and as gifts, my longings remained unsatisfied until one happy day an announcement was made that a guide company was to be formed locally. By this time I was almost seventeen and the oldest of the girls, so I was appointed company leader. At last my ambition was achieved, and I continued in that capacity during holiday breaks from college.

While at training college I opened a cub pack for the church I attended, but my great joy came during my first weeks of teaching in the Ayrshire village, when I had permission to start a guide company. Every girl of appropriate age appeared that first evening. Money was lent from the school fund to buy a complete uniform for each one, payment to be made by instalments or outright, as the parents chose. The large, disused United Free Church was made available as our H.Q., in which we met each Wednesday. Soon the younger girls clamoured for a brownie pack, while the older ones could not bear to leave and decided to form a ranger group instead.

I was delighted to discover that my guide captain from Colmonell was our District Commissioner, coming often to visit us and also welcoming us on day trips to her home. The county president's home was only a few miles from the village and we were given permission to hold our summer camp in the grounds of the dower house. By using local bus services we were also able to have weekend camps and outings, most of which were memorable for various reasons. During her visit to Ayr, our rangers were asked to act as guard of honour to Lady Baden-Powell as she arrived at the station. Many years later, when attending a chief scout's conference at Skegness, I had the pleasure of joining her for breakfast. To my surprise she smiled and said, "I've met you before, haven't I? Let me see - in Scotland with your rangers at Ayr." Her memory was noted for its accuracy, but to be able to pinpoint that meeting so swiftly and correctly left me speechless!

I still maintain contact with these girls, many of them now grandmothers and in that same village. Their letters and Christmas cards are addressed to 'Dear Captain'. A few years ago we had a reunion: they were all wearing their shining, well-worn trefoil badges. It was a very humbling experience that evening to realise just what their guiding had meant to those girls since last we had met thirty-eight years before. There were tears in our eyes as we sang 'Taps' - we were once again ending our meeting round a camp-fire or in a grove of trees above a stream, or perhaps under the stars in the ancient ruined castle where many of them made their promise as rangers. The faces to me were those of the teenagers to whom that promise was so important, by which their lives had been guided, who had been such faithful friends, and who now sang with the same youthful fervour, to the tune of *'Londonderry Air'*:

'I would be true, for there are those who trust me.
I would be pure, for there are those who care.
I would be strong, for there is much to suffer.
I would be brave, for there is much to dare.
I would be friend to all – the foe, the friendless.
I would be giving and forget the gift.
I would be humble, knowing all my weakness.
I would look up and laugh and love and lift.'

That song had been their watchword throughout the passing of those years.

Joan MacLachan found much enjoyment in guides and other clubs.

I helped to run the church ranger company, and when the cub master went away to the army I took on the cubs.

From 1936 on the rangers occupied Monday nights -- they became my friends and cheered me up after a long day in school and a long journey home. We had splendid camps at Flamborough Head, on a site near the lighthouse. My college friend joined us and a Finish pen pal from Helsinki came too. The guides were also with us. One big laugh we had was when our very well-to-do Guider was mistaken for the attendant in the ladies' toilet at the station, and a woman handed her a penny!

In the summer of 1939, after my mother's death, our captain, the doctor's wife, took us all down to Hardington Mandeville, near Yeovil. It was a big stone cottage in a huge field, almost unfurnished, and ideal for camping outdoors. We visited Wells and Cheddar Gorge, and had a perfect holiday in summer weather, which was really beautiful. I suppose these were the last carefree days before the trauma of war overtook us.

I also ran a keep fit class in the city of Nottingham for a Girls' Temperance Club and was paid 10 shillings a week for this: a lot of money for me. It was run by a very 'temperate' lady, who wore her guide uniform, including the enormous old-fashioned hat, on many occasions.

In the summer time we had the loan of a tennis court at a private house belonging to a very famous Nottingham grocer. This was a great treat and privilege.

My brother was in the school cricket XI and joined a local cricket club, too.

The school guide company had its disadvantages for Mrs. Betty Forsyth.

I was a member of our school girl guide company, but never felt any great enthusiasm for it, as the officers were teachers, which gave a false atmosphere to our activities and made any sense of camaraderie impossible.

After I left school I did help with the local cub pack as an assistant leader and enjoyed that. We took the cubs to 'camp' - living in a cottage on a remote estate in the country, with no electricity, where they had to dig their own trenches for latrines!

Elsie Dickinson had a happy time with Brownies.

In 1934 when I was eight, my cousin Jose introduced me to her brownie pack. There were groups of pixies, elves, fairies and

Elsie Dickinson -- a Brownie in the Thirties.

gnomes, each called a 'six', although the numbers could vary. Brown Owl put me in the pixies.

We played various games, and sometimes had a scavenger hunt to find interesting objects from the nearby area; in those days the streets were quiet and relatively safe. We spent a session in our six, learning the brownie promise, how to become a second class brownie, to pass badges and later become a first class brownie.

After our working session we made a small circle and each six danced round in turn, singing our particular song, eg:

'We are the little pixies,
Helping people out of fixes.'

Then we made a line and each gave a penny for the brownie funds and sat down in a circle with a toadstool in the centre. Brown Owl, the leader, gave out notices about forthcoming events, like church parades. Tawny Owl, her assistant, sat beside her. She taught us how to knit and sew and pass badges.

I well remember visiting a lady's house and being shown how to make a rice pudding. I still make my puddings that way today! We also learned how to clean shoes properly; to polish the under step between the sole and heel, as well as the top.

A special event was when a few brownies were old enough to join the guides. When the guides arrived they stood in a horseshoe shape. We sat on the floor and made a ladder with our legs outstretched, one brownie on each side. All the first class Brownies were presented with their 'fairy wings' -- a badge which they proudly wore later on their 'guide' uniforms. This enabled them to run up the ladder to join the Guides: we said they flew up to the guides with the help of their fairy wings. It was a special honour – a lovely little ceremony that I remember very well.

The Rev. Alan Sax was the troop leader and his father was the scoutmaster, but he had experience of another club.

I was a member of a boys' club led by a very well known Jewish social worker, Basil L. Q. Henriques. When I wrote and told him that I was going to become a missionary to Jewish people, he was very annoyed and told me that he did not want to have anything more to do with me. He could understand my personal decision but he could not accept that I should propagate the Christian faith.

Lilian Smith learned from the Woodcraft Folk and Sunday School Club how to do many useful things.

My brother played the bugle in the Boys Brigade and nearly drove us mad when he was practising. My sister and I belonged to the Woodcraft Folk. There we were encouraged to make things like wood cuts and raffia work.

At the Sunday School club we did sewing for the Missionary School in Africa. We made tops and trousers for the little boys - horrible stiff calico. They must have been very uncomfortable to wear.

By 1930 many of the Bobs had left school and were at college or university, and as the decade went by many had jobs and some were married with children, so we were not able to meet so regularly. However, we still kept in touch and during the summer holidays at least some of us were able again to go to Marigolds and know the delight of having a week-end together there in the country. Sometimes the more hardy joined for a walking holiday to Holmbury St. Mary or another Youth Hostel, and shared in the singing and fellowship there, including sometimes scrubbing out the burnt porridge pot!

Then there was the Solkhon family camp at Thakeham, where most of us were Bobs, and the weeks at Lucy Summers' cottage at Cudham, Kent, when we could revel in country life and also dip into her intriguing library of books.

It was when war was imminent that we agreed that in 1957, our special Bob year, we would meet at the 19th tree in the New Forest on February 26th. We fell around laughing as we pretended we were old, wheelchaired and toothless!

We did meet that day, after being scattered around the country for many years, but in the comfort of the Burford Bridge Hotel at Box Hill in Surrey. There were twelve of us, each wearing blue, and we astonished ourselves by picking up exactly where we had left off, almost as if there had been no gap in the years. There were cables from those abroad and we sent joint letters to them. In the evening we climbed to the top of Box Hill in pouring rain, laughing as we slipped and almost fell!

From then on we celebrated the 57th birthday of each Bob member in each other's homes; in Cornwall, Devon, Chichester, Birmingham, Surrey, London and Oxfordshire. When we became too old to travel in the cold of February, we changed to May, when many Bobs had birthdays. Now in the Nineties we are depleted in numbers and in our seventies and eighties, so it is the telephone and letters that keep us in touch, with the occasional one-to-one visit. Still the magic remains, and we can laugh at the many wonderful memories we share.

BIBLIOGRAPHY

I am grateful for permission from:

Scottish Local History to reproduce *The Exhibition that was Child's Play*, by Dr. W. G. Jardine, 1988;

North Surrey Libraries (Surrey County Council): Mrs. Ivy Green's article on *'My First Seaside Holiday'*;

also extracts from *Out Of The Doll's House*, by Angela Holdsworth, published by B.B.C. Enterprises Limited; and *Twopence to Cross The Mersey* by Helen Forrester, published by The Bodley Head.

Other books for reference:

Batsford: *Living Through History, Britain In The 1930's*, Charles Freeman.

Crescant Press: *The Thirties - A Dream Revalued*, Julian Symons 1960.

Collins: *British Society 1914-45,* by J. Stevenson 1990.

Harper Collins: *A History of English Christianity*, 1920-1985, 1986.

University Paperbacks: *Britain Between The Wars 1918-1940*, Charles Loch Mowatt 1955.

Macdonald Cardinal: *The Long Weekend*, R. Graves and A Hodge, 1940.

St. Martins Press: *The Hundred Days to Hitler*, Roger Manvell & Heinrich Fraenhols, 1974.

Michael Joseph: *1936 As Recorded by The Spectator*, introduced by Charles Moore and Christopher Howlie 1986.

Faber & Faber *Britain's Locust Years 1918-40*, William McElwee, 1962.

Batsford: *Living Through History, Britain in the 1930's,* Charles Freeman.

British Society 1914-1945, by G.D.H. Cole & M. I. Cole.

Marshall Pickering: *By Grace Alone*, Juliana Ray, 1985.